COERCIVE CONTROL AND THE CRIMINAL LAW

This book considers how a phenomenon as complex as coercive control can be criminalised. The recognition and ensuing criminalisation of coercive control in the UK and Ireland has been the focus of considerable international attention. It has generated complex questions about the "best" way to criminalise domestic abuse. This work reviews recent domestic abuse criminal law reform in the UK and Ireland. In particular, it defines coercive control and explains why using traditional criminal law approaches to prosecute it does not work. Laws passed in England and Wales versus Scotland represent two different approaches to translating coercive control into a criminal offence. This volume explains how and why the jurisdictions have taken different approaches and examines the advantages and disadvantages of each. As jurisdictions around the world review what steps need to be taken to improve national criminal justice responses to domestic abuse, the question of what works, and why, at the intersection of domestic abuse and the criminal law has never been more important. As such, the book will be a vital resource for lawyers, policy-makers and activists with an interest in domestic abuse law reform.

Cassandra Wiener is a senior lecturer in law at The City Law School, City, University of London. She is an expert in the criminal law on coercive control and advises governments and activists around the world on the doctrinal implications of domestic abuse law reform.

COERCIVE CONTROL AND THE CRIMINAL LAW

Cassandra Wiener

Routledge
Taylor & Francis Group

LONDON AND NEW YORK

Designed cover image: © Getty images

First published 2023
by Routledge
4 Park Square, Milton Park, Abingdon, Oxon OX14 4RN

and by Routledge
605 Third Avenue, New York, NY 10158

Routledge is an imprint of the Taylor & Francis Group, an informa business

© 2023 Cassandra Wiener

British Library Cataloguing-in-Publication Data
A catalogue record for this book is available from the British Library

Library of Congress Cataloging-in-Publication Data
Names: Wiener, Cassandra, author.
Title: Coercive control and the criminal law / Cassandra Wiener.
Description: Abingdon, Oxon ; New York, NY : Routledge, 2023.
Identifiers: LCCN 2022036801
Subjects: LCSH: Sex crimes--England. | Sex crimes--Scotland. | Intimate partner violence--England. | Intimate partner violence--Scotland.
Classification: LCC KD7975 .W54 2023 | DDC 345.42/0253--dc23/eng/20220924
LC record available at https://lccn.loc.gov/2022036801

ISBN: 978-0-367-19350-8 (hbk)
ISBN: 978-1-032-42287-9 (pbk)
ISBN: 978-0-429-20184-4 (ebk)

DOI: 10.4324/9780429201844

Typeset in Bembo
by MPS Limited, Dehradun

For Nina and Milto.
I hope that you are both still dancing.

CONTENTS

ACKNOWLEDGEMENTS

Firstly, I would like to thank my interviewees: the survivors, judges, police and domestic abuse advisers who gave up their time so generously. I am grateful to them all, but I am especially grateful to the survivors of abuse who were so bravely willing to talk about their experiences with me.

I owe the most enormous debt to the supervisors of the PhD thesis that inspired this book: Professor Heather Keating and Dr Tanya Palmer. They were patient, persistent, encouraging and demanded the highest standards while letting me find my own way through. Thank you also to my examiners Professor Mark Walters and Professor Vanessa Munro. They were tough – and right – and I am grateful.

I have also been lucky enough to receive significant help and support from academics, lawyers, and activists along the way. Thank you to Dr Marsha Scott (Chief Executive, Scottish Women's Aid) for being so generous with her time, and telling it like it is, Dr Katrin Hohl (City, University of London) and Professor Eugene McLaughlin (City, University of London) for their friendship and constant help and support. Thank you to my colleagues at The City Law School: Professor Richard Ashcroft for his unflappable leadership; Dr John Stanton, Dr Kyle Murray and Dr Maria Kendrick for making everything more fun and to Dr Jonathan Garabette and Colin Passmore for their invaluable professional expertise. Most importantly, thank you to Professor Evan Stark: for friendship, book lists, laughter, 'e-companionship', and generally for pushing me to achieve more than I initially imagined I could.

I would like to thank my friends: firstly and most importantly my London tribe – Anna Minton, Alexander Sainsbury, Gaby Feldman, Jessica Frankopan, Jess Wren, Kate Bone, Patrick Carpenter, Sophie Goodhart and Zoe Burnett – connect me with who I really am. I am grateful to my Sussex sisters – Elly, Lucy, Sally and Tori – for dog walks, companionship, and distraction at the more intense parts of the research journey. Also, not forgetting the overseas contingent: Andy (Boston), Maia

(New York) Jordi (Bangkok) and Kate (Ibitha), and the Hac crew Tim, Giles, Tom, Alex G, Russell ... for keeping me dancing.

I finally want to thank my family: Ken Donner for proofreading services, especially with an early draft of chapter 3, which was particularly helpful as it went on to form the basis of my first publication; ED for invaluable technical support; Barbara Donner, Sue Stansmore, Sebastian and Rose Wiener for essential emotional support and general encouragement. Last of all I want to thank my husband, Barnaby Wiener. He will never read this book, but without him it would not have been written. I dedicate it to him.

PREFACE

Professor Evan Stark

Cassandra Wiener's *Coercive Control and the Criminal Law* compares the application of the new paradigm of abuse to criminal justice reform in England/Wales and Scotland. She traces the differences in approach to the political context in each country, particularly the devolution in Scotland that allowed a fortuitous alignment between activists, women's policy concerns and the opportunities for police and justice reform, and asks how these differences affect the response to survivors. Her analysis explains an unusually positive outcome of our work, when the political stars are aligned, justice outcomes for women improve. Absent these conditions, change is likely to be incremental. This book takes a critical step towards comprehensive social reform.

Starting in the 1970s and building in a groundswell since decades of grassroots pressure worldwide forced governments in dozens of countries to assume responsibility for protecting women from violence in their personal lives. But by 2010, it had become apparent that aggressive law-enforcement was insufficient. Though England was spending more on domestic violence policing annually than on National Defense, for example, abuse in the population continued to increase.[1] Advocacy organizations representing abused women such as Refuge and Women's Aid also pointed to another paradox, that among millions of arrests, only a tiny proportion resulted in a conviction for a crime or a sentence. The criminal justice system had become a revolving door through which the same abusive men passed back into their homes and communities. Abuse remained widespread, ongoing and devastating. These problems can be traced to the restricted definition of the abuse problem as a domestic or partner assault. Since the crimes for which offenders are arrested and charged bear only a slight resemblance to the extensive harms they inflict on victims, criminal justice expenditures on domestic violence are ineffective. In response, we proposed to supplant the prevailing definition of abuse with "coercive control", a serious crime that reflects the scope, duration and consequence of the abuse most victimized women experience and report.

The campaign to publicise coercive control was successful. In December of 2012, the Home Secretary Theresa May, called for a national consultation on the proper definition of domestic abuse. Davina James Hanman, Director of Against Woman Abuse, in London, and I submitted a definition that was selected as the "New Cross-Governmental Definition of Domestic Violence" for England/Wales. This 'Working Definition' explicitly identified coercive control as a form of partner abuse alongside domestic violence, the first formal recognition of coercive control by a major government. The Working Definition recognized coercive control as a "course of conduct" (or 'pattern of incidents of controlling, coercive or threatening behavior, violence or abuse'). *Coercion* is defined broadly as encompassing psychological, physical, sexual, financial and emotional abuse. The Working Definition also adapted my view that the harmful nature of controlling behavior lies in making a person subordinate and dependent, isolating them from sources of support, exploiting their resources for personal gain, depriving them of the means needed for independence, resistance and escape and regulating their everyday lives.

From 2012 to 2014, the Working Definition replaced more than 20 other conflicting definitions that guided the funding and delivery of services to abuse victims throughout Britain. Applying the Working Definition to work with abused women and children immediately broadened the scope of assessment with women to consider a range of harms in addition to violence, look at abuse historically, as a "course of conduct" rather than a single event, like an assault, and to consider the effects of criminal conduct on the victim's rights, liberties and standing as a person as well as physical and psychological effects. Service providers welcomed the Working Definition because it focused attention on facets of their experience with abused women that were already at the periphery of their vision.

Theresa May called a second consultation in 2014, this time, to consider 'whether we should create a specific offence that captures patterns of coercive and controlling behaviour in intimate relationships in line with the Government's non-statutory definition of domestic abuse'.[2] Since the original non-statutory definition referenced here included 'financial, sexual, emotional and physical abuse' as well as isolation, exploitation, deprivation, regulation and making persons 'subordinate,' at the onset of negotiations, a broad type of offense was one option.

Wiener makes a convincing case that this second consultation never seriously considered a broadly worded offense. Suffice it to say here that the new law enacted as 'coercive control' (s 76) was written not as a "bespoke" offense to encompass the pattern of abusive behaviour described in my book but to 'fill a gap in the law – behaviour that we regard as abuse but that did not amount to violence'.[3] In a word, coercive control in England was downsized as "psychological abuse".

Had legal reform ended here, Wiener's monograph would remain an elegant case study with none of the scope or insight afforded by comparison. Fortunately, in no small part in response to the limits Wiener among others had identified in s 76, the

Domestic Abuse (Scotland Act) 2018 created a bespoke offense that specified multiple elements of coercive control, subsumed violence and sexual assault along with controlling behaviour and psychological abuse not currently crimes, extended coverage to former partners, stiffened the top sentence and shifted the weight of evidence to the perceived intent of the offender.

Wiener's monograph presents argument and evidence to support her preference for the Scottish approach. More will be needed before this law becomes permanent. Meanwhile, England can catch up: as victims, police and judges there attempt to use s 76 to manage stalking, sexual abuse, financial exploitation and other elements of coercive control that currently fall outside its purview, greater reform is likely in that country. Wiener's optimism about the prospects for reform in Scotland is refreshing. But even more endearing is her sociohistorical analysis, particularly of how devolution in 1999 allowed 'previously unacknowledged differences between UK jurisdictions in relation to the experience of social problems and the organisation of policy responses to them'[4] to come to the fore. Here, it seems to me, lies the great strength of the book as (feminist) policy analysis. A distinctly Scottish approach to domestic abuse emerged because devolution allowed it to emerge, by allowing elements of the judiciary, the police, the Procurator Fiscal (State Attorney), the women's sector and newly elected members of a supportive Scottish Parliament to work together to prioritise violence against women. In particular the women's sector moved to implement a national partnership approach which, crucially, was based on gendered understandings of domestic abuse. The long-term verdict of the most ambitious effort yet to translate coercive control into the criminal law remains outstanding. But the decentralized approach Wiener features provides an intriguing template for enacting policies elsewhere, particularly in countries like the United States, China or Canada, where local sentiment for gender equity is strong but overall support is not.

I urge readers to mind Wiener's two caveats. The first concerns turning to criminalization of abuse as a path to equity. The State to which we turn for protection is a key source of the inequality and discrimination that underlie women's susceptibility to abuse in the first place. She is also aware that involvement with the criminal justice system is not for all women or equally benign for classes of women whose status is already precarious, immigrants or people of color, for instance. The fact remains – reform is a critical piece of the equity agenda that helps to open up women's opportunities for jobs, housing, health and justice. Wiener's underlying point remains sound. Criminal justice involvement and court protection can be an important step for many women. The moments captured in this book thus have a historical and practical significance in the context of the ongoing reform agenda. Unfortunately, it is a precarious time for women's equity around the world, and this reform agenda has never been more important.

Notes

1 Syliva Walby and Jude Towers, 'Measuring Violence to End Violence; Mainstreaming Gender' (2017) 1(1) Journal of Gender Based Violence 11.
2 Home Office, 'Strengthening the Law on Domestic Abuse: A Consultation' [2014] 5 available at <https://www.gov.uk/government/uploads/system/uploads/attachment_data/file/344674/Strengthening_the_law_on_Domestic_Abuse_-_A_Consultation_WEB.PDF> accessed 30 June 2022.
3 Attorney General Robert Buckland, HC Deb, 20 January 2015, Vol 591, Col 172.
4 Michele Burman and Jenny Johnstone, 'High Hopes? The Gender Equality Duty and Its Impact on Responses to Gender-Based Violence' (2015) 43(1) Policy & Politics 45, 46.

INTRODUCTION

Assessing Coercive Control Law Reform

In early 2013, Rob Titchener, a "tall dark and handsome" dairy farmer arrived in Ambridge. He started an affair with Helen Archer – and began the controversial storyline of the usually staid and very popular BBC Radio Four drama, "The Archers", that 'gripped the UK' for three and a half years.[1] The portrayal of Rob's torturous gaslighting of Helen culminated when Helen "snapped" and stabbed Rob in their family home. Helen was arrested, charged and tried by jury in a Sunday night special episode in September 2016,[2] when the programme was extended to an hour for the first time in the drama's 65-year history. The dramatic Sunday night conclusion – the jury acquitted Helen because of the history of Rob's controlling abuse – prompted a fund-raising campaign, 'Because for every fictional Helen, there are real ones',[3] that raised over £200,000 for domestic abuse charities. The Chief Executives of the two leading women's sector organisations, Sandra Horley (Refuge) and Polly Neate (Women's Aid) made supportive statements, with Horley commenting that 'This story line has saved lives as women reach out and ask for help', and Polly Neate talking about 'the Archers effect' in relation to the 20% increase in calls to the National Domestic Abuse Helpline.[4] There was even a supportive statement from the Prime Minister's Office.[5]

While Helen and Rob's story played out in homes across the country, coercive control laws were making their way through the UK Parliament. On December 27, the Serious Crime Act 2015 received Royal Assent. The Serious Crime Act 2015, s 76 ('section 76') made 'controlling or coercive behaviour' a criminal offence for the first time in England and Wales. The other UK jurisdictions (Northern Ireland and Scotland) and Ireland have followed suit. Now other jurisdictions around the world including New South Wales,[6] South Australia,[7] Hawaii and California,[8] to name but a few, are considering the same.

This is therefore an exciting time for lawyers, policy makers and activists with an interest in domestic abuse law reform. The criminalisation of coercive control

DOI: 10.4324/9780429201844-1

in the United Kingdom and Ireland has been the focus of considerable international attention. It has generated complex questions about the "best" way to criminalise domestic abuse – for example, how do you draft a law that accurately captures a phenomenon as slippery as coercive control? Should new law sit alongside or replace existing laws on interpersonal violence? Is, in fact, 'more law' the answer at all?[9] These are difficult questions, and despite the international focus on coercive control, there is as yet little in the public policy or academic domain which answers them. This book addresses that gap.

Why More Law?

I begin from the practical premise that using the criminal justice system as a response to domestic abuse is necessary, in part because it has the potential to represent an important safety point for vulnerable people. This is especially important in the context of a regime which, historically, has victimised rather than supported those in need of help. This second layer of victimisation, (inflicted by the criminal justice system), took place despite the fact that there has always been a criminal law infrastructure available for the prosecution of some aspects of domestic abuse. Offences such as assault and battery, actual bodily harm and grievous bodily harm, murder, manslaughter, indecent assault and rape outside of marriage[10] were and are available to the police in the context of domestic abuse as well as in non-domestic contexts. But, even in the early 1990s in the United Kingdom, the police were not always willing or able to respond to calls for help. This indifference needs to be understood in the context of unprecedented criminal justice expansion: against the backdrop, in other words, of an era in which the growth in general rates of incarceration were accelerating to a troubling degree.[11] Even during this period of heightened criminal justice activity PC Fromer, who began his career in the police in 1988, summed up the former approach to me as, 'it was literally like you turn up, somebody's got a bloody nose, I'm not interested thank you very much'.[12]

The story of the women's sector's success in addressing what was a disinterested and unresponsive criminal justice system is well known. Reform to sexual offences law in 1992 in England and Wales (and marginally earlier in Scotland), for example, meant that the law no longer recognised a private realm in which a man is free to rape his wife.[13] Or in fact in which to beat her[14] – instead, a Home Office Circular was issued (60/1990) that advised police to treat "domestic violence" as they would any other violent crime.[15] There is now a lively literature around the question of whether the women's sectors' success in this regard represents a welcome or unwelcome contribution to the ever-expanding punitive state. For those for whom this development is unwelcome, 'carceral creep'[16] describes the increasing readiness of governments around the world to take steps to strengthen or replace existing laws on domestic abuse. There is a structural paradox, it is argued, inherent in what is essentially an alignment between those who work for the emancipation of women and the 'state's most masculinist repressive arm'.[17]

I recognise the importance of understanding how women (and men) from diverse backgrounds engage with the criminal law. I am not advocating criminal justice as a route to address broader issues of gender equality,[18] or that criminalising coercive control is in any way a 'quick fix policy option'; the law is a blunt instrument when it comes to achieving social change.[19] Moreover, I accept that asking police for help is not an ideal or even a possible route for many women.[20] Nevertheless, I think it is important to make the point that we are yet to find safe, power-informed alternatives to criminal justice for the victims of domestic abuse. There are suggestions of alternative strategies in the form of transformative justice and restorative justice initiatives.[21] But these have not yet been suitably adapted for use in the context of coercive control, as the safety of using such methods in the context of an abusive and intimate power imbalance is yet to be conclusively established.[22] For the most part this book does not engage with that debate. Instead I take the view that 'more law' should instead be framed as 'different law' – that better understandings of domestic abuse allow us to work for an improved rather than an increased criminal justice response – and that until there are safe alternatives, 'different law' is better than no law at all.

The recognition that coercive control is domestic abuse at its most insidious, in terms of the cost to society and the harm to the victim, is now well supported by the research literature.[23] The cost to society is calamitous however it is "measured" – in terms of its impact on children,[24] on victims' mental health,[25] or in economic terms (estimated at £15.7 billion per year in 2012,[26] and at £66 billion by the Home Office in 2016/7).[27] The financial costs are therefore significant. But, as I show in the next chapter, these pale in comparison to the qualitative harms caused to victims of abuse. The links between coercive control and death are also strong.[28] The most recent figures show that domestic homicides are at an all-time high, and that up to three women lose their lives in this way in England and Wales each week.[29] Not well reported, is that between four and ten victims of domestic abuse in England and Wales take their own lives every week.[30]

In the context of the magnitude of the damage, it is not surprising that the criminalisation of coercive control is moving up policy agendas around the world. It is becoming apparent that the unique qualities of the behviours in, and the harm caused by, coercive control require a bespoke criminal justice approach. And this response needs to sit on the shoulders of specific, appropriate and functioning criminal law doctrine. This is because the criminal law defines what is, and is not, relevant from a criminal justice perspective.[31] One of its most important functions, therefore, is the correct labelling of a crime.[32] It is difficult to label domestic abuse correctly in law without a consideration of coercive control.

Correct labelling facilitates other important improvements, both practical and normative, for the policing and prosecution of coercive control. Domestic abuse is now considered to be an ordinary – and significant – part of the work of the police.[33] Evan Stark observed that the activation of a criminal justice response from the 1970s onwards 'had created a revolving door for a class of chronic of-fenders'.[34] The criminalisation of coercive control allows police and the Crown Prosecution Service to be more efficient with the time and resources that are allocated for this part of their work, by allowing them to treat repeated offences against a victim as a serious crime even when the individual acts themselves may not appear serious. Police and prosecutors respond positively to the opportunity to deal with some of the chronic offenders in their caseloads, and to the ability to take action in the face of serious harm (such as psychological abuse and control) that have not hitherto been actionable. As one Detective Chief Inspector said to me: 'This should be a fantastic new story. And it is. We have got a piece of law that now lets us deal with some of the most nasty people that you could come across'.[35]

There are other practical advantages. I have mentioned the increasing re-cognition of the links between coercive control and homicide[36] – its crim-inalisation therefore offers police valuable tools at a specific point in time when the ability to remove a dangerous perpetrator from a volatile situation can be a life-saving device. More generally speaking, prosecuting coercive control in theory allows for better ongoing safeguarding practice, encouraging more reliable risk assessment practice by the police. It has the potential to remove the illusion, so often present in policing models with an incident-specific focus, that victims of control exercise autonomy "between" episodes by "choosing" to stay, and instead could allow for a risk assessment with a more appropriate orientation to the on-going entrapment experienced by victims of coercive control.

Finally, the criminalisation of coercive control carries an important symbolic message, which has a particular significance in this context. The gaslighting tactics of a controlling regime such as that imposed by Rob Titchener in The Archers story line are a focus in the next chapter. But in the context of behaviour patterns which frequently persuade a victim that it is all her fault, or that she is "going mad", the normative function of criminal censure is of special value. Acknowledging the wrong of domination in personal life in this way sets up a clear counter to the gaslighting that has been in many cases been drip fed over long periods of time. Jen, an Independent Domestic Violence Advisor (IDVA) that I spoke to when researching this book, explains it like this:

> For our sector, it's absolutely a gift because we are now able to turn around to our survivors and say: this is a criminal offence. So it values and puts an evidence-base underneath what they are experiencing. "It is a criminal offence that he was behaving like that." It is just so valuable to us.[37]

The public message contained within, 'It is a criminal offence that he was be-having like that', gives the survivors the possibility of a healthy world view at a time when the very way that they see the world is under attack. The criminal law in this case, as well as containing a warning for potential perpetrators of abuse, allows the victim to tell a different (healthier) story about the abuse she has ex-perienced. IDVAs tell us this is crucial to the recovery process.

The Reform Agenda

As I said above, since at least 2012 a view has been developing in governmental and policy circles that acknowledging coercive control might necessitate some changes in the criminal law used to prosecute it. This sat alongside the recognition that the prevalence of domestic abuse is still unacceptably high. The Office for National Statistics figures show that recorded rates of domestic abuse in England and Wales remain stubbornly high, despite rates of other, related types of crime, (for example, violent crime that is not domestic), continuing to fall. The most recent published figures record an estimated 2.3 million victims of domestic abuse in the year ending March 2021, a figure which Home Office statisticians estimate has remained relatively stable over the last five years.[38] At stated above, recent domestic homicide figures from 2019 are also, unfortunately, at their highest level for five years.[39]

A key difficulty revealed by the statistics is the so-called justice gap.[40] Despite improvements in the criminal justice process, there is a shortfall between estimates of abuse and the number of cases in the legal system.[41] Furthermore, the proportion of cases in the system that result in conviction is very small.[42] While it is clear that this problem remains, there is not an agreed consensus on how best to tackle it, or even from a more systemic perspective, why it persists. But it became increasingly clear through the 2000s that the problem might be at least in part the criminal law itself.[43] Accompanying process driven reforms, in other words, was a growing recognition in the academic and policy/think tank communities of the inadequacy of the criminal law itself in the context of domestic abuse.

Stark published the first edition of his book, *Coercive Control*, in 2007[44] and reinforced what others were also saying, that there are some types of domestic abuse that are *not* just like any other crime. The incident focused nature of the parts of the criminal law that were most often used to prosecute domestic abuse do not "fit" with coercive control, which is a pattern of behaviour that develops over time.[45] The Protection from Harassment Act 1997 was, (before the implementation of specific coercive control legislation), the only piece of criminal legislation in England and Wales that was intended to apply to courses of conduct rather than one-off incidents in this context. However, there was resistance to its use in conjunction with the prosecution of domestic abuse: it was held by the Court of Appeal (*Curtis, Widdows*) that it does not apply in the case where the abuser and the survivor are sharing a living space.[46]

Those two cases, *Curtis* and *Widdows*, in 2010 and 2011 respectively, (which the Government later described as 'unhelpful'),[47] deserve more attention than they get and I analyse them in chapter 3. It is thanks at least in part to these judgments that in 2012, the year before the beginning of The Archers story line referred to above, the UK Government asked the policy development think-tank, The Centre for Social Justice, to review how the response to domestic abuse could be improved. One of its key conclusions was to agree with Stark: the legislative position was inadequate. Its report concluded:

> Fundamentally the law and legal system were not designed with domestic abuse in mind and they still both misapply understandings of other sorts of crime to it … . As the law emphasises incidents, rather than patterns of behaviour, it fails to give adequate recognition to the serious wrongdoing inherent in strategic patterns of control and subjugation.[48]

Three years later, as Rob Titchener's abuse of Helen Archer was reaching its grisly climax, section 76 came into force in England and Wales making 'controlling or coercive behaviour in an intimate or family relationship' a criminal offence, and carrying a penalty of up to five years in prison. In January 2019 Ireland followed suit – the Domestic Violence Act (IR) 2018, s 39 mirrors section 76. Neither of these pieces of law addresses the 'fundamental' point made by the Centre for Social Justice report. Instead, both of these two offences are best understood as parts of a patchwork – coercive control is constructed as psychological abuse, and the inability of the criminal law to prosecute such non-physical abuse is perceived as a "gap" which the new coercive control law is designed to "patch".

Another three years later, Scotland did things very differently. The Domestic Abuse (Scotland) Act 2018 (the DASA) came into force in April 2019. The DASA is not a patch. Instead, it is an overhaul that reflects a paradigm shift: it creates a whole new domestic abuse offence with coercive control at its centre. Finally, Northern Ireland followed Scotland, also creating a new offence with the Domestic Abuse and Civil Proceedings Act 2021.

Section 76 and the DASA are thus used throughout this book to be representative of two very different responses to the challenge of capturing coercive control in the criminal law. Neither statute is perfect, and both are a product of the socio-political conditions that produced them. This book therefore investigates section 76 and the DASA from a doctrinal and a socio-legal perspective. I use the rest of this chapter to explain in more detail how this is done.

My Approach

While the criminalisation of coercive control is being considered by governments around the world, the pioneering steps taken by the jurisdictions of the United Kingdom, and by Ireland, are a relatively recent development. There is not much doctrinal or socio-legal exploration of how these different reforms have played out. This book seeks to address that gap first and foremost by investigating the impact that a recognition of coercive control has on the policing and prosecution of domestic abuse with a view to understanding what this means for the survivors it is meant to protect. With that as the general focus, in particular I drill down to investigate:

1. What was the context for reform in England/Wales and Scotland and why has this produced two such different approaches?

2. What impact does the difference in approach have on the efficacy of the criminal justice response and
3. What does this mean for campaigners who are interested in domestic abuse law reform?

The research was conducted over a four-year period and had three different elements: empirical work, observation and case review and doctrinal research. For the empirical work, I identified four different respondent categories as sources of useful data: survivors, IDVAs, police and the judiciary. I ran interviews and focus groups with survivors and IDVAs, around ten interviews in total that lasted from between one and two hours, in various locations across the United Kingdom. Eight IDVAs and five survivors attended two separate focus groups. This work yielded rich data that allowed me insight into the nature of coercive control – it was deliberately not intended to generate insight that was generalisable in the manner of quantitative research.[49] Instead, the insight into the architecture and impact of coercive control was used to inform my assessment of the efficacy of the law being used to prosecute it.

I used interviews with police (20) and judges (7 – including 4 Crown Court Judges in England and 3 Sheriffs in Scotland), to contextualise my assessment of the doctrinal implications of the criminal law used to prosecute domestic abuse and coercive control. I also ran a focus group for senior police. Fortuitously, (this was not planned), I ended up working with police and the judiciary from the same location in England. This meant that I was able to speak, in two instances, to both the police officer in charge of a case and the Crown Court Judge who presided over it. This generated unique insight into how the different parts of the criminal justice process are fitting together in the context of section 76.

The observations that I had planned were unfortunately impeded by the Covid-19 pandemic. In order to enrich the study further, I wanted to observe several trials, both in England and Scotland, but as court business increasingly moved online from September 2020 this became difficult to arrange. I managed one English trial, and two Scottish, (one pre the DASA, and one post), before September 2020. As section 76 has now been in force for over five years I have been able, however, to supplement trial observations in England/Wales by conducting an extensive search into the early reported cases. The majority of these cases involve sentencing appeals which illuminate how judges in the lower courts are conceptualising section 76 alongside existing offences, one of the key areas of difficulty for the courts that emerged when researching this book.

Finally, the doctrinal review of the existing legal infrastructure in England/Wales and section 76 and the DASA was contextualised with a socio-legal analysis of conditions that lead up to the reforms. This allowed me to understand how and why the reforms were different, and also to assess the repercussions of those differences for the prosecution of abuse.

How the Book Is Organised

Chapter 1 introduces the reader to the theory and practice of coercive control. This ordering is intentional: the normative and descriptive power of the criminal law is well recognised. It is important to establish what coercive control *is* as far as possible *outside* of the domain of the criminal law before assessing (in chapters 2, 3, 4, 5 and 6) to what extent it is properly captured *by* the criminal law. For the theory of coercive control I draw on the academic literature, and in particular the work of Stark[50] and Mary Ann Dutton and Lisa Goodman.[51] As far as possible, my exploration of the practice of coercive control is done from the perspective of the survivors and IDVAs that I worked with when researching this book.

Chapters 2, 3, 4, 5 and 6 then turn to the criminal law in England and Wales, and Scotland. Chapters 2, 3 and 4 tell the story of why a recognition of coercive control matters via an analysis of the pre-section 76 legislative regime. Reform of the criminal law is never a straight forward exercise. Deborah Tuerkheimer describes the way that reality comes to 'bear on legal structures' via a series of 'pressure points'.[52] She says:

> There is both movement and resistance on the part of legal structures subjected to the force of lived experience. Each (movement/resistance) reveals the defects of structures left intact, the remaining doctrinal patchwork a testament to the power of incompatible truths.[53]

Chapters 2, 3 and 4 therefore provide a detailed review of the 'movement and resistance' that led to the construction of section 76 in England and Wales. In these three chapters, I show how each of the three pieces of legislation that were and still are currently used by police and prosecutors in England and Wales have shown themselves to be inadequate – 'defective' – in light of what we now understand about the lived experience of survivors of coercive control (as expressed in chapter 1). I also explain why a recognition of coercive control from a criminal justice perspective is essential for an improved policing response to abuse.

Chapter 5 tracks the passage of section 76 through Parliament, reviews how section 76 is constructed and concludes with an assessment of how it is being implemented. I argue that section 76 itself can only properly be understood as one part of Tuerkheimer's 'doctrinal patchwork'. While section 76 is a progressive and significant step, it is also one which has inadvertently accelerated the "fragmentation" of coercive control into its constituent parts, from a legislative perspective. The new, legal, definition of domestic abuse set out in the Domestic Abuse Act 2021, section 1 cements this fragmentation approach, as I explain in this chapter. My review of the implementation of section 76 suggests that this process of fragmentation has meant that the criminal law still struggles to properly describe or adequately capture the realities of coercive control. This in turn creates safeguarding, evidentiary, narrative and victim-validation limitations that are still, in England and Wales, interfering with the Criminal Justice System response to domestic abuse.

Chapter 6 then looks at the position in Scotland. The socio-political situation in Scotland is very different: devolution in 1999 allowed 'previously un-acknowledged differences between UK jurisdictions in relation to the experience of social problems and the organisation of policy responses to them' to come to the fore.[54] A distinctly Scottish approach to domestic abuse therefore emerged as devolution allowed for an accompanying decentralisation of policy – allowing the women's sector and newly elected members of a supportive Scottish Parliament to work together to prioritise violence against women.[55] In particular the women's sector moved to implement a national partnership approach which, crucially, was based on *gendered* understandings of domestic abuse. The DASA was crafted on the back of this partnership, and represents the most ambitious effort yet to translate coercive control into the criminal law. The gendered understanding of abuse that is reflected in the Act addresses many of the issues raised by the analysis in chapters 2, 3 and 4 of this book.

The conclusion reflects back on the project, and draws together the key findings from the analysis of the lived experience of domestic abuse, and of ap-proaches to domestic abuse law reform taken by England and Wales, and Scotland over the last six years.

Definitions

Definitions in this area are complicated. Domestic abuse, for the purpose of this book, is physical, sexual and/or psychological abuse between people who are in (or who have been in) an intimate relationship. Coercive control is a type of domestic abuse. Domestic abuse and coercive control are therefore not the same thing, and this distinction – between domestic abuse and coercive control – is the focus of examination in the next chapter. While I recognise that, unfortunately, women also abuse men, government statistics now confirm what women's sector research has always suggested – that the perpetrators of coercive control are almost always men.[56] For this reason I have chosen to focus on male perpetrators of abuse for this book. Furthermore, I recognise that coercive control takes place within same-sex relationships but also that research suggests that this kind of abuse is qualitatively and quantitatively different.[57] My focus is on heterosexual couples and I recognise this as an explicit limitation of this research project.

Two further definitions are central to this project. "Victim" is the word most often used in the criminal justice literature to describe people who have suffered as a result of another's criminal behaviour, but it has some unhelpful connotations. To describe all people who have experienced abuse generically as "victims" is not appropriate. Debates over the language of "victim" versus "survivor" have been going on for some time.[58] I recognise that coercive control is a direct attack on agency. The term "victim" suggests passivity that my time spent with survivors showed me does not adequately capture the experiences of people who have been abused. Although it could be said that "survivor" suggests resolution (of the abuse) as a threshold for qualification (as a survivor),[59] due to the special sensitivity around the idea of agency in relation to coercive control, I prefer "survivor" and use it wherever possible. Furthermore, I recognise that not all victims survive in the sense that they do not continue to live: many victims of domestic abuse lose their lives at the hands of their abuser.[60] Domestic homicide is critically important but is not the subject of this research.

Finally, coercive control itself – the most important definition to this project – has already been introduced, above. I draw on Stark's work and on interviews and focus groups with survivors and their closest advisers to provide a detailed exposition of coercive control in the following chapter, and I explain the extent to which it does (and does not) overlap with domestic abuse. The government uses the term 'controlling or coercive behaviour' in section 76, and the fact that the government's construct of controlling or coercive behaviour is not, in fact, the same phenomenon as coercive control is critical and is reviewed in chapter 5.

Conclusion

Coercive control is a significant criminal justice problem and the harm it causes is uniquely damaging. The improvement in public understanding of coercive control as symbolised by the infamous Rob Titchener storyline, combined with awareness of prosecution difficulties resulted in changes to the criminal law at first only in England and Wales, but later throughout the United Kingdom and Ireland that are significant and progressive.

Context matters; jurisdictions work within the confines of their socio-political environments. Nevertheless the very different outcomes for reform programmes in England/Wales and Scotland show that *how the law is drafted* has significant repercussions later on for the efficacy of the police and prosecutors that work to enforce it. This matters: as Stark points out 'A true revolution requires that a credible alternative be put in place of what is torn down'.[61] Getting this right will not always be possible, and any reform program is better than no reform at all. But knowing what matters from a doctrinal perspective in the context of domestic abuse reform is important for the jurisdictions around the world who are considering this step. There will always be movement and resistance in the context of domestic abuse law reform. My hope for this book is that it will help activists and reformers everywhere as they decide what needs to change and how they will change it.

Notes

1 Nicola Slawson, 'The Archers' Verdict on Helen Titchener Concludes' *The Guardian* (12 September 2016) available at <https://www.theguardian.com/tv-and-radio/2016/sep/11/the-archers-verdict-on-helen-tichener-aired> accessed 20 July 2021.

2 Ibid.

3 Paul Kerley and Claire Bates, 'The Archers: What Effect Has the Rob and Helen Story Had?' *BBC News Magazine* (5 April 2016) available at <https://www.bbc.co.uk/news/magazine-35961057> accessed 20 July 2021.

4 Ibid.

5 Evan Stark and Marianne Hester, 'Coercive Control: Update and Review' (2019) 25(1) Violence against Women 81, 85.

6 Parliament of New South Wales, 'Coercive Control in Domestic Relationships' (June 2021) available at <https://www.parliament.nsw.gov.au/ladocs/inquiries/2626/Report %20-%20coercive%20control%20in%20domestic%20relationships.pdf> accessed 9 July 2021.

7 Amy Dale, 'Criminalising Coercion' Law Society Journal Online (1 September 2020) available at <https://lsj.com.au/articles/criminalising-coercion/> accessed 7 July 2021.

8 America's Conference to End Coercive Control, 'Hawaii and California Lead the Way Signing the First Coercive Control Bill in the Americas' available at <https://www.theacecc.com/post/hawaii-and-california-lead-the-way-signing-the-first-coercive-control-bills-in-the-americas> accessed 9 July 2021.

9 Sandra Walklate, Kate Fitz-Gibbon and Jude McCulloch, 'Is More Law the Answer? Seeking Justice for Victims of Intimate Partner Violence through the Reform of Legal Categories' (2017) Criminology & Criminal Justice 1; Julia Tolmie, 'Coercive Control: To Criminalize or Not to Criminalize?' (2018) 18(1) Criminology & Criminal Justice 50; Michelle Burman and Oona Brooks-Hay, 'Aligning Policy and Law? The Creation of a Domestic Abuse Offence Incorporating Coercive Control' (2018) 18(1) Criminology & Criminal Justice 67.

10 The ruling in *R* ([1992] 1AC 599 HL) which overturned the marital rape exemption in England and Wales was confirmed by the Criminal Justice and Public Order Act 1994, s 142 – this step is reviewed in detail in chapter four. The equivalent step in Scotland came earlier – see HM Advocate v Duffy 1983 SLT 7, HM Advocate v Paxton 1984 JC 105 and S v HM Advocate 1989 SLT 469.

11 David Garland, *The Culture of Control: Crime and Social Order in Contemporary Society* (University of Chicago Press 2001).

12 Interview with PC Fromer (13 November 2017) 2. The names of all interview respondents have been changed to protect anonymity.

13 R [1992] 1AC 599 HL.

14 Antonia Cretney and Gwynn Davis, 'Prosecuting "Domestic" Assault' [1996] Criminal Law Review 162, 162.

15 Nichola Groves and Terry Thomas, *Domestic Violence and Criminal Justice* (Routledge 2014).

16 Elizabeth Bernstein develops 'carceral feminism' as a lens through which to view feminist movements' commitment to carceral paradigms of social justice in the context of the anti-trafficking and anti-prostitution movement. See Elizabeth Bernstein, 'Militarized Humanitarianism Meets Carceral Feminism: The Politics of Sex, Rights, and Freedom in Contemporary Antitrafficking Campaigns' 2005 36(1) Signs 45. This idea is used by later writers such as Mimi Kim to apply to the violence against women movement more generally. See Mimi Kim, 'The Carceral Creep: Gender-Based Violence, Race, and the Expansion of the Punitive State, 1973–1983' (2020) 67 Social Problems 251. Sandra Walkgate and Kate Fitz-Gibbon develop this further as 'coercive control creep' in Sandra Walklate and Kate Fitz-Gibbon, 'The Criminalisation of Coercive Control: The Power of the Law' (2019) 8(4) International Journal for Crime, Justice and Social Democracy 94.

17 Kim, The Carceral Creep n16 252.

18 See Alison Phipps, *Me Not You the Trouble with Mainstream Feminism* (Manchester University Press 2020).

19 Charlotte Barlow and Sandra Walklate, *Coercive Control* (Routledge 2022).

20 Kimberle Crenshaw, 'Mapping the Margins: Intersectionality, Identity Politics, and Violence against Women of Color' 1991 (43) Stanford Law Review 1241.

21 Marilyn Fernandez, *Restorative Justice for Domestic Violence Victims* (Lexington Books 2011): but Fernandez is careful to advocate restorative justice as an add on, rather than a replacement, for traditional criminal justice processes. See also Sarah Curtis-Fawley and Kathleen Daly, 'Gendered Violence and Restorative Justice the Views of Victim Advocates' (2005) 11(5) Violence against Women 603 who conclude that while there are 'positive elements' to using restorative justice for gendered violence there are also 'concerns and reservations'.

22 Ruth Busch, 'Domestic Violence and Restorative Justice Initiatives: Who Pays if We Get It Wrong?' in Heather Strang and John Braithwaite (eds), *Restorative Justice and Family Violence* (Cambridge University Press 2002); Julie Stubbs, 'Domestic Violence and Women's Safety: Feminist Challenges to Restorative Justice' in Heather Strang and John Braithwaite (eds), *Restorative Justice and Family Violence* (Cambridge University Press 2002) and James Dignan, 'The Victim in Restorative Justice' in Sandra Walkgate (ed.) *Handbook of Victims and Victimology* (Routledge 2007).

23 Holly Johnson, 'Rethinking Survey Research on Violence against Women' in Rebecca Dobash and Russell Dobash (eds) *Rethinking Violence against Women* (Sage 1998) 23.

24 Jane Callaghan et al, 'Beyond "Witnessing": Children's Experiences of Coercive Control in Domestic Violence and Abuse' (2018) 33 Journal of Interpersonal Violence 1551. See also Susan Heward Belle, '"Exploiting the Good Mother" as a Tactic of Coercive Control: Domestically Violent Men's Assaults on Women as Mothers' (2017) 32 Journal of Women and Social Work 374 and Office for National Statistics, 'Domestic Abuse in England and Wales for the Year Ending March 2021', available at <https://www.ons.gov.uk/peoplepopulationandcommunity/crimeandjustice/articles/domesticabuseprevalenceandtrendsenglandandwales/yearendingmarch2021> accessed 1 December 2021.

25 Cathy Humphries and Ravi Thiara, 'Mental Health and Domestic Abuse: "I Call It Symptoms of Abuse"' (2003) 33 British Journal of Social Work 209.

26 Sylvia Walby, *The Cost of Domestic Violence* (Women and Equality Unit 2004) available at <www.devon.gov.uk/cost_of_dv_report_sept04.pdf> accessed 1 September 2019.

27 Rhys Oliver et al, *The Economic and Social Cost of Domestic Abuse* (Home Office 2019).

28 Jane Monckton Smith, Karolina Szymanska and Sue Haile, *Exploring the Relationship between Stalking and Homicide* (Homicide Research Group, University of Gloucestershire 2017).

29 Thomas MacIntosh and Steve Swann, 'Domestic Violence Killings Reach Five Year High' *BBC News* (13 September 2019) available at <https://www.bbc.co.uk/news/uk-49459674> accessed 6 October 2019.

30 Sylvia Walby and Jonathan Allen, 'Domestic Violence, Sexual Assault and Stalking: Findings from the British Crime Survey' (Home Office 2004) available at <http://eprints.glos.ac.uk/4553/1/NSAW%20Report%2004.17%20-%20finalsmall.pdf> accessed 7 September 2018; Jane Monkton-Smith, 'Intimate Partner Femicide: Using Foucauldian Analysis to Track an Eight Stage Progression to Homicide' (2020) 26(11) Violence against Women 1267. For the most recent intimate partner homicide statistics see Office for National Statistics, Domestic Abuse in England and Wales for the Year Ending March 2021 n24. For a more recent analysis of the links between domestic abuse and suicide see Vanessa Munro and Ruth Aitken, 'Adding Insult to Injury? The Criminal Law's Response to Domestic Abuse Related Suicide in England and Wales' (2018) 9 Criminal Law Review 732; Vanessa Munro and Ruth Aitken, 'From Hoping to Help: Identifying and Responding to Suicidality amongst Victims of Domestic Abuse' (2020) 26(1) International Review of Victimology 29.

31 Deborah Tuerkheimer, 'Recognising and Remedying the Harm of Battering: A Call to Criminalize Domestic Violence' (2004) 94(4) Journal of Criminal Law and Criminology 959, 974.

32 James Chalmers and Fiona Leverick, 'Fair Labelling in Criminal Law' (2008) 71(2) Modern Law Review 217.

33 Heather Douglas, *Women, Intimate Partner Violence, and the Law* (Oxford University Press 2021).

34 Evan Stark, 'Forward' in Evan Stark, *Coercive Control: How Men Entrap Women in Personal Life* (Oxford University Press 2022) 20.

35 Interview with Detective Chief Inspector Richards (23 March 2016) 1.

36 Jane Monkton Smith's research into the links between coercive control and homicide – see n28 – have been widely reported in the popular press: see, for eg Jane Wharton, 'Killers Follow Eight Stage Pattern of Domestic Abuse' *Metro* (30 August 2019) available at <https://metro.co.uk/2019/08/30/killers-follow-eight-stage-pattern-domestic-abuse-10655805/> accessed 26 July 2021.

37 Interview with Jen (15 January 2016) 8.

38 Office for National Statistics, Domestic Abuse 2021 n24.

39 MacIntosh and Swann, Domestic Violence Killings Reach Five Year High n29.

40 Sonia Harris-Short and Joanna Miles, *Family Law Text, Cases and Materials* (Oxford University Press 2011) 210.

41 Office for National Statistics, Domestic Abuse 2021 n24.

42 Office for National Statistics, Domestic Abuse 2021 n24; Marianne Hester and Nicole Westmarland, *Tackling Domestic Violence: Effective Interventions and Practice* (Home Office Research Study 290, Home Office 2005).

43 Tuerkheimer, Recognising and Remedying the Harm of Battering n31; Alafair Burke, 'Domestic Violence as a Crime of Pattern and Intent: An Alternative Reconceptualization' (2007) 75 George Washington Law Review 558.

44 Evan Stark, *Coercive Control: How Men Entrap Women in Personal Life* (Oxford University Press 2007).

45 Ibid.

46 *Curtis* [2010] EWCA Crim 123; *Widdows* [2011] EWCA Crim 1500. This is discussed in detail in chapter three.

47 'Even where stalking and harassment legislation may be the appropriate tool to tackle domestic abuse, Court of Appeal case law is an unhelpful barrier.' (R v Curtis 1 Cr. App. R.31, and R v Widdows (2011) 175J.P. 345).' Home Office, *Strengthening the Law on Domestic Abuse Consultation Summary of Responses* (December 2014) 11 available at <https://www.gov.uk/government/uploads/system/uploads/attachment_data/file/389002/StrengtheningLawDomesticAbuseResponses.pdf> accessed 31 July 2019.

48 Samantha Callan and Ellie Farmer, *Beyond Violence, Breaking Cycles of Domestic Abuse* (Centre for Social Justice 2012) available at <www.centreforsocialjustice.org.uk/UserStorage/pdf/Pdf%20Exec%20summaries/DA%20Exec%20Sum.pdf> accessed 1 May 2013, 24.

49 Brent Flyvbjerg, for example maintains that it is perfectly possible to draw general conclusions, even from a single case study: Brent Flyvbjerg, *Making Social Science Matter Why Social Inquiry Fails and How It Can Succeed Again* (Cambridge University Press 2011) chapter six.

50 Stark, Coercive Control n44.

51 Mary Ann Dutton and Lisa Goodman, 'Coercion in Intimate Partner Violence: Toward A New Conceptualization' (2005) 52(11/12) Sex Roles 744.

52 Tuerkheimer, Recognizing and Remedying the Harm of Battering n31 990.

53 Ibid.

54 Michele Burman and Jenny Johnstone, 'High Hopes? The Gender Equality Duty and Its Impact on Responses to Gender-Based Violence' (2015) Policy & Politics 43 (1) 45 46.

55 Burman and Brooks-Hay, Aligning Policy and Law n9.

56 The most recent Ministry of Justice quarterly statistics bulletin records that between 97% and 99% of defendants convicted of controlling or coercive behavior from

2017–2019 were male. See Office for National Statistics, 'Criminal Justice System Statistics Quarterly: December 2019' available at <https://www.gov.uk/government/statistics/criminal-justice-system-statistics-quarterly-december-2019> accessed 6 August 2021.

57 Catherine Donovan, Marianne Hester, Jonathan Holmes and Melanie McCarry, 'Comparing Domestic Abuse in Same Sex and Heterosexual Relationships' (Initial Report, University of Bristol 2006).

58 Michelle Fine, 'The Politics of Research and Activism: Violence against Women' (1989) 3 Gender and Society 549; Jenny Davis and Tony Love, 'Women Who Stay: A Morality Work Perspective' (2018) 65(2) Social Problems 251.

59 See Liz Kelly and Jill Radford, 'Sexual Violence against Women and Girls' in Russell Dobash and Rebecca Dobash (eds), *Rethinking Violence against Women* (Sage 1998) for an example of this critique of the term 'survivor'.

60 Between two and three women lose their lives each week to domestic abuse. Office for National Statistics, Domestic Abuse 2021 n24. Statistics suggested the numbers were increasing, even before lockdown: MacIntosh and Swann, Domestic Violence Killings Reach Five Year High n29.

61 Stark, Coercive Control 2022 n34 19.

Bibliography

America's Conference to End Coercive Control, 'Hawaii and California Lead the Way Signing the First Coercive Control Bill in the Americas' available at <https://www.theacecc.com/post/hawaii-and-california-lead-the-way-signing-the-first-coercive-control-bills-in-the-americas> accessed 9 July 2021.

Barlow C and Walklate S, *Coercive Control* (Routledge 2022).

Bernstein E, 'Militarized Humanitarianism Meets Carceral Feminism: The Politics of Sex, Rights, and Freedom in Contemporary Antitrafficking Campaigns' (2005) 36(1) Signs 45.

Burke A, 'Domestic Violence as a Crime of Pattern and Intent: An Alternative Reconceptualization' (2007) 75 George Washington Law Review 558.

Burman M and Brooks-Hay O, 'Aligning Policy and Law? The Creation of A Domestic Abuse Offence Incorporating Coercive Control' (2018) 18(1) Criminology & Criminal Justice 67.

Burman M and Johnstone J, 'High Hopes? The Gender Equality Duty and Its Impact on Responses to Gender-Based Violence' (2015) 43(1) Policy & Politics 45.

Busch R, 'Domestic Violence and Restorative Justice Initiatives: Who Pays if We Get It Wrong?' in Heather S and Braithwaite J (eds), *Restorative Justice and Family Violence* (Cambridge University Press 2002).

Callaghan J, Alexander J, Sixsmith J and Fellin L, 'Beyond "Witnessing": Children's Experiences of Coercive Control in Domestic Violence and Abuse' (2018) 33 Journal of Interpersonal Violence 1551. DOI: 10.1177/0886260515618946

Callan S and Farmer E, *Beyond Violence, Breaking Cycles of Domestic Abuse* (Centre for Social Justice 2012) available at <www.centreforsocialjustice.org.uk/UserStorage/pdf/Pdf%20Exec%20summaries/DA%20Exec%20Sum.pdf> accessed 1 May 2013, 24.

Chalmers J and Leverick F, 'Fair Labelling in Criminal Law' (2008) 71(2) Modern Law Review 217.

Crenshaw C, 'Mapping the Margins: Intersectionality, Identity Politics, and Violence against Women of Color' (1991) 43 Stanford Law Review 1241.

Cretney A and Davis G, 'Prosecuting "Domestic" Assault' (1996) 28(4) Criminal Law Review 162.

Curtis-Fawley S and Daly K, 'Gendered Violence and Restorative Justice The Views of Victim Advocates' (2005) 11(5) Violence against Women 603.

Dale A, 'Criminalising Coercion' Law Society Journal Online (1 September 2020) available at <https://lsj.com.au/articles/criminalising-coercion/> accessed 7 July 2021.

Davis J and Love T, 'Women Who Stay: A Morality Work Perspective' (2018) 65(2) Social Problems 251. DOI: 10.1093/socpro/spx016.

Dignan J, 'The Victim in Restorative Justice' in Walkgate S (ed.), *Handbook of Victims and Victimology* (Routledge 2007).

Dutton M and Goodman L, 'Coercion in Intimate Partner Violence: Toward A New Conceptualization' (2005) 52(11/12) Sex Roles 744.

Donovan C, Hester M, Holmes J and McCarry M, 'Comparing Domestic Abuse in Same Sex and Heterosexual Relationships' (Initial Report, University of Bristol 2006).

Douglas H, *Women, Intimate Partner Violence, and the Law* (Oxford University Press 2021).

Fernandez M, *Restorative Justice for Domestic Violence Victims* (Lexington Books 2011).

Fine M, 'The Politics of Research and Activism: Violence against Women' (1989) 3 Gender and Society 549.

Flyvbjerg B, *Making Social Science Matter Why Social Inquiry Fails and How It Can Succeed Again* (Cambridge University Press 2011).

Garland D, *The Culture of Control: Crime and Social Order in Contemporary Society* (University of Chicago Press 2001).

Groves N and Thomas T, *Domestic Violence and Criminal Justice* (Routledge 2014).

Harris-Short S and Miles J, *Family Law Text, Cases and Materials* (Oxford University Press 2011).

Hester M and Westmarland N, *Tackling Domestic Violence: Effective Interventions and Practice* (Home Office Research Study 290, Home Office 2005).

Heward Belle S, '"Exploiting the Good Mother" as a Tactic of Coercive Control: Domestically Violent Men's Assaults on Women as Mothers' (2017) 32 Journal of Women and Social Work 374.

Home Office, *Strengthening the Law on Domestic Abuse Consultation Summary of Responses* (December 2014) available at <https://www.gov.uk/government/uploads/system/uploads/attachment_data/file/389002/StrengtheningLawDomesticAbuseResponses.pdf> accessed 31 July 2019.

Humphries C and Thiara R, 'Mental Health and Domestic Abuse: "I Call It Symptoms of Abuse"' (2003) 33 British Journal of Social Work 209.

Johnson H, 'Rethinking Survey Research on Violence against Women' in Dobash R and Dobash R (eds), *Rethinking Violence against Women* (Sage 1998).

Kelly L and Radford J, 'Sexual Violence against Women and Girls' in Russell Dobash and Rebecca Dobash (eds), *Rethinking Violence against Women* (Sage 1998).

Kerley P and Bates C, 'The Archers: What Effect Has the Rob and Helen Story Had?' *BBC News Magazine* (5 April 2016) available at <https://www.bbc.co.uk/news/magazine-35961057> accessed 20 July 2021.

Kim M, 'The Carceral Creep: Gender-Based Violence, Race, and the Expansion of the Punitive State, 1973–1983' (2020) 67 Social Problems 251.

MacIntosh M and Swann S, 'Domestic Violence Killings Reach Five Year High' *BBC News* (13 September 2019) available at <https://www.bbc.co.uk/news/uk-49459674> accessed 6 October 2019.

Monckton Smith J, Szymanska K and Haile S, *Exploring the Relationship between Stalking and Homicide* (Homicide Research Group, University of Gloucestershire 2017) <http://eprints.glos.ac.uk/4553/1/NSAW%20Report%2004.17%20-%20finalsmall.pdf> accessed 7 September 2018.

Monkton-Smith J, 'Intimate Partner Femicide: Using Foucauldian Analysis to Track an Eight Stage Progression to Homicide' (2020) 26(11) Violence against Women 1267.

Munro V and Aitken R, 'Adding Insult to Injury? The Criminal Law's Response to Domestic Abuse Related Suicide in England and Wales' (2018) 9 Criminal Law Review 732.

Munro V and Aitken R, 'From Hoping to Help: Identifying and Responding to Suicidality amongst Victims of Domestic Abuse' (2020) 26(1) International Review of Victimology 29.

Office for National Statistics, 'Criminal Justice System Statistics Quarterly: December 2019' available at <https://www.gov.uk/government/statistics/criminal-justice-system-statistics-quarterly-december-2019> accessed 6 August 2021.

Office for National Statistics, 'Domestic Abuse in England and Wales for the Year Ending March 2021', available at <https://www.ons.gov.uk/peoplepopulationandcommunity/crimeandjustice/articles/domesticabuseprevalenceandtrendsenglandandwales/yearending march2021> accessed 1 December 2021.

Oliver R, Alexander B, Roe S and Wlasny M, *The Economic and Social Cost of Domestic Abuse* (Home Office 2019).

Parliament of New South Wales, 'Coercive Control in Domestic Relationships' (June 2021) available at <https://www.parliament.nsw.gov.au/ladocs/inquiries/2626/Report %20-%20coercive%20control%20in%20domestic%20relationships.pdf> accessed 9 July 2021.

Phipps A, *Me Not You the Trouble with Mainstream Feminism* (Manchester University Press 2020).

Slawson N, 'The Archers' Verdict on Helen Titchener Concludes' *The Guardian* (12 September 2016) available at <https://www.theguardian.com/tv-and-radio/2016/sep/11/the-archers-verdict-on-helen-tichener-aired> accessed 20 July 2021.

Stark E, *Coercive Control: How Men Entrap Women in Personal Life* (Oxford University Press 2007).

Stark E, 'Forward' in Evan Stark, *Coercive Control: How Men Entrap Women in Personal Life* (Oxford University Press 2022).

Stark E and Hester M, 'Coercive Control: Update and Review' (2019) 25(1) Violence against Women 81.

Stubbs J, 'Domestic Violence and Women's Safety: Feminist Challenges to Restorative Justice' in Heather Strang and John Braithwaite (eds), *Restorative Justice and Family Violence* (Cambridge University Press 2002).

Tolmie J, 'Coercive Control: To Criminalize or Not to Criminalize?' (2018) 18(1) Criminology & Criminal Justice 50.

Tuerkheimer D, 'Recognizing and Remedying the Harm of Battering: A Call to Criminalize Domestic Violence' (2004) 94(4) Journal of Criminal Law and Criminology 959.

Walby S, *The Cost of Domestic Violence* (Women and Equality Unit 2004) available at <www.devon.gov.uk/cost_of_dv_report_sept04.pdf> accessed 1 September 2019.

Walby S and Allen J, 'Domestic Violence, Sexual Assault and Stalking: Findings from the British Crime Survey' (Home Office 2004) available at <http://eprints.glos.ac.uk/4553/1/NSAW%20Report%2004.17%20-%20finalsmall.pdf> accessed 7 September 2018.

Walklate S and Fitz-Gibbon K, 'The Criminalisation of Coercive Control: The Power of the Law' (2019) 8(4) International Journal for Crime, Justice and Social Democracy 94.

Walklate S, Fitz-Gibbon K and McCulloch J, 'Is More Law the Answer? Seeking Justice for Victims of Intimate Partner Violence through the Reform of Legal Categories' (2017) 18(1) Criminology & Criminal Justice 1.

Wharton J, 'Killers Follow Eight Stage Pattern of Domestic Abuse' *Metro* (30 August 2019) available at <https://metro.co.uk/2019/08/30/killers-follow-eight-stage-pattern-domestic-abuse-10655805/> accessed 26 July 2021.

Cases

Curtis [2010] EWCA Crim 123.
Duffy [1983] SLT 7.
Paxton [1984] JC 105.
R [1992] 1AC 599 HL.
Sv HM Advocate [1989] SLT 469.
Widdows [2011] EWCA Crim 1500.

Legislation

Criminal Justice and Public Order Act 1994.
Domestic Abuse and Civil Proceedings Act 2021.
Domestic Abuse (Scotland) Act 2018.
Domestic Violence Act (IR) 2018.
The Protection from Harassment Act 1997.
Serious Crime Act 2015.

1

THE ARCHITECTURE AND PREVALENCE OF COERCIVE CONTROL SEEING WHAT IS 'INVISIBLE IN PLAIN SIGHT'[1]

Introduction: 'Because for Every Fictional Helen, There Are Real Ones'[2]

Sally Challen, a quietly spoken middle-class Surrey housewife, became in 2011 a real-life Helen Titchener, and 'one of the most reported cases of the year'.[3] On 14 August 2010, Sally prepared lunch for her husband. As he ate it in their family kitchen in the wealthy suburb of Clayton, she killed him in a frenzied attack with a claw hammer. Sally was convicted at Guildford Crown Court in June 2011. She was sentenced to 22 years imprisonment, later reduced to 18 years on appeal.

In 2017, the campaigning group Centre for Women's Justice took on her case. Their campaign drew on its similarities with the Helen story-line, 'it was dramatised very well in Helen's storyline in Radio 4's The Archers back in 2016',[4] and emphasised that Sally's "from nowhere" crime could only be understood in the context of the horrific abuse that had preceded it. It said that Sally killed Richard only after years of being abused and humiliated by him. The abuse was continuous:

> He bullied and belittled her, controlled their money and who she was friends with, not allowing her to socialise without him. But, whilst he forced strict restrictions on her behaviour, he himself, would flaunt his money, have numerous affairs and visit brothels. If she challenged him, he would turn it back on her and make her feel she was going mad.[5]

Gaslighting, economic abuse, and isolation are all hallmarks of coercive control. The Centre for Women's Justice submitted grounds of appeal highlighting new psychiatric evidence and an expert's report showing how coercive control provides a better framework for understanding Sally's out-of-character attack. Professor Evan Stark and Dr Gwen Adeshead gave expert evidence on coercive control and

DOI: 10.4324/9780429201844-2

Sally's mental health respectively at the appeal. Sally's conviction was quashed and a retrial was ordered. In June 2019, the Crown Prosecution Service decided against a retrial, accepted Sally's manslaughter plea, and substituted her sentence for one of 14 years. She walked free due to time already being served.

The Sally Challen case is an important landmark despite what it did not achieve. The Court of Appeal was clear in the judgment that, 'We must emphasise that we were not persuaded that had it stood alone the general theory of coercive control on the facts as presented to us would have afforded the appellant a ground of appeal'.[6] Coercive control was not and still is not a defence to murder. Nevertheless, the Court of Appeal *did take coercive control into account*. The hurdle for the defence in persuading the Court of Appeal that a conviction is unsafe on the grounds of new evidence is a high one, and the Centre for Women's Justice success in this regard is significant. The Court of Appeal was prepared to accept, in other words, that 'the understanding of what has been labelled "coercive control" has improved over the years, so much so that Parliament enacted section 76 of the Serious Crime Act 2015 to make it a criminal offence'.[7] It then considered that coercive control is relevant as a framework within which to understand Sally's deteriorating mental health. In this way, the door as to its relevance to the defences recognised by the criminal law could be said to have been left ajar.

Understanding of coercive control has indeed improved over the years. In this chapter, I consider coercive control from two different perspectives – theoretical/empirical (understanding coercive control) and quantitative (measuring coercive control). In other words, I answer the questions: How is a coercively controlling strategy successful? And: How present are these strategies within what we label as domestic abuse? The first question is easier to answer than the second: when considering the theory and practice of coercive control I draw on my empirical work with survivors of abuse, and also on a rich body of research detailing 'powerful, vivid accounts of sexual violence and battering relationships'.[8] But if understandings of control have improved, prevalence estimates have not. The question of how much domestic abuse is coercive control is still a challenge, as I explain in the second half of this chapter. Progress has, as Andy Myhill of the College of Policing puts it, 'stalled',[9] and until the Crime Survey of England and Wales has questions in its interpersonal violence module that more reliably capture coercive control, estimates of its prevalence are, at best, precarious.

Understanding Coercive Control

In the evidence which Stark gave to the Court of Appeal in the Sally Challen case, Stark explained that:

> In coercive control, abusers deploy a broad range of non-consensual, non-reciprocal tactics, over an extended period of time to subjugate or dominate a partner, rather than merely to hurt them physically. Compliance is achieved by making victims afraid and denying basic rights, resources and liberties

without which they are not able to effectively refuse, resist or escape demands that militate against their interests.[10]

Stark conceptualises coercive control as a 'capture crime', analogous to other capture crimes such as hostage-taking and kidnapping.[11] Using human rights discourse, Stark explains perpetrator success by their use of tools more familiar as used to break the will of kidnap victims, prisoners, hostages and prisoners of war. In this way, the gaslighting tactics of a coercively controlling regime are brought into sharp focus, dimensions of domestic abuse that Stark points out, 'have gone largely unnoticed and are not normally associated with assault'.[12] Stark therefore frames perpetrator behaviour, (including physical/sexual violence), as compliance ensuring tactics – by making victims afraid and denying basic rights, perpetrators make coercive demands which they can ensure their victims obey.

Stark's paradigm is as much about the victim's response as it is about the actions of a perpetrator. Coercive control incorporates perpetrator behaviour and victim response. The 'capture crime' perspective incorporates a victim's response to the abuse. He points out that 'thinking of women as victims of capture crimes also helps reframe their reactions'.[13] If a woman is seen pacing backwards and forwards in a small space, he suggests, you need to 'see' the jail cell to account for her behaviour. The fact that coercive control encompasses perpetrator behaviour and victim response is one of the reasons it does not easily translate, as a label, into the criminal law. The criminal law, with its distinct specificity requirements,[14] defines perpetrator behaviour and victim response separately, as two (separate) parts of an actus reus. I said in the previous chapter that I wanted to look at coercive control outside the framework of the criminal law, in order to then go on and assess its construction by/in the criminal law. As these are empirically distinct (perpetrator behaviour and harm) for ease of comparison with later criminal law definitions in this chapter I will review them in turn.

Perpetrator Behaviours

Making the Victim Afraid

The first time a perpetrator demonstrates his physical power, aggressively, is often when a victim realises how vulnerable they really are. Jessica (an Independent Domestic Violence Adviser [an IDVA]) told me the disturbing story of a client who was badly frightened on her honeymoon:

> Her story was that everything was groovy, no issues, they got married, they went on their honeymoon, and he strangled her with the bathroom towel. Really, really badly. There was a horrific, traumatic incident when he strangled her almost to death with the bathroom towel … So then after that for six years of their relationship – … he never ever again used physical violence on her but whenever there was a moment of tension, he would go

to the bathroom and he would bring out a towel, and he would put it on the table. And that was the sign: and then she would just be, like, "and then I would just give in - I would just do whatever it is he was trying to get me to do".[15]

Sexual and physical violence are not always present as perpetrator behaviours, but violence − or the fear of it − usually underpins control. It's an easy way to make a victim afraid. With fear comes credibility: when a threat is credible, a demand is coercive. For many survivors, the onset of fear comes as a transformative moment.

The towel incident is a good example of the enabling role that the onset of a demonstration of physical power can have. The strangling with the towel happened once, but the placing of the bathroom towel on the kitchen table throughout the six years of their relationship became a long-term instrument of terror with no more actual physical violence needed.

Sexual violence is used in the same way as physical violence. There can be a transformative moment; this can be a rape, or rough unwanted handling or touching, for example, and this gives credibility to later sexual demands and threats. Louise Plummer, an Australian researcher and survivor, writes of her experience of living with a coercively controlling perpetrator. She explains in detail how her recognition of what her abusive partner, Richard, was capable of gave credibility to his threats. This meant that, for the duration of their relationship, she had sex whenever and however he wanted it.

Louise explains:

> Richard seemed to believe that in order to keep me, he needed to rule me. Early in our relationship, we argued and he called me degrading names. I angrily expressed regret for becoming involved with him, and said, "You will never touch me again. Now, get out." Richard sneered, "I can fuck you whenever I want to." I raised my voice, reiterating that he should leave. Richard pushed me to the floor and sat on me, delivering repeated hard slaps across my face, and then raped me, taunting me with the fact that he could and would do what he liked, when he liked. I actually did feel like conquered property: worthless. The rape ended - at least for the time being - further talk of leaving.[16]

In this scenario, Richard makes a threat, 'I can fuck you whenever I want to', which he carries out with a violent attack. He slaps her, pushes her to the floor and then rapes her. Louise feels 'conquered' and is coerced into staying with him. For the rest of their time together Richard only needed to warn, 'don't make me come and get you', and she would submit to sex. His threat had credibility. She knew what he would do if she did not submit. The regular (unwanted) sex that they had was Richard exercising sexual control: having sex when and how he wanted.

Sally Challen had a similar story of sexual abuse. She said:

> After we returned from America Richard started calling me slut, and other horrible things. He did anally rape me a few more times. I didn't resist, I just let him do it, but it would have been clear that I didn't want it. Occasionally I tried to get out of sex, by saying that I had a headache, but he would proceed anyway. He would tell me to "Go upstairs and get ready", which would mean being clean and washed, and sometimes he would leave me waiting for ages.[17]

Most of the survivors I spoke to, (but not all), gave an account of the role that physical and/or sexual violence played in their abusive relationship as an enabler, as at least in part responsible for the fear that ensured their compliance. Aggressive physical force (whether sexual or non-sexual) gave credence to threats, much in the same way as the towel on the kitchen table in Jessica's example, the menacing, 'don't make me come and get you', in Louise's example, or Richard's, 'go upstairs and get ready', above. Violence of any kind, in other words, gives credibility to the relationship between the demand and the threat by demonstrating to the victim what can happen if she does not comply. This is what Stark refers to as the 'or else' proviso that colours every demand.[18]

In her piece 'Failing to See the Wood for the Trees', Tanya Palmer argues that sexual violation can take both 'acute' and 'chronic' forms.[19] Her intentionally medical terminology is chosen because, 'both terms have connotations of seriousness', and neither one is more serious than the other. Palmer states that she wants to 'deliberately resist placing these two types of sexual violation in a hierarchy'.[20] Palmer explains that when framing sexual violence as 'acute', she is drawing on 'medical understandings of an acute illness, symptom etc as being of rapid onset and short duration, an episode of crisis in which the patient is in serious and immediate danger, as well as more general uses of 'acute' to refer to a situation that is severe, intense and urgent'.[21] In essence she is referring to 'an identifiable event or encounter' which frames the violation of a person's sexual autonomy.[22]

Palmer articulates 'chronic' sexual violation as taking place where a victim's autonomy is 'gradually eroded over a longer period of time'.[23] A perpetrator who is expressing dominance over, and control of, his victim via what might present as "low-level" sexual violence is, with behaviour that is at once menacing and strategic, inflicting violence that is chronic. In this case, the survivor might find it difficult to isolate any one of the supposedly "low-level" attacks, rather she articulates the abuse as an everyday backdrop, as part of the fabric of her life.

Palmer and I develop Stark's model of control in the specific context of sexual abuse in our article 'Telling the Wrong Stories'[24], and point out that Louise's rape ordeal functions as both an acute incident of violation, and as part of the fabric of the chronic abuse that she was subjected to every single day. The sexual violence cemented an understanding of ownership – of the total control that Richard had over her. Louise explains how Richard 'needed to rule me', and how, after the first rape, she felt like 'conquered property: worthless'. Once ownership has been asserted, apparently "low-level" sexual violence can serve as insidious reminders. Not all of the violence that Louise experienced in the following years of her abusive relationship with Richard was as extreme, but the expression of ownership was ever-present in gestures such as forced touching/grabbing.

Stark said of Sally's experiences of anal rape that 'for me those incidents are the context within which she experiences repeated sexual aggression on his part. The staging of sex, waiting for him – she experiences that as a repetitive assault. It's an example of what I call 'rape as routine'.[25] Chronic sexual violence of this type – 'rape as routine' is no less serious than a one-off attack. In many ways it is worse, because it is experienced as a constant. Even apparently "low-level" forced touching and grabbing, when imbued with menace because of the credibility-threat nexus, is a visible manifestation of the worst kind of ever-present coercive demand. In this way, especially behaviour such as Richard's forced touching and grabbing of Louise functions as 'an assertion of ownership – a frequent reminder that her body is not her own'.[26]

I think that Palmer's concepts of 'acute' and 'chronic' violence are a helpful lens through which to understand not only the sexual but also the physical violence inflicted by perpetrators of abuse.[27] Survivors I spoke to described physical abuse that took both of these forms. Some incidents stood out as acute – one example of an incident which stood out is Jessica's story of the near strangulation with the bathroom towel. Another survivor I spoke to, Karen, remembers one or two incidents where the violence she experienced in her relationship escalated into something that she remembered in a more incident-specific way. She said: 'But the big incident that stood out for me was when I was breast feeding my boys, and he head butted me'.[28]

Karen also described chronic, ongoing physical abuse that accompanied life as a kind of backdrop. Jessica described this as 'the usual'. She said, 'there was occasionally hitting and punching – the usual'.[29] Describing this kind of physical abuse as 'the usual' suggests that it is inconsequential or not serious, which is where Palmer's construction of violence that is 'chronic' is particularly helpful.[30] Karen, for example, interjected her narrative with almost casual references to physical abuse. She said, 'But then we would be walking on the road and he would just punch me in the face',[31] and, 'He could just be violent for no apparent … he could just be violent'.[32]

Karen described how her partner would decide on her supper, and if she refused to eat it immediately he would shout at her and throw it at her.[33] All of these examples, the punching in the face, the violence for no reason and the throwing of the dinner plate are typical of how survivors can articulate day-to-day physical abuse, in a general way, as a backdrop that had to be accepted and navigated. This is no less serious – when seen as part of a chronically abusive strategy its significance as a constant chipping of a survivor's autonomy comes into focus.

Denying Basic Rights, Resources and Liberties

Perpetrators deny survivors' rights, resources and liberties that in "normal" life are taken for granted. This makes them less able to resist or escape. The demands that take these rights, resources and liberties away are myriad and bespoke. To the outsider, they can seem bizarre. One IDVA I interviewed told me about a survivor whose partner hid gold coins around the house before he left for work in the morning. When he returned home in the evening he held out his hand for the coins. If she had not found them all, it meant she had not cleaned the house properly and she was punished.[34] The demands can be humiliating. A police officer I spoke to, Detective Constable Stephens, described an incident that had been attended by a colleague. The victim had reported a domestic rape, and the colleague had gone to the victim's house to interview her. The interview took place in the kitchen, and Detective Constable Stephen's colleague noticed a dog bowl on the floor by the fridge. She noticed that the victim did not appear to have a dog, so she asked about the bowl. The victim explained that that was where she ate her supper.[35] Denying this victim the right that most of us take for granted – the ability to eat from a plate at a table – acted as a continuous reminder of the perpetrator's dominance, a visceral, humiliating and continual reminder of the impossibility of resistance.

Denying survivors access to family and friends is another tool – it has a profound and long-term effect on a survivor in the way that it increases her vulnerability. Without support, it is difficult for her to resist the worldview that he has and wants her to share.[36] This has emotional and cognitive repercussions that are discussed in relation to the survivor response, below.

Denying survivors the freedom to go about their daily lives without surveillance takes away another "for granted" freedom – which adds credibility to the perpetrator threat. The survivor has reason to be fearful that her partner will know if she disobeys his demands because she knows that he is spying on her. Technology is the perpetrator's friend. IDVAs I spoke to such as Annie spoke about the technology available to perpetrators for surveillance purposes as one of the biggest challenges facing survivor support workers.[37] Survivors were monitored everywhere, at the pub, at work; one perpetrator even monitored the time his victim spent on the toilet.[38] Some form of surveillance was present in the lives of all of the survivors that I interviewed. As with everything else, it can seem innocuous if it is not contextualised. Kim explained how she herself did not realise that she was being stalked to start with. She said, 'He would just appear where I was, so I wasn't actually aware, prior to that, that he was actually doing that?' She then went on to explain:

> If I had planned to meet anyone from work, which didn't happen very often, because I chose not to do that, he would – I mean a friend reminded me recently about it – he would just – then if we went to the pub, or wherever we were, he would then be there. He would then watch me.[39]

Post Separation Abuse

The sensation of being watched, as with so much of the coercive behaviours, does not end with the relationship. Kim spoke about the post-separation presence of her former partner:

> And there were incidents at the house that were happening to make me feel scared, I couldn't prove it was him. I'd come home and there was a big footprint at the front door, it was like someone had kicked the door, because it was like rubber. And in the middle of the night, I've got a little dog, and he was barking, and I came downstairs and the back door was open. And things like my washing line - I really like hanging washing out, and he knew that, and the washing line had been cut.[40]

Her relationship with her abusive partner had ended, but he still knew where she lived, and knew enough about her personally to continue to terrorise her. He knew, for example, that she likes to hang out her washing, so the cutting of the washing line had a personalised (frightening) significance. It is interesting that survivors are aware that the end of the relationship is not necessarily a solution for them. This is despite the expectations of the criminal justice system that 'Women who are abused should leave their abuser'.[41] Sadia, for example, said, 'He always said ... if I ever leave him, that he will continue for the rest of his life and he will make my life hell – that's his exact words'.[42] Separation is the subject of a more detailed analysis in chapter 6, but the survivors I spoke to were aware that the controlling behaviours continue much as before.[43]

To summarise: the dimensions of coercive control are best seen as a strategy of domination. The strategy involves making the victim afraid – which usually, but not always, involves the fear of physical and/or sexual violence. The taking away of 'for granted' rights and freedoms makes it harder for the victim to resist. The totality of the harm experienced by the survivor can only be understood with an appreciation of this infrastructure and context. The next section of this chapter explores the harm by reviewing the impact that coercive behaviour has on its victims.

The Harm

The survivor experience of coercive control is a 'condition of unfreedom that is experienced as *entrapment*'.[44] In the context of this 'state of siege',[45] survivors make it clear that they do not generally consider physical injury to themselves to be of much consequence. Maya explained:

> Physical pain was the least of my worries. When it comes to the rest of his abuse. I wouldn't even notice. It wouldn't even concern me. It is not something that really bothers you so much as all those other aspects of abuse which are preoccupying your mind. You are more likely to ask for help

when it comes to other parts of abuse than physically. Physically, I never thought, "oh, I need to go and do something about this bruise", or about him grabbing me here or kicking me, but about other aspects, his drinking threats, legal threats. Reflections on my child's life. Those are things about which I wanted to ask for help, and eventually did.[46]

IDVAs also comment on the relative unimportance of physical violence to their clients. Annie explained: 'Some of the women that come in here say that they can deal with the physical part, because the body heals, but it's the emotional part that they can't deal with'.[47] Fear, (and in particular fear for the safety of children), instability and personality change are all much more important to the survivor than physical injuries.

Fear is expressed as the generalised fear of an innominate event, a terror of something that might happen, rather than the fear of something specific. Susan Edwards distinguishes between 'immediate fear, fear of future harm or being *in fear*'.[48] This distinction becomes important in later chapters in the context of what the law is prepared to recognise as "fear". Every single survivor spoke of the instability generated by having a *generalised fear* at the core of every lived day.[49] To use Edwards' terminology, this is the 'fear of future harm' and/or being 'in fear' rather than 'immediate fear'.[50] Immediate fear was also experienced by survivors in relation to specific incidents such as the head-butting incident described by Karen above. The important point to recognise is that there is no hierarchy here – living 'in fear'[51] is as destabilising as the fear of an immediate threat. In some ways it is more so because it is ongoing – and does not end with the relationship.

Fear continues not only as a response to continuing perpetrator behaviours, but even if/when the abuse does cease. Singer and songwriter FKA Twigs spoke to Louis Theroux of the post-traumatic stress she experienced long after she had successfully ended all contact with her abusive ex-partner Shia Labeouf:

> You were asking what have you been doing over lockdown? For me I've just been like - I've been trying not to wake up between three and seven in a panic attack. That's what I have been trying to do. And I am there now. You know - just. But for a long time anything that woke me up in the night, whether it was my dog, or just a noise outside or needing to go to the bathroom it could trigger a really intense panic attack, because I was left with PTSD - from that which, again, is just something that I don't think we really talk about as a society. Just in terms of the healing, and how much work that has to be done to get back to the person that you were before.[52]

Post-traumatic stress is a common long-term repercussion of coercive control that means the shadows of living 'in fear'[53] can stretch far into a survivor's future life.

Instability is also generated by changes in a perpetrator's mood. Sarah reported that 'It was very much setting up this sense of "here are my rules", and immediately, although you can't see them, you are walking on eggshells'.[54] Sadia commented that:

> It's like living on a rollercoaster. It's like going on a train journey and never knowing which stop you are going to get off - if it's going to be a nice stop? Or a bad stop? And the day is like that every day. Basically. You don't know how the day is going to start. And you don't know how the day is going to end.[55]

For most survivors, accompanying the instability rollercoaster is an elusive sense of personal control: if only they could behave differently, the perpetrator's abusive behaviour would stop. FKA Twigs speaks, for example, of 'things that you could do wrong that could take away from the happiness of where things could be'.[56] This perception on the part of the victim of the link between what she does and how he might react goes to the core of the relationship between a victim's generalised fear and the impact it has on her daily life. The day is spent trying to keep him from exploding, keeping everyone safe, and trying not to crush the eggshells underfoot. Kim explained it thus: 'There were warning signs, and because I felt that I kind of got the measure of him, I felt that I could kind of adapt things, almost appease him, make sure the kids were safe, which obviously was the main thing'.[57] At another point in the interview she said, 'I would always try to make it OK'.[58]

Linked to the desire to 'adapt things', 'appease him', 'make it OK', comes an assumption of responsibility for the consequences if she doesn't succeed. Sue, an IDVA, elaborated on this:

> One of the reasons that they blame themselves is that they feel then like they have a degree of control, like they can prevent it from happening again. So it's like, "I was raped because I did X. So if I don't do X again, then I won't get raped. Which means that I can now have control over my life so that I don't get raped." The reality is that's not why she got raped. She got raped because he's a perpetrator. Part of blaming yourself is about giving yourself back a degree of control.[59]

The most significant short-term part of the impact that the control has on the survivor is therefore the way that she moderates her behaviour: the "X" in 'so if I don't do X again', but the long-term context is more profound. FKA Twigs speaks about how she was berated for hours, and made to feel like she was 'the worst person ever, so cold and so awful and such a terrible girlfriend' if/when she didn't manage to meet Laboeuf's demands for frequent displays of affection throughout the day.[60] Sarah explained how she blames herself for the abuse, 'and of course anything I did or didn't do, wasn't just wrong whether I did it or didn't do it, but it was also an example of my badness, my passive aggression, my withholding, my darkness ...'. Sarah internalised the abuse even as she was describing it in an interview environment: 'my badness, ... my darkness'.[61] This internalisation goes to the heart of the impact that coercive control has on its victims as it affects the way that they see themselves and the world around them. As Anita, an IDVA, put it: 'underneath something emotional about you has changed'.[62] In another IDVA's words:

> They are at a point where they are pretty much believing what has been said over a period of time to the extent that they found it hard to see him as guilty of a crime because the blame was entirely on themselves and it informed who they were. (Jessica).[63]

FKA Twigs said simply, 'everything that I was, was somehow tied to him'.[64] Stark puts it thus: 'he changes who and what she *is*'.[65]

The impact of the control on the victim is devastating. She exists in a constant state of generalised anxiety that she has not moderated her behaviour sufficiently to avert catastrophe for herself and her children. Her fear is real and not imagined as it is based on a realistic appraisal of the perpetrator's capabilities. As Kim put it: 'and then obviously when the boys came along I just wanted everything to be OK so ... treading on eggshells, and trying to make it OK. But it wasn't OK. And, so, it's like trying to paper the cracks, and there is only so many times that you can keep doing that before they start ...'[66] (she trailed off).

For the survivor respondents, however, even the crippling anxiety is not the worst effect of the abuse. US psychologist Mary Ann Dutton talks about the way in which the psychological impact of abuse goes beyond symptom-focused conditions such as anxiety to include 'the ways in which battered women have come to think about the violence, themselves, and others as a result of their experiences'.[67] Survivors explain that worst of all was how they learn to blame themselves for the position in which they find themselves, and lose confidence in their ability to make decisions about their own and their children's lives. Stark says, 'what is taken away from the women whose stories I tell ... is the capacity for independent decision making in the areas by which we distinguish adults from children and free citizens from indentured servants'.[68] Sue (IDVA) gave an example of this:

> I had one woman in particular who told me in the beginning like "I don't know what to eat, I don't know how to get dressed in the morning I don't know ... because for so long he made every decision in my life, and now I don't know how to make any decisions anymore."[69]

IDVAs emphasise that the survivor will not always be aware of these changes in herself when she first reaches out for help: 'the time when they are first talking to us they are probably not the person who they really are but I don't know if they are able to identify if that is the case'.[70]

"Counting" Coercive Control

It is not yet clear how much of what gets picked up by general omnibus crime surveys, such as the Crime Survey of England and Wales (the CSEW), as domestic abuse is coercive control. This is in part because the measurement of coercive control has a fraught history. The long-term argument between competing schools of research on the fundamental issue of the prevalence of domestic abuse was resolved, up to a point, by Michael Johnson in 1995. A group of predominantly feminist scholars and activists have, he explained, historically described a lower prevalence rate of abuse that is perpetrated almost entirely by men against a backdrop of an imbalance of power and control.[71] The "family violence" school, by contrast, has measured abuse that is much more prevalent, and which is part of what they framed as "conflict" within families, and is perpetrated by women as much as by men.[72] Positions became increasingly acrimonious and entrenched.[73] Both, according to Johnson, are 'right'.[74] They both measure "real" phenomena. Crucially, they measure *different* phenomena.

Johnson introduced typologies that clarify the differences in prevalence rates from the different research perspectives. 'Situational couple violence' is the gender-neutral 'conflict' measured by family violence researchers. Some people resort to violence to resolve their differences, and this results in one-off violence that is incident specific. The archetypal fight over the remote would be an example of this kind of violence. 'Intimate terrorism', on the other hand, refers to the phenomenon articulated by the feminist school which is qualitatively and quantitatively different. It is highly gendered, and embedded in a pattern of power and control. Johnson's key insight is that, 'In order to understand the nature of an individual's use of violence in an intimate relationship, you have to understand its role in the general control dynamics of that relationship'.[75] In other words, at the heart of the distinction between the feminist school's and the family violence researchers' assessment of intimate partner abuse is the presence or absence of Stark's 'coercive control'.[76] How much "domestic abuse" you find depends on what you are looking for.

Johnson's recognition of different typologies of intimate partner abuse is becoming accepted on both sides of the Atlantic.[77] This goes some way to explaining why, as set out above, recognition of the significance and ubiquity of coercive control is no longer confined to a school of feminist researchers and activists. But it is frustrating that this recognition has not yet resulted in better quantitative measures. The lack of specificity in the data generated by the CSEW is hampering our understanding of, and therefore our criminal justice response to, abuse.

The CSEW is the primary source for government estimations of the scope of domestic abuse in England and Wales. According to the most recent count, in the year ending March 2020 an estimated 1.6 million women experienced domestic abuse.[78] But the CSEW still does not reliably measure coercive control. Any attempt to calculate how many of the 1.6 million women are experiencing coercive control is therefore still speculative, to some degree.

A self-completion module on inter-personal violence was introduced in 2001.[79] Since 2004/05,[80] a similar module has been included every year. Detailed questions on the nature of domestic abuse are included every second year. Questions are asked around some aspects of coercive control; there are questions on threats, stalking, sexual assault, and, to an extent, emotional abuse. However, as a recent Office for National Statistics analysis on CSEW statistics explains:

> The CSEW estimates do not currently completely capture the offence of "coercive or controlling behaviour", which was introduced on 29 December 2015. This new offence captures coercive control through psychological and emotional abuse that can stop short of physical violence. The CSEW has measured some elements of such non-physical abuse since April 2004, but this doesn't exactly match the offence ... New survey questions to better estimate experiences of this type of abuse are still under development.[81]

I conduct a review of the 'controlling or coercive behaviour' offence in chapter 5. Its construction, and the incorrect positioning of coercive control as "psychological" or "non-physical" abuse has caused difficulties for the prosecution of coercive control that are felt right the way through the Criminal Justice System. The CSEW has launched a consultation to develop better survey questions on coercive control.[82] If drafted properly, these could be critical to an improved understanding of its prevalence.

Most recently, in March 2021, the Home Office weighed into the debate. It published a review of the section 76 offence. In it, the Home Office comments that, 'At present there is no robust measure of the prevalence of controlling or coercive behaviour specifically',[83] and suggests as the first key research recommendation that, 'robust estimates of the prevalence and characteristics of [coercive or controlling behaviour] should be developed'.[84]

In 2015, Andy Myhill of the College of Policing published an analysis of the 2008/9 Crime Survey of England and Wales data. He estimated then, (and was clear to emphasise the precarious nature of the estimate), that around a third of the women reporting violence to the survey were experiencing coercive control.[85] More recently, Charlotte Barlow et al's analysis of assault occasioning actual bodily harm cases, recorded by one partner police force over an 18-month period, found that in 87% of those cases, 'there was evidence of coercive control identifiable through victim witness statements and previous occurrence records detailing repeat victimisation'.[86] The Home Office review of the section 76 offence found in 2021 that there was significant variability in data provided by the sector, with estimates of coercive control varying from 30% to over 90%.[87]

All in all, this means that the most recent formulations of the self-completion modules *still* do not allow for estimates to be anything other than precarious. The key issue raised by Johnson – that at the heart of the distinction between typologies is the presence or absence of coercive control – has not moved on since the introduction of the 2001 module referred to above. They still do not allow for clear distinctions to be made between the different typologies of abuse suggested by Johnson 25 years ago. As a consequence, 'Attempts to categorise victims in these data sets as having experienced either situational violence or coercive control can be regarded as speculative, at least to some extent'.[88] The perpetrator's behaviour and harm of coercive control are still not captured in anything like enough detail. Coercive control remains 'invisible in plain sight'.[89]

Conclusion

The hidden nature of coercive control is a challenge to the way in which the criminal law articulates crime. Structurally, much of the criminal law focuses on acute incidents and uses a calculus of injuries arising from specific encounters to determine the seriousness of those incidents. As discussed above, the extent of physical violence at any one point in time within coercive control is not a reliable indicator of the seriousness of the offence. When physical or sexual abuse forms part of coercive control it is chronic:[90] it often presents as supposedly (in terms of injuries) "low-level", but constant. When it is assessed in the context of, for example, the Offences against the Person Act 1861, reviewed in the following chapter, it appears not to be serious if no one individual incident causes significant physical injury. Furthermore, Stark observes that this pattern of supposedly "low-level" physical abuse causes difficulties within a criminal justice system that assumes victims are lying, or exaggerating, if they articulate a level of danger that appears disproportionate in the context of the immediately preceding incident alone.[91]

It is the fluidity, as well as the invisibility, of coercive control that challenges the way in which the criminal law categorises criminal behaviour. The interplay between violent and non-violent, sexual and non-sexual tactics is symbiotic, complex and thus problematic in the context of a lexicon which groups crimes in a binary manner as physical or non-physical, as sexual or not-sexual. Coercive control doesn't "fit" binary categories in this way as the behaviour undermines a victim's physical, sexual, psychological and emotional integrity and is not limited to one at the expense of others but blends the different domains in a way that defies such categorisations. In this book, I argue that this has repercussions for any attempts in the criminal law to fragment aspects of control and thereby to criminalise them separately. Finally, the fact that it is not yet possible to be clear about how many women are experiencing coercive control is impeding criminal justice process from both a safeguarding and a prosecution perspective, as my review in the following chapters makes clear.

In the following chapters of this book I therefore review the development of the legislation and common law that is currently used to prosecute coercive control in England and Wales, and Scotland. Throughout, I return to the model of coercive control set out in this chapter as I assess the extent to which the wrongful behaviours and harms inflicted by the perpetrators of coercive control as articulated by the survivors of abuse are translated into criminal law. I also illustrate how an understanding of control has the potential to improve the criminal justice decision-making process.

In the next chapter, I focus on domestic assault, which is still, despite the introduction of coercive control legislation, by far and away the most common domestic abuse-related offence prosecuted in England and Wales. I begin this assessment with a review of the case of Caroline Flack, the TV presenter who committed suicide after being charged with the common assault of her then partner, Lewis Burton. If the police and prosecutors working on her case had taken the kind of coercive control informed approach to decision-making that I set out in this chapter, I argue it may well have saved her life.

Notes

1 Evan Stark, *Coercive Control: How Men Entrap Women in Personal Life* (Oxford University Press, 2007) 203.
2 Paul Kerley and Claire Bates, 'The Archers: What Effect Has the Rob and Helen Story Had?' *BBC News Magazine* (5 April 2016) available at <https://www.bbc.co.uk/news/magazine-35961057> accessed 20 July 2021.
3 BBC2, 'The Case of Sally Challen' available at <www.bing.com> accessed 20 July 2021.
4 Justice for Women, 'Sally Challen' available at <https://www.justiceforwomen.org.uk/sally-challen-appeal> accessed 21 July 2021.
5 Ibid.
6 *Challen* [2019] EWCA Crim 916 [65].
7 Ibid [35].
8 Holly Johnson, 'Rethinking Survey Research on Violence against Women' in Rebecca Dobash and Russell Dobash (eds), *Rethinking Violence against Women* (Sage 1998) 23.
9 Andy Myhill, 'Measuring Coercive Control: What Can We Learn from National Population Surveys?' (2015) 21(3) Violence against Women 355, 372.
10 *Challen* n6 [38].
11 Stark, Coercive Control n1 203.
12 Ibid. 205.
13 Ibid. 205.
14 James Chalmers and Fiona Leverick, 'Fair Labelling in Criminal Law' (2008) 71(2) Modern Law Review 217.
15 Interview with Jessica (16 August 2016) 6.
16 Louise McOrmond-Plummer, 'Lucky to Be Alive: A Battering Partner Rapist' in Louise McOrmond-Plummer et al (eds), *Perpetrators of Intimate Partner Sexual Violence: A Multidisciplinary Approach to Prevention, Recognition and Intervention* (Routledge 2016) 99.
17 BBC 2, Sally Challen n3.
18 Evan Stark, 'Forward' in Louise McOrmond-Plummer et al (eds), *Perpetrators of Intimate Partner Sexual Violence: A Multidisciplinary Approach to Prevention, Recognition and Intervention* (Routledge 2016) xxvii.
19 Tanya Palmer, 'Failing to See the Wood for the Trees: Chronic Sexual Violation and the Criminal Law' 2020 84(6) The Journal of Criminal Law 573, 573.
20 Ibid. 578.
21 Ibid. 574.
22 Ibid. 575.
23 Ibid. 573.
24 Tanya Palmer and Cassandra Wiener, 'Telling the Wrong Stories: Rough Sex, Coercive Control and the Criminal Law' [2021] Child and Family Law Quarterly 331.

25 BB2, Sally Challen n3.
26 Palmer, Wood for the Trees n17 579.
27 Ibid.
28 Interview with Karen (24 November 2016) 4.
29 Jessica n15 10.
30 Palmer, Wood for Trees n17 579.
31 Karen n28 4.
32 Ibid.
33 Ibid.
34 Interview with Meghan (2 June 2015).
35 Detective Constable Stephens, Focus Group with Police (30 November 2016) 13.
36 Stark, Coercive Control n1.
37 Interview with Annie (4 December 2015) 3. See also Bridget Harris and Delani Woodlock, 'Digital Coercive Control: Insights from Two Landmark Domestic Violence Studies' (2018) 59(3) The British Journal of Criminology 530.
38 Interview with Anita (6 June 2015) 10.
39 Interiew with Kim (24 November 2016) 11.
40 Ibid. See also Survivors Focus Group (8 September 2016).
41 Heather Douglas, *Women, Intimate Partner Violence and the Law* (Oxford University Press 2021).
42 Survivors Focus Group n40 5.
43 See also Elizabeth Vivienne, 'Custody Stalking: A Mechanism of Coercively Controlling Mothers Following Separation' (2018) 25 Feminist Legal Studies 185.
44 Evan Stark and Marianne Hester, 'Coercive Control: Update and Review' (2019) 25(1) Violence against Women 81, 89 (emphasis in original).
45 Mary Ann Dutton, 'Understanding Women's Responses to Domestic Violence: A Redefinition of Battered Woman Syndrome' (1992) 21 Hofstra Law Review 1191, 1208.
46 Maya, Survivors Focus Group n40 16.
47 Annie n37 2.
48 Susan Edwards, 'Recognising the Role of the Emotion of Fear in Offences and Defences' (2019) 83(6) The Journal of Criminal Law 450, 461 (my italics).
49 See, for example the conversation between Zara, Mahira and Sadia at the Survivors Focus Group n40 4.
50 Edwards, Recognising the Role of the Emotion of Fear n48 461.
51 Ibid.
52 FKA Twigs, Interview with Louise Theroux, *Grounded* Podcast Audio.
53 Edwards, Recognising the Role of the Emotion of Fear n48 461.
54 Interview with Sarah (29 June 2016) 8.
55 Sadia, Survivors Focus Group n40 1.
56 FKA Twigs n52 5.
57 Kim n39 8.
58 Kim n39 9.
59 Interview with Sue (16 August 2016) 3.
60 FKA Twigs n52.
61 Sarah n54 7.
62 Anita n38 10.
63 Jessica n15 6.
64 FKA Twigs n52.
65 Stark, Coercive Control n1 262 (emphasis mine).
66 Kim n39 5.
67 Dutton, Understanding Women's Responses to Domestic Violence n45 1217.
68 Evan Stark, 'Introduction' in Stark E, *Coercive Control: How Men Entrap Women in Personal Life* (Oxford University Press 2022) 29.

69 Sue n59 6.
70 Ibid. 6.
71 Rebecca and Russell Dobash, *Violence against Wives* (The Free Press 1979); Rebecca and Russell Dobash, 'Women's Violence to Men in Intimate Relationships: Working on a Puzzle' (2004) 44 British Journal of Criminology 324; Stark, Coercive Control n1, Stark and Hester, Update and Review n44.
72 Murray Straus, 'Measuring Intrafamily Conflict and Violence: The Conflict Tactics (CT) Scales' (1979) 41(1) Journal of Marriage and Family 75; Murray Straus and Richard Gelles, *Violence in American Families: Risk Factors and Adaptions to Violence in 8,145 Families* (Transaction Publishers 1990).
73 Michael Johnson reported that the debate was so 'acrimonious' that in the late 1990s he was unable to persuade the protagonists to take part in a conference, as they refused to be in the same room as each other. Michael Johnson, *A Typology of Domestic Violence Intimate Terrorism, Violent Resistance, and Situational Couple Violence* (University Press 2008).
74 Michael Johnson, 'Patriarchal Terrorism and Common Couple Violence: Two Forms of Violence against Women' (1995) 57(2) Journal of Marriage and the Family 283.
75 Johnson, A Typology n73 5.
76 Stark, Coercive Control n1; Stark and Hester, Update and Review n44.
77 Nicole Conroy, Clare Crowley and Daniel DeSanto, 'Assessing the State of Empirical Research on Johnson's Typology of Violence: A Systematic Review [2022] Journal of Family Violence (forthcoming); Myhill, Measuring Coercive Control n9.
78 Office for National Statistics, 'Domestic Abuse in England and Wales Overview: November 2020' available at <https://www.ons.gov.uk/peoplepopulationandcommunity/crimeandjustice/bulletins/domesticabuseinenglandandwalesoverview/november2020> accessed 16 July 2020.
79 This module targeted what it referred to as 'intimate partner violence', 'sexual assault', and 'stalking', drawing these three areas into a single interpersonal violence module. See Sylvia Walby and Jonathan Allen, 'Domestic Violence, Sexual Assault and Stalking: Findings from the British Crime Survey' (Home Office 2004) 15.
80 Andrea Finney, 'Domestic Violence, Sexual Assault and Stalking: Findings from the 2005/5 British Crime Survey' (Home Office 2006).
81 Office for National Statistics, 'Domestic Abuse: Findings from the Crime Survey for England and Wales: Year Ending March 2018' available at <https://www.ons.gov.uk/peoplepopulationandcommunity/crimeandjustice/articles/domesticabusefindings-fromthecrimesurveyforenglandandwales/yearendingmarch2018#prevalence-of-domestic-abuse> accessed 16 July 2021.
82 Office for National Statistics, Redevelopment of Domestic Abuse Statistics: November 2021 available at <https://www.ons.gov.uk/peoplepopulationandcommunity/crimeandjustice/articles/redevelopmentofdomesticabusestatistics/researchupdatenovember2021> accessed 5 June 2022.
83 Home Office, *Review of the Controlling or Coercive Behaviour Offence* (Home Office Research Report 122 2021) 11.
84 Ibid.
85 Myhill, Measuring Coercive Control n9.
86 Charlotte Barlow et al, 'Putting Coercive Control into Practice: Problems and Possibilities' (2020) 60(1) The British Journal of Criminology 160.
87 Home Office, Review of the Controlling or Coercive Behaviour Offence n83 13.
88 Sylvia Walby and Andy Myhill, 'New Survey Methodologies in Researching Violence against Women' in Martin Freeman (ed), *Domestic Violence* (Ashgate 2002) 369.
89 Stark, Coercive Control n1.
90 Palmer, Wood for Trees n17 573.
91 Ibid. 94.

Bibliography

Barlow C, Johnson K, Walklate S and Humphries L, 'Putting Coercive Control into Practice: Problems and Possibilities' (2020) 60(1) The British Journal of Criminology 160.

BBC2, 'The Case of Sally Challen' available at <www.bing.com> accessed 20 July 2021.

Chalmers J and Leverick L, 'Fair Labelling in Criminal Law' (2008) 71(2) Modern Law Review 217.

Conroy N, Crowley C and DeSanto D, 'Assessing the State of Empirical Research on Johnson's Typology of Violence: A Systematic Review' (2022) Journal of Family Violence (forthcoming).

Dobash R and Dobash R, *Violence against Wives* (The Free Press, 1979).

Dobash R and Dobash R, 'Women's Violence to Men in Intimate Relationships: Working on a Puzzle' (2004) 44 British Journal of Criminology 324.

Douglas H, *Women, Intimate Partner Violence and the Law* (Oxford University Press 2021).

Dutton M, 'Understanding Women's Responses to Domestic Violence: A Redefinition of Battered Woman Syndrome' (1992) 21 Hofstra Law Review 1191.

Edwards S, 'Recognising the Role of the Emotion of Fear in Offences and Defences' (2019) 83(6) The Journal of Criminal Law 450.

Finney A, 'Domestic Violence, Sexual Assault and Stalking: Findings from the 2005/5 British Crime Survey' (Home Office 2006).

FKA Twigs, 'Interview with Louise Theroux', *Grounded* Podcast Audio.

Harris B and Woodlock D, 'Digital Coercive Control: Insights from Two Landmark Domestic Violence Studies' (2018) 59(3) The British Journal of Criminology 530.

Home Office, *Review of the Controlling or Coercive Behaviour Offence* (Home Office Research Report 122 2021).

Johnson H, 'Rethinking Survey Research on Violence against Women' in Dobash R and Dobash R (eds), *Rethinking Violence against Women* (Sage 1998) 23.

Johnson M, 'Patriarchal Terrorism and Common Couple Violence: Two Forms of Violence against Women' (1995) 57 Journal of Marriage and the Family 283.

Johnson M, *A Typology of Domestic Violence Intimate Terrorism, Violent Resistance, and Situational Couple Violence* (University Press 2008).

Justice for Women, 'Sally Challen' available at <https://www.justiceforwomen.org.uk/sally-challen-appeal> accessed 21 July 2021.

Kerley P and Bates C, 'The Archers: What Effect Has the Rob and Helen Story Had?' *BBC News Magazine* (5 April 2016) available at <https://www.bbc.co.uk/news/magazine-35961057> accessed 20 July 2021.

McOrmond-Plummer L, 'Lucky to Be Alive: A Battering Partner Rapist' in McOrmond-Plummer L, Levy-Peck J and Easteal P (eds), *Perpetrators of Intimate Partner Sexual Violence: A Multidisciplinary Approach to Prevention, Recognition and Intervention* (Routledge 2016).

Myhill A, 'Measuring Coercive Control: What Can We Learn from National Population Surveys?' (2015) 21(3) Violence against Women 355. DOI: 10.1177/1077801214568032.

Office for National Statistics, 'Domestic Abuse: Findings from the Crime Survey for England and Wales: Year Ending March 2018' available at <https://www.ons.gov.uk/peoplepopulationandcommunity/crimeandjustice/articles/domesticabusefindingsfromthecrimesurveyforenglandandwales/yearendingmarch2018#prevalence-of-domestic-abuse> accessed 16 July 2021.

Office for National Statistics, 'Domestic Abuse in England and Wales Overview: November 2020' available at <https://www.ons.gov.uk/peoplepopulationandcommunity/crimeandjustice/bulletins/domesticabuseinenglandandwalesoverview/november2020> accessed 16 July 2020.

Office for National Statistics, Redevelopment of Domestic Abuse Statistics: November 2021 available at <https://www.ons.gov.uk/peoplepopulationandcommunity/crimeandjustice/articles/redevelopmentofdomesticabusestatistics/researchupdatenovember2021> accessed 5 June 2022.

Palmer T, 'Failing to See the Wood for the Trees: Chronic Sexual Violation and the Criminal Law' (2020) 84(6) The Journal of Criminal Law 573.

Palmer T and Wiener C, 'Telling the Wrong Stories: Rough Sex, Coercive Control and the Criminal Law' (2021) Child and Family Law Quarterly 331.

Stark E, *Coercive Control: How Men Entrap Women in Personal Life* (Oxford University Press 2007).

Stark E, 'Forward' in Louise McOrmond-Plummer et al (eds), *Perpetrators of Intimate Partner Sexual Violence: A Multidisciplinary Approach to Prevention, Recognition and Intervention* (Routledge 2016).

Stark E, 'Introduction' in Stark E, *Coercive Control: How Men Entrap Women in Personal Life* (Oxford University Press 2022).

Stark E and Hester M, 'Coercive Control: Update and Review' (2019) 25(1) Violence against Women 81. DOI: 10.1177/1077801214521324.

Straus M, 'Measuring Intrafamily Conflict and Violence: The Conflict Tactics (CT) Scales' (1979) 41(1) Journal of Marriage and Family 75.

Straus M and Gelles R, *Violence in American Families: Risk Factors and Adaptions to Violence in 8,145 Families* (Transaction Publishers 1990).

Vivienne E, 'Custody Stalking: A Mechanism of Coercively Controlling Mothers Following Separation' (2018) 25 Feminist Legal Studies 185.

Walby S and Myhill A, 'New Survey Methodologies in Researching Violence against Women' in Freeman M (ed), *Domestic Violence* (Ashgate 2001).

Walby S and Allen J, 'Domestic Violence, Sexual Assault and Stalking: Findings from the British Crime Survey' (Home Office 2004).

Cases

Challen [2019] EWCA Crim 916.

Legislation

Offences against the Person Act 1861.
Serious Crime Act 2015.

2

DOMESTIC ASSAULTS AND COERCIVE CONTROL

Introduction

Domestic assaults form the part of domestic abuse that is by far the most often investigated by the police. In the year ending March 2021, nearly half of the 1,459,663 domestic abuse-related offences recorded by the police were for violence against the person offences.[1] These offences include all physically abusive acts that do not result in a death and are not sexual in nature. Police and prosecutors use the Offences against the Person Act 1861[2] (the OAPA) and the associated common-law offences of assault and battery, (together, the 'offences against the person regime'), to prosecute domestic assault, whether or not the assault also forms part of a coercively controlling strategy.

Domestic assault must always be taken seriously. Not all domestic assault, however, is coercive control. In the last chapter, I explained how coercive control and violence that is situationally specific (Johnson's 'situational couple violence')[3] are not the same thing, and do not have the same risk profile. Coercive control is always dangerous – situational couple violence not necessarily so. I said that an ability to distinguish between the two would greatly improve the criminal justice response to domestic abuse and that the introduction of coercive control laws would to some extent enable this to happen. In my view, so-called low-level domestic assault that is part of a coercively controlling strategy is anything but. It must always be considered to be high risk and should be prosecuted as coercive control. Situationally specific violence may or may not be high risk, and is better prosecuted using the offences against the person regime.

This review of the offences against the person regime is divided into three parts. In the first part, I use the case study of celebrity TV presenter Caroline Flack to show how a failure to recognise situational violence can result in poor charging and safeguarding decisions on the part of prosecutors and police, sometimes (as in

DOI: 10.4324/9780429201844-3

Caroline's case) with tragic consequences. In the second part, I focus on violence that is part of a controlling strategy, and show how the offences against the person regime causes problems for police, prosecutors, the judiciary and survivors themselves. In the final part of the chapter, I look at developments in the criminal law that tested the offences against the person regime and that ultimately resulted in law reform that is the subject of the following chapter.

Situational Assault vs Coercive Control: The Tragic Case of Caroline Flack

The first difficulty with the offences against the person regime in the context of domestic assault is therefore that it does not distinguish between assaults that are situationally specific and those that are not. The Caroline Flack case – which ended with her suicide on 15 February 2020 – is a good example of what can go wrong when police use a "level of violence" rather than a "level of control" measure to assess risk in domestic abuse cases. It is a good example, in other words, of the confusion caused by current police and Crown Prosecution Service (the CPS) (non-control informed) practice, and of the potentially devastating repercussions for risk assessment that this can have.

Caroline Flack's boyfriend, Lewis Burton, called police to Caroline's house in Stoke Newington at 5:25 am on 12 December 2019. It is not clear exactly what took place. Both Caroline and Lewis had been drinking all of the previous day and evening, and there had been an argument over some text messages that Caroline found on Lewis's phone. It was said later in court that the transcript of Lewis' call to the police was incoherent and confused because he was drunk.[4] Initially, Lewis alleged that Caroline hit him with a lamp while he was sleeping, although he later retracted this. Caroline said she hit him accidentally with her phone. Caroline's phone was later taken by police. It had blood on it and there was a crack on one of the corners, which suggests it was indeed the phone that was used.[5]

In any event, what is clear, is that Caroline hit Lewis with an object that caused a minor cut to his head. She also cut herself in one or both arms, in an act of self-harm, immediately afterwards. The cut to Caroline's arm bled profusely, resulting in distressing photographs circulating in the tabloid press of blood-soaked sheets. The cut to Lewis's head was later described as 'minor' and he was not given any medical treatment.[6] Caroline was arrested, taken to Holborn police station for questioning, and then straight to hospital for an assessment at a psychiatric unit.

Detective Inspector Lauren Bateman was the most senior Metropolitan Police detective on duty for the Holborn area on the night of 12 December 2019.[7] Initially, the CPS prosecutor who considered the evidence supplied by the police decided that a caution would be appropriate, but this was overturned when Bateman authorised an appeal of that initial CPS decision. Caroline was charged with common assault, and she was bailed to return to court on 23 December, with a police bail condition that she was not to contact Lewis before then. The decision to charge Caroline with common assault was reviewed and confirmed by CPS prosecutor Kate Weiss a week later. Weiss said in her report that Caroline demonstrated a 'lack of remorse' by breaching her bail condition not to contact Lewis. In fact, rather than "contacting" Lewis, Caroline had posted a picture of Lewis on her public Instagram page with a caption which said, 'I love you'.[8]

The CPS were operating within their guidelines to charge Caroline with assault, although a caution would arguably have been more appropriate in the circumstances. The coroner found at the later coroner's hearing that Weiss' review, and decision to proceed with the charge the week after the incident were woefully inadequate. The self-harming and fragility of Caroline's mental health were not fully taken into account. Instead, 'The significance of one paragraph detailing that the star suffered from numerous mental health conditions, including a condition recognisable in the US but not in the UK'[9] was completely overlooked. In conclusion, the coroner observed that the CPS review:

> Gives a flavor of wanting to find reasons to continue the prosecution rather than looking at this afresh. It would be easy to gain an impression from this that for whatever reason, Caroline isn't liked – "She's a celebrity and she must be dealt with severely." I can understand why that impression could be gained by this document.[10]

Certainly, the injury was minor, the action was not pre-meditated, Caroline had no previous convictions, there was no history of violence between her and Lewis and no history of domestic abuse from Caroline.[11] Lewis was adamant: he did not support the prosecution and asked that the action be discontinued. The likelihood of repeat offending was low and Caroline had admitted the offence. These mitigating factors would all suggest that a caution would have been the better charging decision, as in fact was admitted by senior CPS prosecutor Alison Wright at the inquest hearing. Sections of Wright's evidence were read in court as follows:

> [Caroline] has repeatedly admitted she assaulted him. I do not believe that the case is in the public interest to prosecute as the injured party does not support the allegation, there is no domestic violence history, the suspect is 40 with no previous convictions. There is nothing so serious about this incident which means the guidelines (to issue a caution) need to be diverted from.[12]

Detective Inspector Lauren Bateman also gave evidence at the inquest. She told the court that another reason that the incident was not suitable for a caution was because officers were looking at 'domestic abuse guidelines'. She explained that, in her mind, 'Domestic abuse is an "umbrella term" covering not just violence but also harassment and other things'. She said, 'by no means am I saying Caroline is a domestic abuser'.[13] *This is confused and confusing.* Bateman was the most senior Metropolitan Police police officer on duty that night. It seems unfortunate that she was unable, or unwilling, at the coroner's hearing to be reflective about the absurdity of relying on domestic abuse guidelines to assess a suspect who she had identified as *not* a domestic abuser.

If we bring a consideration of coercive control into the equation then much of the muddle is resolved. Bateman is right to consider domestic abuse an "umbrella term". It covers both abuse that is controlling and that which is not. The use of it as an umbrella term means that, in the context of domestic assault, Bateman was not encouraged to consider risk in terms of the presence or absence of coercive control. The decision facing Bateman and her team on the evening of 12 December was whether or not to charge Caroline with common assault, an offence that has remained unchanged for more or less 150 years. It would have been better if, as part of that decision-making process, Bateman had given more priority to the consideration that on the evidence that was available to her Caroline was unlikely to be an abusive and controlling perpetrator of coercive control. This would have led to more appropriate decision-making and may have ultimately saved Caroline's life.

The domestic abuse guidelines referred to by Bateman are 'The Offences against the Person, Incorporating the Charging Standard', which has a section on 'Charging Offences Involving Domestic Abuse',[14] and the CPS 'Domestic Guidelines For Prosecutors'.[15] The underlying assumption in both of these documents is that 'domestic abuse' is the same thing as 'coercive control'. For example,

> Domestic abuse is rarely a one-off incident and is the cumulative and interlinked physical, psychological, sexual, emotional or financial abuse that has a particularly damaging effect on the victim.[16]

The difficulty with this advice is that as I explained in the previous chapter, domestic abuse can, absolutely be a one-off incident. The incident at Caroline Flack's house on 12 December, described at the coroner's hearing as an 'impulsive action'[17] is most likely to have been just such a one-off incident. This would explain all of the other variables, that Caroline was 40 with no previous convictions, that there was no evidence of previous domestic abuse between the parties and that the assault took place in a situationally specific context. The confusing nature of the guidelines is in fact perfectly reflected in the ambiguities present in Bateman's evidence to the court: Caroline needed to be charged because the domestic abuse guidelines say that domestic abuse is serious, but she is not a 'domestic abuser'.

Three days later Caroline filmed herself tearfully saying she had lost her job. Of the incident, she said 'It was a fight. I have never hurt anyone in my life. The only person I ever hurt is myself'. Things deteriorated quickly from that point. On 17 December 2019, Tamsin Lewis, a medical practitioner, was called to see Caroline and described her as distressed and tearful. Tamsin Lewis explained that Caroline was apologetic about what happened, and felt it was a lovers' tiff which had been heightened by alcohol. Tamsin Lewis reported that Caroline's mood was low and she seemed anxious, Caroline said sleep had been 'impossible' and kept asking for 'reassurance that "everything would be okay"'. She was prescribed sleep medication and also an antibiotic for a wound – which suggests she may have still been self-harming.[18]

Caroline was also assessed by leading Harley Street consultant psychiatrist Dr Jonathan Garabette, who expressed concerns about the likely impact of the ongoing court case on Caroline's mental health. He reported that she was clinically vulnerable and that it was likely this would worsen while the case against her was ongoing. Interestingly, the evidence given in court suggests that Garabette refers in his report to 'old traumatic events' including an 'earlier abusive relationship' (not Lewis) and 'alleged ongoing harassment', which would all suggest further concern for her mental health.[19] It is not clear whether or not Caroline had involved the police with her concerns about any ongoing harassment from a former partner. The CPS were sent a copy of Garabette's report by Caroline's legal team. This was the last communication made by Caroline's legal team which specifically referred to her mental health.[20]

Caroline attended Westminster Magistrates Court on 23 December where she pleaded not guilty to the single charge of common assault. Lewis arrived separately, (the police bail condition meaning that they were unable to arrive together), to show his support for Caroline. Prosecutor Kate Weiss told the court about the original incident and said that, 'Both were covered in blood and in fact one of the police officers likened the scene to a horror movie'. Weiss did not clarify that much, if not most, of the blood at the scene belonged to Caroline.

As I said above, any domestic abuse, whether it is part of a coercive controlling strategy or not, must always be taken seriously. Charging Caroline with assault was harsh, in the circumstances, but not necessarily incorrect. She applied force to his head, and he called for emergency assistance. But what happened next would not have been possible in the context of a properly domestic abuse-informed CPS response. Caroline applied to have her bail conditions lifted – arguing that she did not want to spend Christmas alone, without her boyfriend – but the CPS opposed the application and the judge refused it. Caroline put her head in her hands, as she knew that this meant that she was prevented from contacting Lewis directly or indirectly, and from attending his address, (or he attending hers), until trial.

It is unfortunate that this bail condition would in all likelihood have put particular pressure on Caroline. Caroline's response to the ending of intimate relationships was known to be problematic; the emotional upset she experienced being outside the realm of what would normally be considered a healthy response. Jody Flack, Caroline's twin sister, said in her statement to the coroner that 'heartbreak' was something that [Caroline] found extremely difficult to cope with emotionally.[21] There was speculation in online spaces (never substantiated) that she may have been suffering with borderline personality disorder. An inability to end relationships healthily is often referred to as one of the hallmarks of borderline personality disorder. The contents of the medical report that was served on the CPS before the 23 December hearing are, of course, confidential. Whether or not the CPS had notice of Caroline's particular vulnerability in this regard it is unlikely that Lewis was in need of the protection offered by a non-contact order, which is designed for high-risk victims of coercive control.

In January, Caroline's defence team made an application to the CPS for the case to be dropped. The CPS emailed Caroline's defence team to confirm that they would be continuing with the prosecution on 13 February.[22] In the early hours of Saturday, 15 February an ambulance was called from Caroline's flat. Two paramedics assessed her and advised her to attend hospital out of concern for her mental health. Caroline refused,[23] and took her own life later on Saturday morning.

Lewis had described in his statement to the coroner that Caroline was 'very upset, in fact devasted' the last time he was allowed to see her. She was 'not in a good place emotionally … and what was upsetting her most was the police case, the thought of losing her job on Love Island, the hostile media attention and not being able to see him'.[24] On the evening of the day following Caroline's death Lewis broke his silence to express his regret via an Instagram post: 'I know you felt safe with me … and I was not allowed to be there this time'.[25] With a coercive control informed police response, the chances are he would have been.

Situational Assault vs Coercive Control: The Inadequacy of the Offences against the Person Regime in the Context of Coercive Control

To be clear, the problem with the Flack case was not the offences against the person regime itself. Charging Caroline with the common law offence of 'assault by beating' may have been severe, but the law itself, (the unwanted infliction of contact), is an appropriate enough fit for the situationally specific crime that took place. The problem in Caroline's case was that the police and CPS used guidelines designed for coercive control in the context of her situationally specific assault. There *is*, however, a fundamental difficulty with the offences against the person regime itself, and that is its lack of suitability for the prosecution of assault that is also coercive control.

As I showed in the previous chapter, an assault that is part of a coercively controlling strategy is often dismissed incorrectly as "low-level" when assessed by police. This is because it is measured as 'acute' rather than 'chronic' – to use Tanya Palmer's terminology as explained in the last chapter.[26] Assessing assault as a one-off incident (acute), rather than as part of a domination strategy (chronic), abstracts the assault from much of what makes it dangerous. Instead, police focus on the severity of the physical harm caused. The offences against the person regime's "ladder" of offences is structured according to a hierarchy of physical harm caused, and this is therefore how police are trained to assess assault. One of the hallmarks of chronic abuse is that the level of physical harm caused is, ironically, the worst possible indicator of risk. Chronic abuse, irrespective of physical harm, is usually high risk, and it must always be taken seriously. Viewing coercive control through the lens of legislation that was designed to prevent 'brawls and street fights'[27] in Victorian times has negative consequences for effective policing, effective prosecution and also undermines rather than validates the victims' own experience of the crime.

Thus, from a policing perspective the apparently "low-level" nature and regularity of abuse which is chronic interferes with risk assessment processes, as it means that much of what makes it dangerous gets overlooked. Framing 'chronic' abuse as 'acute' incidents also makes it harder for police to empathise with a victim's plight: encouraging police to assume a kind of decisional autonomy "between incidents" on the part of victims that victims tell us does not exist. From a prosecution perspective, the evidential requirements of the offences against the person regime are targeted, again, towards abuse that is acute (one-off incidents), and are inappropriate in the context of an abusive regime. Finally, from a victim's own perspective, the offences against the person regime overlooks much of what makes the offending behaviour insidious; she can feel that her perspective gets lost altogether. I will look at each of these problem areas in turn.

Risk Assessment

Perhaps the most significant negative consequence of the trivialisation of abuse, when viewed through the incident-specific lens, is the impact on the risk assessment process that police utilise to try to keep the most vulnerable victims safe. High profile homicide cases such as the death of Daniela Espirita Santo in 2020, who called police seven times for help before she was eventually murdered,[28] reinforce the dangers of what Stark refers to as the way that 'domestic violence policing' creates 'a revolving door for a class of chronic offenders'.[29] In the focus group that I ran with senior police officers, for example, one Detective Chief Inspector explained that: 'it always surprises first responders and front-line officers, when you have a "low-risk" they are likely to be the murders'.[30] Two other senior officers in the room agreed that domestic homicides are almost always initially (incorrectly) assessed as 'low-risk' cases.[31] When I asked the Detective Chief Inspector to explain what he meant, he gave me an example. Recently, he said, there had been a domestic homicide in a neighbouring town. He said: 'It was a female who reported on six or seven occasions low risk harassments ... when I say "low-risk" it sounds so wrong ... every job, every contact that she had with this particular force was "low-risk"'. I asked: 'What made them "low-risk?', and he responded: 'because they were looked at as individual isolated incidents ... but, she's now dead'. He concluded: 'So, now it's easy to say, well, six different incidents ... when officers are presented with just that "low" thing – it's "low-risk"'.[32] As I have argued elsewhere, risk assessments are a necessarily evil – a way to ration finite police resources.[33] But as Stark points out: 'The level of control an offender is exercising is a far better way to ration scarce police resources than the level of violence'.[34]

Decisional Autonomy

Feeding into the impact on the risk assessment process, and another consequence of the incident-specific focus of the offences against the person regime, is 'the assumption [by police] that victims ... exercise decisional autonomy "between" episodes'.[35] This means that victims who fail to capitalise on that (assumed) autonomy can be perceived as responsible, at least in part, for the ongoing abuse that they experience. Being *trapped*, in other words, is mis-construed as a *decision* to stay. An understanding of the coercive control back-drop allows police to understand that each acute, violent incident is, to many women, relatively unimportant in the context of the chronic 'state of siege'[36] imposed by their abuser.

In fact, there is no "between" episodes: while the violence might be intermittent, the fear it engenders is chronic – ongoing. Stark describes the effect of this kind of mismatch between police assumptions and empirical reality as follows: 'Some police officers attribute the woman's apparent inability to "leave" to a deficit in her character and consider her expressions of fear exaggerated, fabricated, or as the by-product of mental illness, particularly in contrast to the relatively minor nature of the incident to which they are responding'.[37] One Detective Chief Inspector commented to me simply that he understood that, 'By and large if you've got physical injuries with no psychological effect it's easier to leave'.[38] Getting his officers to understand was more of a challenge: 'How can we get them to know that?'.[39]

Prosecution Difficulties

Frustration with victims who are "un-cooperative", difficulties with risk assess-ment and mistakes with safeguarding all have an effect on the ability of police to prosecute offenders and keep victims safe.

Survivors rarely trivialise the abuse they experience. But it is exactly the un-importance of each individual act of physical violence to the survivor that causes difficulties for prosecutors when they have to frame assaults in an incident-specific way. Survivors understandably find it difficult to pinpoint chronic abuse to specific dates on which particular assaults took place. One of the first trials I observed – before the introduction of the coercive control legislation – involved an abusive relationship between a student and an older man. After three hours of cross-examination the exhausted student had still failed to locate this particular attack in time and space. Was she in front of the coffee table or behind it? Was it mid-morning, or early afternoon?

To the student, these details seemed unimportant in the context of the chronic, ongoing abuse to which she had been subjected over a 12-month period.[40] The defence barrister was attacking her credibility in a way that is reasonable in light of the evidential requirements of the OAPA, but that was unreasonable in the context of what she could be expected to remember. While the date of a one-off incident, such as a mugging by a stranger, is memorable, dates of attacks that occur regularly are not. Instead, the nature of living with attacks that are continuous is a tendency on the part of victims (such as this student) to 'blend, generalise and summarise'.[41]

In the last chapter, I described how Jessica, for example, referred to this kind of physical abuse as 'the usual'. She said, 'There was occasionally hitting and punching – the usual'.[42] Another example is Karen, who interjected her narrative with almost casual references to physical abuse. She said, 'but then we would be walking on the road and he would just punch me in the face'[43] and, 'he could just be violent for no apparent ... he could just be violent'.[44] If you had asked Jessica or Karen to particularise any of the 'usual' attacks, (I did not, because it would have felt insensitive and inappropriate), they would have found it difficult.

Frustration from the judiciary, that this inability to locate specific attacks makes it difficult to prove domestic abuse offences in court, can also be found in the case law.[45] In *Hills*, for example, a case which is the subject of a detailed review below, the judge discounts much of the victim's evidence of assaults because, despite her saying that 'over a period of time and on a fairly regular basis, she had been ill-treated by the appellant', none of the complainant's witness statements referred to the dates of the allegations.[46] Furthermore, 'The complainant could not recall specific dates when she had been assaulted'.[47]

Cloaking

It is not surprising that legal provisions introduced in the nineteenth century 'to address bar brawls and street fights'[48] are ill-suited for the prosecution of coercive control well over a 100 years later. The non-fatal offences against the person regime reflects a Victorian preoccupation with 'men's security of property and persons',[49] and with that a certain understanding of what constitutes a crime. This understanding rests on assumptions that are not appropriate in the context of coercive control. A transactional focus places an emphasis on the boundary pre-servation of property or a person. The crime is conceived of as a violation of that boundary that takes place at a particular instant in time. Another inappropriate assumption is that the boundaries in need of policing are physical in nature. In other words, violations are conceived of as physical harm to person or to property. This emphasis on transactional specificity and physical harm means that much of the harm experienced by survivors of coercive control is excluded altogether. Deborah Tuerkheimer refers to this exclusion as 'cloaking'.[50]

Cloaking is an example of what Tuerkheimer refers to as the 'disconnect between life and law'[51] that is particularly acute for survivors of coercive control engaging with criminal justice systems such as those in the United States and in England and Wales. She argues that the transactional crime paradigm is not a good framework from within which to prosecute coercive control.[52] There is a "disconnect" because, as has been explained, 'abusive behaviour does not occur as a series of discrete events'.[53]

Individual incidents of physical violence are not always memorable, but the same cannot be said for the fear (and loss of autonomy) engendered as a result. Indeed, 'The battered woman's fear, vigilance, or perception that she has few options may persist, even when long periods of time elapse between physically or sexually violent episodes'.[54] In chapter 3, I gave the example of the survivor who spent the six years following an attack experiencing trauma and loss of autonomy every time her abusive partner put a bathroom towel on the kitchen table. Ten years elapsed, but she described how 'he was never physically violent to me ever again. He would just always bring out the towel'.[55]

Historically, there has been limited analysis in the legal literature of fear and trauma, and none of loss of autonomy.[56] This is linked to the fact that, 'There is no consistent legal framework or doctrinal coherence within the law regarding this emotion (fear)'.[57] As I review in more detail below, recent developments mean that a clinical mental health condition can amount to bodily harm for the purposes of the OAPA.[58] Otherwise, traditionally, and prior to the legislative developments described in the following chapters, what Hobhouse LJ referred to as '*mere* emotions such as fear or distress or panic'[59] are irrelevant: 'cloaked'.[60]

Downgrading 'extreme fear or panic'[61] to 'something which is not more than a strong emotion'[62] trivialises the responses of women in domestic abuse cases. Severe and sustained 'living in fear'[63] usually has significant consequences, whether or not there is a clinical diagnosis.[64] Moving beyond 'medicalised, trauma-based accounts of harm'[65] is especially important in the context of domestic abuse. Victims with dependent children understandably fear the ramifications of a diagnosis of a psychiatric illness.[66]

Conclusion on the Inadequacies of the Offences against the Person Regime

In summary, the crimes prosecuted under the non-fatal offences against the person regime account for over 75% of the domestic abuse offences recorded by the police, and yet are uniquely ill-suited to prosecuting violence that is part of a controlling strategy. The offences against the person regime conceives of crimes as incident-specific and transactional in nature, and the prosecution of coercive control as offences against the person puts unreasonable pressure on victim-survivors, and 'cloaks' both aspects of perpetrator behaviour and the harm experienced by the victim.[67] Harm that is not physical is often overlooked, and much of the "everyday" violence goes uncharged.

The offences against the person regime thus causes problems for police, prosecutors, the judiciary and survivors themselves. In the late 1990s, three important cases came before the courts which exposed many of these shortcomings in a way that made legislative reform inevitable. That legislative reform is the subject of the following chapter. In the final part of this chapter I will explain how the offences against the person regime was tested, via the recognition of criminal behaviours that came to be known as "stalking".

Stalking and the Offences against the Person Regime

Stalking

In this book, I use the term "domestic stalking" to refer to stalking that takes place where there has been an intimate relationship between perpetrator and victim, whether or not that relationship is ongoing. I use the term "non-relational stalking" to refer to all other stalking, i.e. where the victim and perpetrator are known to one another but have never been intimately involved, or where the victim and perpetrator have never met. These definitional issues are important, as they have not always been clear to Parliament, and developments in the criminal law have suffered as a result.

The stalking that first became recognised as a serious social problem in the United States was non-relational.[68] Research tracking the development of the concept of stalking in the United Kingdom, via content analysis of newspaper articles in the 1990s, concludes that the media portrayal of stalking in the United Kingdom followed a similar trajectory.[69] A Home Office review conducted in 2000 supports these conclusions: 'Public perceptions of stalking have been coloured by the media attention given to high profile cases involving public figures or personalities'.[70]

Non-relational stalking can involve the obsessive pursuit of victims by people who are mentally ill. The media focused on stalkers as 'dangerous and mentally ill with a tendency towards the commission of violent crime',[71] and this fed a public preoccupation with celebrity victims who were in need of protection from delusional strangers.[72] In fact, it is now recognised that the most common form of stalking is domestic; it takes place where the victim and perpetrator know one another and are, or have been, in an intimate relationship.[73] The situation with regards to the mental health of perpetrators of domestic stalking is discussed below. It is possible that a percentage of such perpetrators are mentally ill but this has not been established. The inaccurate colouring of the public perception of stalking by the media attention given to non-relational celebrity cases had an impact on the Protection from Harassment Act 1997 (the 'PHA'), which I explore in the following chapter.

Stalking is important because it often forms part of the behaviour patterns that make up coercive control, as I explained in chapter 3. It is usually one of the tactics utilised by perpetrators of coercive control. Certainly most, if not all, of the survivors that I interviewed described stalking as a key constituent of the abuse that they experienced. In chapter 3, I gave examples of how perpetrators tracked survivors' movements and spied upon them. Karen spoke about how:

> If I had planned to meet anyone from work, which didn't happen very often, because I chose not to do that, he would - I mean a friend reminded me recently about it - he would just then if we went to the pub, or wherever we were, he would then be there. He would then watch me.[74]

By watching Karen in the pub, the perpetrator made his presence felt when they are not ostensibly together. This demonstrates how stalking is the mechanism within control that a perpetrator uses to extend his control through time and space to make that control "complete". Kim described similar behaviour: 'He used to come to my work – he knew where the kids were at nursery – so he used to go to their schools. Everywhere I went, he was there'.[75] Sarah used the term 'complete control' when describing the stalking behaviours she experienced. She said:

> He was in complete control. He was a very Mac man - iMac all that kind of stuff, really early adopter of all that technology. And so basically he - I actually had to have a police cyber detective set up new emails for me. He was the administrator of all the accounts. So even though I sought help, of course, anything that was on the computers - he could see it all. And he knew where I was, because of the "find my phone" tracker, which he delighted in proving.[76]

There is no doubt that stalking and coercive control are highly correlated in that they are often simultaneously present and the one "completes" the other.[77] Two points are important here, however. Firstly, stalking forms *part* of the controlling or coercive behavioural repertoire of a perpetrator within an abusive intimate relationship; *it is not the same thing as coercive control*. Secondly, as reflected by the early media reports of stalking referred to above, non-relational stalking exists as a typology completely outside of coercive control.

From 1994 to 1997 there was extensive media coverage of the perceived inadequacies of the offences against the person regime in the context of non-relational stalking.[78] From a legal perspective, the difficulties faced by the courts coalesced around both the nature of stalking (the act), and its effect (the harm). In both cases, the difficulty for the criminal law was the 'cloaking'[79] caused in part by the lack of an incident-specific physical dimension to perpetrator behaviour and victim response. In 1997, three important stalking cases came before the courts: *Constanza*,[80] *Ireland and Burstow*.[81] In all three cases the courts grappled with the inadequacies of the offences against the person regime in the context of what was becoming increasingly clear about stalking.

Constanza[82]

The judgment in *Constanza* was handed down first, in March 1997. The stalking was non-relational: the perpetrator (Mr Constanza) and his victim (Miss Wilson) were acquaintances, but were not, nor had they ever been, in a relationship. They both worked for the same company. Constanza wished to form a relationship with Wilson, and resorted to increasingly intrusive behaviour in pursuit of her. Schiemann LJ summarised his behaviour:

> Between October 1993 and June 1995 the Appellant (Constanza) indulged in the following unusual behaviour: - following her home from work, making numerous silent telephone calls to her at work and at home as well as some telephone calls in which he spoke, sending and delivering over 800 letters to her home over a period of 4 months, sitting in his car outside her home in the early hours of the day, driving past her home and circling on

occasion, visiting her home in April 1995 and talking to her and her mother for long periods on the doorstep when asked not to do so, and daubing the words "no guts, coward" on her door in marker pen on three occasions.[83]

Schiemann LJ explained that by June 1995, Wilson 'felt that all the actions of Constanza were such that he posed a threat to her personal safety. She had told him that his behaviour was making her ill and he had told her that if he could not have her nobody else could'.[84]

Constanza was originally convicted at first instance of assault occasioning actual bodily harm further to the OAPA, s47. This offence is satisfied where the defendant commits a common assault or a battery, and the victim has suffered actual bodily harm as a result. As there had been no physical contact between Constanza and Wilson there could be no question of a battery. Both parties at first instance agreed on the legal definition of common assault,[85] and on the actual bodily harm that Constanza accepted he had caused Wilson to suffer. Wilson was diagnosed with clinical depression and chronic anxiety by a psychiatrist in July 1995; Constanza accepted the psychiatrist's conclusion that it was Constanza's relentless pursuit of her that had caused her to be seriously, clinically ill. Nevertheless, Constanza appealed his conviction on the basis that his actions could not, in law, amount to an assault. The essential issue for the Court of Appeal was a question of fact: whether or not he had committed the common assault that forms the basis of the OAPA, s47 offence. Had he caused the victim to apprehend *immediate* violence?

The action of Constanza that was singled out for the OAPA, s47 charge was his hand-delivery of a letter on 12 June which contained the following wording: 'After that no more excuses, no more being the child. Or we play games my way'.[86] It is an illustration of Tuerkheimer's 'disconnect between life and law'[87] that, having outlined the shocking extent of the perpetrator's campaign of intimidation, and the ensuing destruction of Wilson's life, the essential question before the Court of Appeal was whether or not he had caused the victim to apprehend immediate violence. Was the victim in fear of *immediate* violence on the 12 June, at the moment when she opened and read the letter from Constanza? If not, there could be no common assault, and thus no assault occasioning actual bodily harm.

The court ruled that Constanza's actions could amount to an assault because Wilson *had* been in fear of immediate violence. Schiemann LJ explained that it was enough if the victim was in fear of violence, 'at some time not excluding the immediate future'.[88] Schiemann LJ had to be creative if he was to assist a victim of stalking within the offences against the person regime framework. The OAPA, s47 requirement that "fear" must be "fear-of-imminent-violence" makes it ill-suited for the prosecution of stalking. Susan Edwards' distinction between 'immediate fear, fear of future harm or being in fear' is relevant here.[89] Critics argued that Schiemann LJ's creativity in this regard distorted the meaning of the OAPA, s47. Wilson was certainly living in fear, and she feared future harm, but was she really in fear of immediate violence from Constanza when she opened his letter? Or, is it more that, 'This case ... seems to provide another example of the courts distorting the law of assault in an attempt to counter the problem of stalking'.[90] Another commentator went further: 'The approach of the court verges on the cavalier'.[91]

As I stated above, fear is under-theorised from a legal perspective.[92] Instead, a hierarchy is assumed, which privileges immediate fear of a specific violent event at the expense of a more generalised fear of future harm. In fact, research shows that high levels of fear – 'living in fear'[93] – leads to states of "hyper-vigilance" in victims that can have a serious and detrimental effect on their health.[94] Survivors that I interviewed described a generalized anxiety that they said was far more devastating, in terms of the impact on their day-to-day life, than fear that is limited in time and space to a single physically violent event.[95] At the time of *Constanza*, resistant commentators were correct to suggest that, 'The victim's fear may not have been "of" any specific future event, but rather a generalised state of acute anxiety. And that ... has not sufficed'.[96] The fact that fear must be "of" a specific imminent future event in order to "count" for the purposes of the OAPA is one of the many reasons the OAPA is ill-suited to the prosecution of stalking.

At the time Wilson received the 12 June letter, she, just like Karen, was experiencing high levels of fear arousal for much of the time. Whether or not that fear arousal was linked to an expectation of violence at a particular moment on 12 June might have seemed irrelevant to her, in the context of how it felt to live in its grip. Despite the best efforts of the Court of Appeal, in other words, the totality of the psychiatric distress experienced by Wilson was "fragmented" in a way that led to the "cloaking" of much of the harm she experienced. This had repercussions for the validity of the criminal sanction, (OAPA, s47), in the stalking context that had already become the subject of a high-profile media debate.[97]

Ireland, Burstow[98]

Ireland and *Burstow* were heard together in the House of Lords, and fed into the debate. *Ireland* involved non-relational stalking. The case against Robert Ireland was that, during a period of three months in 1994, he made repeated silent telephone calls to three different women. Sometimes he breathed heavily down the phone. The calls were mostly made at night. One of his victims was diagnosed with a psychiatric illness, (anxiety and depression), that her psychiatrist determined was caused by Robert Ireland's behaviour. *Burstow* was concerned with domestic stalking. Anthony Burstow had an intimate relationship with his victim. She ended the relationship, and he proceeded to harass her over a lengthy period of time. During the eight-month period covered by the indictment under consideration he made silent telephone calls to her, made abusive telephone calls to her, distributed offensive cards (about her) in the street where she lived and was frequently at her home and place of work. He took photographs of her without her permission and sent threatening letters. She suffered a severe depressive illness.

Robert Ireland was convicted at first instance of assault occasioning actual bodily harm (OAPA, s47); Anthony Burstow was convicted of inflicting grievous bodily harm (OAPA, s 20). Both men appealed their convictions and both appeals were dismissed. Leave was granted to appeal to the House of Lords in both cases, and the appeals were heard together. The question of public importance to be decided in *Ireland* was, 'whether the making of silent telephone calls can amount in law to an assault'.[99] The point of general public importance in *Burstow* related to a different offence but amounted to essentially the same question: 'whether the offence of inflicting grievous bodily harm ... can be committed where no physical violence is applied directly or indirectly to the body of the victim'.[100] Both questions are, in fact, dealing with the same point that was looked at in *Constanza*:[101] could the nefarious behaviour of stalkers be captured by the law on offences against the person? Also at issue in *Burstow* and *Ireland* was a question as to whether psychiatric illness could constitute bodily harm.

The House of Lords ruled in the affirmative on both points. It held that the making of silent telephone calls could constitute assault occasioning actual bodily harm further to OAPA, s47. Furthermore, 'in light of contemporary knowledge covering recognisable psychiatric injuries, and bearing in mind the best, current scientific appreciation of the link between the body and psychiatric injury', a recognisable psychiatric condition could amount to bodily harm.[102] This ruling is progressive from the survivor perspective, but it highlights the limitations of the criminal law as it then stood, in the context of a growing awareness of an insidious wrong. While the ruling in *Ireland* and *Burstow* represented a creative attempt to accommodate the act and harm of stalking, it was somewhat akin to fitting a 'square peg' (stalking) into a 'round hole' (the criminal law).[103]

Stalking Is Not Assault

The artificial nature of the "fit" between "life" and "law" exemplified by *Constanza, Ireland* and *Burstow* was observed by commentators at the time, both in the legal and psychological literature, and in the media.[104] One commentator concluded that:

> The cases of *Ireland* and *Constanza* involved a deliberate restatement of the immediacy requirement in cases of psychiatric harm, a situation which led to the accusation that the courts were distorting the law of assault in an attempt to counter the problem of stalking.[105]

Heather Keating et al state: 'This whole approach adopted by the House of Lords is misguided and involves stretching the existing concept of assault too far'.[106] Of particular concern was the tension that was perceived between behaviour that is ongoing, and the incident-specific focus of the OAPA. The mismatch between the ongoing nature of the fear generated by stalking and the requirement for fear that is linked to the anticipation of an imminent violent event has already been referred to above. Lawyers also argued that adapting the incident-specific OAPA, s47 offence in this way gives rise to difficulties with the correspondence principle:

when did the assault in *Constanza* begin? For how long did it continue? 'Does the actus reus have intermissions when the perpetrator is asleep?'[107] Psychologists pointed out that it is difficult to pin generalised disorders such as depression or anxiety that are ongoing to single abusive incidents.[108]

Data from my interviews with police support Keating's view that this approach is misguided. Detective Constable Shell, for example, spoke about a case he had investigated involving a woman who had had a nervous breakdown as a result of her abusive partner's behaviour. Detective Constable Shell explained 'I tried to run with mental ABH, but in the end, I couldn't get enough medical evidence to show that she was ... we couldn't document that he was causing this. Rather than that she was suffering for a different reason'.[109] In other words, Detective Constable Shell tried to persuade the CPS to charge the perpetrator in question with causing the victim to suffer actual bodily harm. The harm in this case constituted the victim's recognised psychiatric disorder. This attempt failed because it was difficult for Detective Constable Shell, as the officer in charge of the investigation, to get expert evidence that established a conclusive link between the psychiatric illness of the victim and specific acts of the perpetrator.

Conclusion

In conclusion, the crimes that constitute the offences against the person regime are the fragments of domestic abuse that are most often prosecuted by police. Unfortunately, police are not encouraged to distinguish between assaults that are situationally specific (as in the case of Caroline Flack) and assaults that are part of a controlling strategy, and the criminal justice response to domestic abuse suffers as a result. The resulting muddle has an impact on risk assessment, on the ability of police to understand and thus respond sensitively to, survivors of abuse, on the prosecution of abuse in the courts and finally on the survivor experience of engaging with the law. Much abuse does not get prosecuted at all. Even when an assault is successfully prosecuted, the severe and sustained emotional suffering experienced by survivors is not recognised as legally significant, unless and until it is diagnosed as a clinical medical condition. Even where there is such a diagnosis, establishing legal causation – pinpointing a psychiatric condition to a single event – is difficult.

In the late 1990s, there was extensive media coverage of the inability of the offences against the person regime to accommodate the harms and behaviours associated with non-relational stalking. The Court of Appeal responded by "stretching" the offences against the person regime to allow stalking behaviours, (such as the making of silent telephone calls), to constitute common assault. In Ireland, Burstow it was held that psychiatric injury could amount to bodily harm for the purposes of an OAPA, s47 assault. These steps were criticised by the legal community. Andrew Simester and others summed it up thus: 'Psychiatric injury may have devastating consequences but it is *different* from physical injury. Policing the causing of psychiatric injury by way of nineteenth century laws focused on matters physical is not the way forward'.[110] Against this backdrop of media attention, controversial judicial expansion and accompanying critique, the PHA was making its way through the House of Commons. This is the subject of the following chapter.

Notes

1 Office for National Statistics, 'Domestic Abuse in England and Wales: Year ending March 2021' available at <https://www.ons.gov.uk/peoplepopulationandcommunity/crimeandjustice/articles/domesticabuseprevalenceandtrendsenglandandwales/yearendingmarch2021> accessed 13 May 2022.

2 Specifically, assault occasioning actual bodily harm contrary to section 47 of the Offences against the Person Act 1861 ('ABH'), and wounding with intent and/or causing grievous bodily harm with intent contrary to section 18 of the Offences against the Person Act 1861 ('GBH').

3 Michael Johnson, *A Typology of Domestic Violence Intimate Terrorism, Violent Resistance and Situational Couple Violence* (University Press 2008).

4 Sky News, Caroline Flack Inquest at Poplar Coroner's Court 1 July 2021 – Evidence of Mrs Flack given to coroner Mary Hassell at 13:28. Available at <https://news.sky.com/story/caroline-flack-inquest-resumes-into-death-of-love-island-presenter-12041677> accessed 29 September 2021 (hard copy of Sky News report on file with me).

5 Evidence of Detective Inspector Lauren Bateman, Metropolitan Police given to coroner Mary Hassell at 10:26 on 1 July 2021 ibid.

6 Witness Statement of Kate Weiss, CPS read out by coroner Mary Hassell at 12:23 on 01 July 2021 ibid.

7 Evidence of Detective Inspector Lauren Bateman given to coroner Mary Hassell at 15:18 on 30 June 2021 at Poplar Coroner's Court. Available at <https://news.sky.com/story/caroline-flack-inquest-resumes-into-death-of-love-island-presenter-12041677> accessed 29 September 2021 (hard copy of Sky News report on file with me).

8 Evidence of Detective Inspector Lauren Bateman given to coroner Mary Hassell at 15:18 on 30 June 2021 (n7), and evidence of Mrs Flack at 13:28 on 1 July 2021 (n3).

9 Coroner's questions to CPS prosecutor Lisa Ramsmarran, CPS prosecutor at 12:54 on 1 July n4.

10 Ibid.

11 Coroner Mary Hassell's submissions, 10:53 on 1 July 2021 ibid.

12 Witness Statement of Senior CPS Prosecutor Alison Wright, read by coroner Mary Hassell at 10:58 on 01 July 2021 ibid.

13 Evidence of Detective Inspector Lauren Bateman, given to coroner Mary Hassell at 10:58 on 01 July 2021 ibid.

14 CPS, 'Offences against the Person, Incorporating the Charging Standard' available at <https://www.cps.gov.uk/legal-guidance/offences-against-person-incorporating-charging-standard> accessed 5 August 2021.

15 CPS, 'Domestic Abuse Legal Guidance' available at <https://www.cps.gov.uk/legal-guidance/domestic-abuse> accessed 7 April 2022.

16 Ibid.

17 Coroner Mary Hassell's questions to Detective Inspector Bateman, at 10:53 on 1 July 2021 n4.

18 Jonathan Garabette, *Medical Report on Caroline Flack*, read by coroner Mary Hassell at 15:13 on 30 June 2021 n7.

19 Statement from Tamsin Lewis medical practitioner, read by coroner Mary Hassell at 11:02 30 June 2021 ibid.

20 Evidence of Lisa Ramsarran CPS, given to coroner Mary Hassell at 16:12 on 30 June 2021 ibid.

21 Statement from Jody Flack, read by coroner Mary Hassell at 11:24 on 30 June 2021 n7.

22 Evidence of Lauren Bateman, given to coroner Mary Hassell at 15:18 on 30 June 2021 ibid.

23 Evidence of Lisa Ramsarran CPS, given to coroner Mary Hassell at 15:56 on 30 June 2021 ibid.

24 Statement from Lewis Burton, read by coroner Mary Hassell at 11:10 on 30 June 2021 ibid.

25 Cassandra Wiener, 'Caroline Flack's Death Shows Why Police and Prosecutors Need More Training in Domestic Abuse Cases' *The Conversation* (19 February) 2020 available at <https://theconversation.com/caroline-flacks-death-shows-why-police-and-cps-need-more-training-in-domestic-abuse-cases-131955> accessed 11 October 2021.

26 Tanya Palmer, 'Failing to See the Wood for the Trees: Chronic Sexual Violation and the Criminal Law' 2020 84(6) The Journal of Criminal Law 573, 573.

27 Charlotte Bishop 'Domestic Violence: The Limitations of a Legal Response' in Sarah Hilda and Vanessa Bettinson (eds), *Interdisciplinary Perspectives on Protection, Prevention and Intervention* (Palgrave Macmillan 2016) 66.

28 Jane Bradley, 'A Year Long Cry for Help, and Then Death after an Assault' *New York Times* (New York 10 August 2021).

29 Evan Stark, 'Introduction' in Evan Stark, Coercive Control: How Men Entrap Women in Personal Life (Oxford University Press 2022) 9.

30 Focus Group with Senior Police (30 November 2016) 22.

31 Ibid.

32 Ibid.

33 Cassandra Wiener, 'Seeing What Is Invisible in Plain Sight: Policing Coercive Control' (2017) Howard Journal of Crime and Justice 500.

34 Evan Stark, 'Looking beyond Domestic Violence: Policing Coercive Control' 2012 (12) Journal of Police Crisis Negotiations 199, 202.

35 Ibid. 200.

36 Mary Ann Dutton, 'Understanding Women's Responses to Domestic Violence: A Redefinition of Battered Woman Syndrome' (1992) 21 Hofstra Law Review 1191, 1208.

37 Stark, Looking beyond Domestic Violence n34 205.

38 Interview with Detective Chief Inspector Roberts (23 March 2016) 14.

39 Ibid.

40 Trial at Brighton Magistrates Court on 9 May 2016 (notes of trial on file with me).

41 Deborah Tuerkheimer, 'Recognizing and Remedying the Harm of Battering: A Call to Criminalize Domestic Violence' (2004) 94(4) Journal of Criminal Law and Criminology 959, 979.

42 Interview with Jessica (26 May 2016) 10.

43 Interview with Karen (24 November 2016) 4.

44 Ibid.

45 Alafair Burke, 'Domestic Violence as a Crime of Pattern and Intent: An Alternative Reconceptualization' (2007) 75 George Washington Law Review 558, 577; Heather Douglas, 'Do We Need a Specific Domestic Violence Offence?' (2016) 39 Melbourne University Law Review 435.

46 *Hills* [2001] 1FLR 580 [10].

47 Ibid. [13].

48 Bishop, Domestic Violence n27 66.

49 Nagire Naffine, Criminal Law and the Man Problem (Hart 2019) 23.

50 Tuerkheimer, Recognizing and Remedying the Harm of Battering n41 980; see also Vanessa Bettinson and Charlotte Bishop, 'Evidencing Domestic Violence, Including Behaviour That Falls under the New Offence of "Controlling or Coercive Behaviour"' (2017) 22(1) The International Journal of Evidence and Proof 3, for an English perspective.

51 Ibid.

52 Ibid.

53 Dutton, Understanding Women's Responses to Domestic Violence n36 1208.

54 Ibid. 1209.

55 Interview with Sue (16 August 2016) 6.

56 Jeremy Horder, 'Reconsidering Psychic Assault' [1998] Criminal Law Review 392, 400.

57 Susan Edwards, 'Recognising the Role of the Emotion of Fear in Offences and Defences' (2019) 83(6) Journal of Criminal Law 450, 450 (my brackets). As Edwards acknowledges in this paper, fear has been afforded a degree of recognition in the context of the law on defences to a crime.

58 The rulings in *Ireland; Burstow* [1997] UKHL 34 are considered in detail below.

59 *Chan-Fook* [1994] 1 WLR 695 (CA) [696] (my emphasis).

60 See, for example *Dhaliwal* [2006] 2 Cr App R 24, where the Court of Appeal dismissed the impact of domestic abuse on a victim despite evidence of depression because there was no clinical diagnosis. For commentary on this case see Bishop, Domestic Violence (n25) 70, and more generally see Mandy Burton, 'Commentary on *R v Dhaliwal*' in Rosemary Hunter et al (eds), *Feminist Judgments: From Theory to Practice* (Oxford 2010). For a more recent critique see Emily Finch, 'Psychological Injury: Where's the Harm in It?' 2022 (5) Criminal Law Review 358.

61 *Chan-Fook* n56 [696].

62 Ibid.

63 Edwards, Recognising the Role of the Emotion of Fear n57 450.

64 Vanessa Munro and Sangeeta Shah, 'R v *Dhaliwal* Judgment' in Rosemary Hunter et al (eds), *Feminist Judgments: From Theory to Practice* (Oxford 2010) 264.

65 Clare McGlynn et al. '"It's Torture for the Soul": The Harms of Image-Based Sexual Abuse' (2021) 30(4) 541, 541.

66 Marianne Hester, 'Making It through the Criminal Justice System: Attrition and Domestic Violence' (2006) 5(1) Social Policy and Society 79.

67 Tuerkheimer, Recognizing and Remedying the Harm of Battering n41 980.

68 Michael Sazl, 'The Struggle to Make Stalking a Crime: A Legislative Road Map of How to Develop Effective Stalking Legislation in Maine' (1998) 23 Seton Hall Legislative Journal 57.

69 Emily Finch, *The Criminalisation of Stalking: Constructing the Problem and Evaluating the Solution* (Cavendish 2001).

70 Jessica Harris, *An Evaluation of the Use and Effectiveness of the Protection from Harassment Act 1997* (Home Office Research Study 203, Home Office 2000) 1.

71 Finch, Criminalisation of Stalking n67 109.

72 Kenneth Campbell, 'Stalking around the Main Issue' (1997/8) 8 Kings College Law Journal 128, 128.

73 Laurie Salame, 'A National Survey of Stalking Laws: A Legislative Trend Comes to the Aid of Domestic Violence Victims and Others' (1993) 27 Suffolk University Law Review 67.

74 Karen n43 3.

75 Interview with Kim (6 October 2016) 2.

76 Interview with Sarah (29 June 2016) 7.

77 In a study in Maine, stalking was found to occur within 80% of domestic abuse cases: Sazl, The Struggle to Make Stalking a Crime n68. This finding was mirrored by Jane Monkton-Smith in the UK: see Jane Monkton-Smith et al, 'Exploring the

Relationship between Stalking and Homicide' (Suzy Lamplugh Trust 2017) and also by Charlotte Barlow et al 'Putting Coercive Control into Practice: Problems and Possibilities' (2020) 60(1) British Journal of Criminology 160.

78 Finch, Criminalisation of Stalking n69.

79 Tuerkheimer, Recognizing and Remedying the Harm of Battering n41 980

80 *Constanza* [1997] Crim LR 576 (CA).

81 *Ireland, Burstow* n58.

82 *Constanza* n80.

83 Ibid. 493.

84 Ibid.

85 Glanville Williams states 'It has been settled law since the middle ages that the actus reus of assault has a technical meaning, different from battery, and focuses on the apprehension that unlawful force is about to be applied to the victim' Glanville Williams, *Textbook of Criminal Law* (Sweet and Maxwell 1983) 172 as cited by Horder, Reconsidering Psychic Assault n56 393.

86 *Constanza* n80 493.

87 Tuerkheimer, Recognizing and Remedying the Harm of Battering n41 980.

88 *Constanza* n80 [492].

89 Edwards, Recognising the Role of the Emotion of Fear n57 461.

90 David Cowley, 'Assault by Letter *R v Constanza*' (1998) 62(2) The Journal of Criminal Law 155, 156. See also Campbell, Stalking n66. This point was also made in relation to the later House of Lords judgment in *Ireland, Burstow*: see Faye Boland, 'Psychiatric Injury and Assault the Immediate Effect of *R v Ireland, R v Burstow*' (1997) 19(2) The Liverpool Law Review 231.

91 Campbell, Stalking n72 131.

92 Horder, Reconsidering Psychic Assault n56; Bishop, Domestic Violence n27.

93 Edwards, Recognising the Role of the Emotion of Fear n57 461.

94 Paul Mullen et al, *Stalkers and their Victims* (Cambridge University Press 2000); Jane Monckton Smith et al, *Exploring the Relationship between Stalking and Homicide* (Report by the Homicide Research Group, University of Gloucestershire, 2017) available at <http://eprints.glos.ac.uk/4553/> accessed 2 October 2017.

95 Sadia, Zara and Maia in particular described their experiences of fear, Focus Group with Survivors (8 September 2016).

96 Simon Gardner, 'Case Comment Stalking' [1998] Law Quarterly Review 33, 36.

97 Finch, The Criminalisation of Stalking n69 104 who cites: 'Police Lack Powers over Dangerous Obsession' *The Daily Telegraph* (London 30 January 1996); 'Can Laws Stop the Obsessed?' *The Times* (London 22 February 1993); 'Men Who Must Pursue Women' *The Guardian* (London 26 June 1993); 'The Law and the Stalker' *The Independent* (30 January 1996).

98 *Ireland, Burstow* n58.

99 Ibid. 149.

100 Ibid.

101 *Constanza* n80.

102 *Ireland, Burstow* n58 147.

103 Tuerkheimer, Recognizing and Remedying the Harm of Battering n39 566.

104 'Call for Tighter Law as Victim Tells of Stalking Campaign' *The Times* (London 3 September 1996); 'Law Change after Stalking Case Acquittal' *The Guardian* (London 18 September 1996); 'Law in Urgent Need of Reform' *The Independent* (London 19 September 1996); 'Stopping Stalkers: How Would the Law Change?' *Daily Telegraph* (London 16 October 1996). For further examples and analysis see Finch, Criminalisation of Stalking n69 111.

105 Finch, Criminalisation of Stalking n69 203.

106 Heather Keating et al, *Clarkson and Keating: Criminal Law* (Sweet and Maxwell 2014)

565. See also Paul Andrew, 'Assault Occasioning Actual Bodily Harm – Stalking over Period of Nine Months' [1998] Criminal Law Review 810.

107 'Case Comment Assault: Whether Committed by Words Alone' [1997] Criminal Law Review 576, 577.

108 Dutton, Understanding Women's Responses n36.

109 Interview with Detective Constable Shell (4 December 2017) 12.

110 Andrew Simester et al, *Simester and Sullivan's Criminal Law: Theory and Doctrine* (Oxford 2010) 440 cited by Judith Garland, 'Comment: Protection from Harassment Act 1997: the 'New' Stalking Offences' (2013) 77 Journal of Criminal Law 387, 388 (emphasis in original).

Bibliography

Andrew P, 'Assault Occasioning Actual Bodily Harm – Stalking over Period of Nine Months' (1998) Criminal Law Review 810.

Barlow C, Johnson K, Walklate S and Humphries L, 'Putting Coercive Control into Practice: Problems and Possibilities' (2020) 60(1) British Journal of Criminology 160.

Bettinson V and Bishop C, 'Evidencing Domestic Violence, Including Behaviour That Falls under the New Offence of "Controlling or Coercive Behaviour"' (2017) 22(1) The International Journal of Evidence and Proof 3.

Bishop C, 'Domestic Violence: The Limitations of a Legal Response' in Hilda S and Bettinson V (eds), *Interdisciplinary Perspectives on Protection, Prevention and Intervention* (Palgrave Macmillan 2016).

Boland F, 'Psychiatric Injury and Assault the Immediate Effect of *R v Ireland, R v Burstow*' (1997) 19(2) The Liverpool Law Review 231.

Bradley J, 'A Year Long Cry for Help, and Then Death after an Assault' *New York Times* (New York 10 August 2021).

Burke A, 'Domestic Violence as a Crime of Pattern and Intent: An Alternative Reconceptualization' (2007) 75 George Washington Law Review 558.

Burton M, 'Commentary on *R v Dhaliwal*' in Rosemary Hunter et al (eds), *Feminist Judgments: From Theory to Practice* (Oxford 2010).

Campbell K, 'Stalking around the Main Issue' (1997/8) 8 Kings College Law Journal 128.

Cowley D, 'Assault by Letter *R v Constanza*' (1998) 62(2) The Journal of Criminal Law 155.

CPS, 'Domestic Abuse Legal Guidance' available at <https://www.cps.gov.uk/legal-guidance/domestic-abuse> accessed 7 April 2022 accessed 5 August 2021.

CPS, 'Offences against the Person, Incorporating the Charging Standard' available at <https://www.cps.gov.uk/legal-guidance/offences-against-person-incorporating-charging-standard> accessed 5 August 2021.

'Call for Tighter Law as Victim Tells of Stalking Campaign' *The Times* (London 3 September 1996).

'Case Comment Assault: Whether Committed by Words Alone' (1997) Criminal Law Review 576.

Dutton M, 'Understanding Women's Responses to Domestic Violence: A Redefinition of Battered Woman Syndrome' (1992) 21 Hofstra Law Review 1191.

Douglas H, 'Do We Need a Specific Domestic Violence Offence?' (2016) 39 Melbourne University Law Review 435.

Edwards S, 'Recognising the Role of the Emotion of Fear in Offences and Defences' (2019) 83(6) Journal of Criminal Law 450.

Finch E, *The Criminalisation of Stalking: Constructing the Problem and Evaluating the Solution* (Cavendish 2001).

Finch E, 'Psychological Injury: Where's the Harm in It?' (2022) (5) Criminal Law Review 358.

Gardner S, 'Case Comment Stalking' (1998) Law Quarterly Review 33.

Garland J, 'Comment: Protection from Harassment Act 1997: The 'New' Stalking Offences' (2013) 77 The Journal of Criminal Law 387.

Harris J, *An Evaluation of the Use and Effectiveness of the Protection from Harassment Act 1997* (Home Office Research Study 203, Home Office 2000).

Hester M, 'Making It through the Criminal Justice System: Attrition and Domestic Violence' (2006) 5(1) Social Policy and Society 79.

Horder J, 'Reconsidering Psychic Assault' (1998) Criminal Law Review 392, 400.

Johnson M, *A Typology of Domestic Violence Intimate Terrorism, Violent Resistance and Situational Couple Violence* (University Press 2008).

Keating H, Kyd Cunningham C, Elliott S and Walters M, *Clarkson and Keating: Criminal Law* (Sweet & Maxwell 2014).

'Law Change after Stalking Case Acquittal' *The Guardian* (London 18 September 1996).

'Law in Urgent Need of Reform' *The Independent* (London 19 September 1996).

McGlynn C, Johnson K, Rackley E, Henry N, Gavey N, Flynn A and Powell A, '"It's Torture for the Soul": The Harms of Image-Based Sexual Abuse' (2021) 30(4) Social and Legal Studies 541.

Monckton Smith J, Szymanska K and Haile S, *Exploring the Relationship between Stalking and Homicide* (Report by the Homicide Research Group, University of Gloucestershire, 2017) available at <http://eprints.glos.ac.uk/4553/> accessed 2 October 2017.

Mullen P, Pathe M and Purcell R, *Stalkers and their Victims* (Cambridge University Press 2008).

Munro V and Shah S, 'R v *Dhaliwal* Judgment' in Rosemary Hunter et al (eds), *Feminist Judgments: From Theory to Practice* (Oxford 2010).

Naffine N, *Criminal Law and the Man Problem* (Hart 2019).

Office for National Statistics, 'Domestic Abuse in England and Wales: Year ending March 2021' <https://www.ons.gov.uk/peoplepopulationandcommunity/crimeandjustice/articles/domesticabuseprevalenceandtrendsenglandandwales/yearendingmarch2021> accessed 13 May 2021.

Palmer T, 'Failing to See the Wood for the Trees: Chronic Sexual Violation and the Criminal Law' (2020) 84(6) The Journal of Criminal Law 573.

Salame L, 'A National Survey of Stalking Laws: A Legislative Trend Comes to the Aid of Domestic Violence Victims and Others' (1993) 27 Suffolk University Law Review 67.

Sazl M, 'The Struggle to Make Stalking a Crime: A Legislative Road Map of How to Develop Effective Stalking Legislation in Maine' (1998) 23 Seton Hall Legislative Journal 57.

Sky News, 'Caroline Flack Inquest at Poplar Coroner's Court 30 June 2021' available at <https://news.sky.com/story/caroline-flack-inquest-resumes-into-death-of-love-island-presenter-12041677> accessed 29 September 2021 (hard copy on file with me).

Sky News, 'Caroline Flack Inquest at Poplar Coroner's Court 1 July 2021' available at <https://news.sky.com/story/caroline-flack-inquest-resumes-into-death-of-love-island-presenter-12041677> accessed 29 September 2021 (hard copy on file with me).

Stark E, 'Looking beyond Domestic Violence: Policing Coercive Control' (2012) 12 Journal of Police Crisis Negotiations 199.

Stark E, 'Introduction' in Evan Stark, *Coercive Control: How Men Entrap Women in Personal Life* (Oxford University Press 2022).

'Stopping Stalkers: How Would the Law Change?' *Daily Telegraph* (London 16 October 1996).

Tuerkheimer D, 'Recognizing and Remedying the Harm of Battering: A Call to Criminalize Domestic Violence' (2004) 94(4) Journal of Criminal Law and Criminology 959.

Wiener C, 'Seeing What Is Invisible in Plain Sight: Policing Coercive Control' (2017) 56(4) Howard Journal of Crime and Justice 500.

Wiener C, 'Caroline Flack's Death Shows Why Police and Prosecutors Need More Training in Domestic Abuse Cases' *The Conversation* (19 February 2020) available at <https://theconversation.com/caroline-flacks-death-shows-why-police-and-cps-need-more-training-in-domestic-abuse-cases-131955> accessed 11 October 2021.

Cases

Chan-Fook [1994] 1 WLR 695 (CA).
Constanza [1997] Crim LR 576 (CA).
Dhaliwal [2006] 2 Cr App R 24.
Hills [2001] 1FLR 580.
Ireland, Burstow [1997] UKHL 34.

Legislation

Offences against the Person Act 1861.
Protection from Harassment Act 1997.

3

'AN UNPLEASANT, CLOSED-OFF WORLD'[1]

Domestic Stalking and the Protection from Harassment Act 1997

Introduction

In the last chapter, I explained that this book tells the story of criminal law reform in the context of domestic abuse. In particular, I have said that I am interested in how the criminal law has been adapted to reflect improved understanding of perpetrator behaviour in coercive control. Deborah Tuerkheimer describes how legal reform is achieved via:

> Both movement and resistance on the part of legal structures subjected to the force of lived experience. Each (movement/resistance) reveals the defects of structures left intact, the remaining doctrinal patchwork a testament to the power of incompatible truths.[2]

'Reality', in other words, comes to 'bear on legal structures' via a series of 'pressure points' resulting in legal reform.[3]

The difficulties experienced by judges in the face of the perpetrator behaviour exhibited in cases such as *Ireland* and *Burstow* is an example of just such a reality. The pressure that these cases put upon the criminal law did not go unnoticed. In fact, articles in all of the leading newspapers called specifically for a change in the law.[4] Pressure mounted on the Government to make stalking a bespoke criminal offence. Home Secretary Michael Howard responded by introducing a draft Bill in December 1996. He explained as he did so that, 'In the past year, a number of highly publicised stalking cases have come to public attention. They have high-lighted the need to give the courts more effective powers to deal with stalkers'.[5]

Framing the legislation turned out to be a difficult exercise; the issues were novel and the Protection from Harassment Bill was a ground-breaking and in-novative piece of law. In this chapter, I look at what Parliament was trying to achieve with the Protection from Harassment Act 1997 (the 'PHA'), firstly by

DOI: 10.4324/9780429201844-4

looking at the relevant parliamentary debates, and secondly with a doctrinal review of the PHA itself. In the final part of the chapter I assess how the PHA came to be used in practice. This is where the domestic abuse context becomes important. Parliament had not specifically considered the use of the PHA in the context of domestic abuse, but once again "reality" intruded even in the very early days of the new law. The PHA quickly came to be what Detective Constable James told me was 'bread and butter'[6] for police investigating domestic abuse.

As I explained in the last chapter, the media portrayal of stalking in the 1990s was sensationalist, misleading and overly preoccupied with non-relational stalking.[7] By "non-relational" I mean stalking that occurs between people who are not, nor ever have been in, an intimate relationship. Reflecting this preoccupation, parliamentary debates were concerned only with non-relational stalking. But as soon as the PHA was in force, in the 2000s, it was used by police and prosecutors mostly to prosecute *domestic* stalking. Once again, police and prosecutors had to be creative in order to tackle behaviour that, importantly for this book, is often a manifestation of coercive control. This quickly became a 'pressure point'[8] for the courts, as it fell to them to decide how far the PHA could be "stretched" to cover domestic stalking. Three key decisions demonstrate how the Court of Appeal drew boundaries in relation to the application of the PHA – boundaries that eventually led to the passage of Serious Crime Act 2015, s 76 (section 76), and which therefore have had serious repercussions for the prosecution of coercive control in England and Wales.

The Parliamentary Debates

In March 1996, six months prior to Michael Howard's introduction of the draft bill referred to above, what was originally the 'Stalking Bill' was introduced by backbench Labour MP, Janet Anderson, under the ten-minute rule.[9] The Stalking Bill is interesting both because of the way in which it was structured and for the reasons it was rejected. The Stalking Bill defined stalking using what has been referred to since as the "list" approach; it lists the prohibited behaviour types such as "following", "interfering with property", etc that often manifest as stalking. The official Home Office news release contained a number of criticisms, including the fact that the definition of stalking was too wide and that legitimate activities would be curtailed as a result.[10]

The first controversial decision made by the parliamentary committee responsible for the drafting of the PHA was to abandon any attempts to define stalking. In fact, the word "stalking" is not mentioned anywhere in the bill. The rationale for its absence, (and the abandonment of the list approach adopted by the Stalking Bill), was that 'The behaviour engaged in by stalkers was so diverse that it was impossible to formulate a definition which encompassed all such activities'.[11] Instead, criminal liability is based upon the wider notion of harassment.

Harassment is similarly not defined by the Act. Howard explained that there was no need for such a definition because 'Harassment as a concept has been interpreted regularly by the courts since 1986'.[12] The lack of a definition of stalking was opposed by the shadow Home Secretary, Jack Straw, at the time[13] and later considered to be a mistake. It was reversed by the 2012 amendments to the PHA, which are reviewed below.[14] Curiously, a similar "mistake" was made with section 76; there is no attempt to define 'controlling or coercive behaviour', whether by list or otherwise.

The Government criticised the list approach for being 'too wide in one respect, and too narrow in another'.[15] It was felt to be too narrow because of the nefarious nature of stalking. Anthony Burstow, for example, spoke publicly of his knowledge of the criminal law and the way that he used that knowledge, strategically, to adapt his behaviour.[16] For example, in later interviews he reveals his outrage at the decision by the House of Lords in his case, thus showing that he was well aware that the Offences against the Person Act 1861, s 20 did not cover psychological harm until the courts decided to extend it in order to convict *him*.[17] If the list approach was felt to be narrow in that it left gaps for stalkers to exploit, it also managed to be "wide" by leaving open the possibility that innocuous behaviour would be criminalised. Stalking often involves behaviour that is, in and of itself, seemingly innocent: it is the context that renders it criminal. The Government felt that it would be inappropriate to try to capture context in a definition.[18]

One question that became critical subsequently is the extent to which Parliament intended the PHA to apply to domestic stalking. The fact that stalking can be relational or non-relational is not explicitly discussed in the parliamentary debate that took place on 17 December 1996. Instead, there seems to be an assumption throughout the debate that references to stalking are to non-relational stalking. As he introduced the bill, for example, Howard explained: 'The Bill covers not only stalkers but disruptive neighbours and those who target people because of the colour of their skin'.[19] The ensuing discussion in Parliament centred on stranger stalking, neighbourhood disputes, and nuisance neighbours.[20] The popular portrayal of stalkers in the 1990s as dangerous and mentally ill strangers, in other words, was reflected by an Act that was designed for harassment outside of an intimate relationship. Certainly, this was the conclusion drawn later by the Court of Appeal.[21]

The PHA introduces two new criminal offences (section 2 and section 4). The lesser of the two offences, the section 2 summary offence, is actually set out in section 1 *and* section 2. This is because the PHA creates (in section 1) a prohibited course of conduct which is made both a crime (section 2) and a tort (section 3). I am only concerned with the crime. Section 1 states that 'A person must not pursue a course of conduct (a) which amounts to harassment of another and (b) which he knows or ought to know amounts to harassment of the other'. Section 2 states that 'A person who pursues a course of conduct in breach of section 1 is guilty of an offence'. The maximum sentence is six months' imprisonment. The more serious section 4 offence is triable either way, and appears under the heading 'Putting people in fear of violence'. Section 4, which had a maximum prison sentence of five years at the time,[22] states that

A person whose course of conduct causes another to fear, on at least two occasions, that violence will be used against him is guilty of an offence if he knows or ought to know that his course of conduct will cause the other so to fear on each of those occasions.

Actus Reus of the Protection from Harassment Act 1997: Course of Conduct

As I said at the beginning of this chapter, Tuerkheimer's conceptualisation of the way in which reality comes to bear on legal structures via a series of pressure points, and thus promotes 'movement and resistance'[23] is a useful framework within which to understand the novel terminology of the PHA. This is especially true of the idea of the 'course of conduct' which is central to both the section 2 and the section 4 offences. As I have said in previous chapters, crimes that constitute the non-fatal offences against the person are conceived as transactional. They are conceived of as a single incident in part because this kind of specificity is an important part of the ideology of the criminal law.

This focus on specificity reflects the fact that 'The function of the criminal law is not to judge a person's general character or behaviour over a period of time; its concern is only with the distinct criminal conduct charged'.[24] This links in with the emphasis on choice, control and the rule of law summed up by the correspondence principle. The correspondence principle states that the *actus reus* of the crime must take place at the same moment in time (i.e. the time of the single incident) as the *mens rea* in order to amount to a criminal offence. Only if the defendant's mental state could be said to relate to the proscribed harm should he be held to have "chosen" and thus be liable for his criminal act.[25]

The difficulty with stalking is that, just as with coercive control, it does not occur as a discrete event. This empirical reality is Tuerkheimer's 'pressure point'.[26] 'Course of conduct' is defined in s. 7(3): 'A "course of conduct" must involve (a) in the case of conduct in relation to a single person, conduct on at least two occasions in relation to that person'. The idea of a 'course of conduct' crime is thus a concession to the *ongoing* nature of the behaviour patterns that constitute stalking, but an insistence on specificity is the 'resistance'.

In fact, defining a crime by reference to two related but separate incidents instead of just one incident did not "move" the transactional nature of the legal structure very far − in some ways it had the unintended effect of increasing the incident-specific focus yet delaying a police response. Police Constable South gave an example of this when he explained to me in an interview that 'Often things will come in as harassment, but actually when you look at them you think this doesn't qualify ... it's a first-time harassment and that's your first one for the next time, which is almost inevitably going to happen'.[27] Forcing police and a victim to watch and wait for the next "inevitable" harmful episode is far from ideal.

Other ways in which the "course of conduct" requirement has unintended effects include both the way in which 'judicial decisions interpreting the Act ... lapse back into an examination of individual incidents of assault and battery', and also confusion over the "nexus" that is required to give rise to the course of conduct.[28] Hills[29] is an example of the "lapsing" into an incident focus. There was evidence before Otton LJ of the abusive nature of the relationship in that case, with multiple incidents of abuse that the victim found it difficult (in court) to pin to specific times and dates. Otton LJ held, for example, that: 'The learned judge ruled that the complainant had said that, over a period of time and on a fairly regular basis, she had been ill-treated by the appellant'.[30] The particulars on the indictment included the fact that:

> The appellant assaulted the complainant on a number of occasions by throwing a stool at her, hitting her, restricting her breathing by putting his hands over her mouth or around her throat and attempting to smother her with a pillow.[31]

Otton LJ nevertheless found that the two incidents of assault that formed the basis of the section 4 case could not constitute a course of conduct. Otton LJ was influenced by the fact that the two incidents were isolated and separated by six months, and 'The prosecution might have been wiser to have abandoned the harassment count and to have concentrated on the two substantive counts of violence, and with more prospects of success'.[32] The alleged behaviour between the two incidents was not legally relevant.[33] Otton LJ, correctly, focuses on an examination of the two individual incidents of assault. This examination is abstracted from the abusive backdrop that the prosecution tried to argue demonstrated the necessary course of conduct for the section 4 harassment offence.

Actus Reus of the Protection from Harassment Act 1997: The Result

The second unusual or innovative aspect of the *actus reus* of both section 2 and section 4 is the conceptualisation of the harm that is a constituent part of the offence. Emotional distress that does not necessarily constitute a clinical disorder (but can do) forms the result component of the crime. Section 7(2) is the closest the PHA comes to a definition of harassment, and it states, 'References to harassing a person include alarming the person or causing the person *distress*'.[34] Section 4 criminalises causing a *fear* of violence in another person. Thus, there is no requirement with either of the two offences that the course of conduct is unlawful in itself: it is the emotional reaction of the victim that determines its criminality. This links with the decision described above not to define stalking with a list of stalking behaviours – Howard explained: 'The Bill overcomes the difficulty of defining stalking by focusing on the harmful effect that this activity has on its victims'.[35]

The PHA is structured in this way to address the limitations that the Offences against the Person Act 1861 previously presented to police and prosecutors. Legal intervention was only possible if the stalker committed a substantive criminal offence, which often he deliberately did not, and harm only "counted" if it amounted to a diagnosed clinical condition. The approach taken in the PHA was criticised at the time; concern was expressed at the way that the nature of the offences is left open.[36]

The reason this is a concern, some argued, is because it means that almost anything could constitute harassment. As different individuals will react differently to similar events, and conduct that might alarm one person might not alarm another, the imposition of criminality becomes contingent upon an unknown variable: the emotional response of the recipient.[37] While this is technically correct I do not think it is important in the context of the domestic stalking which is my focus here. This is because the majority of such defendants prosecuted under the PHA are well acquainted with the emotional responses of their victims. The behaviour manifested by perpetrators is a cynical exploitation of their prior knowledge of these emotional responses. For this reason, I find it difficult to imagine a case of domestic harassment or stalking where the emotional response of the recipient is unknown.

The *Mens Rea*

The principle of *mens rea* honours the importance of autonomy in that it states that defendants should be held criminally responsible only for consequences that they 'intended or knowingly risked'.[38] This is often referred to as subjective rather than objective *mens rea*, meaning that the criminal law should only hold individuals liable on the basis of their informed choices. In other words, to be liable, a defendant must be aware of what he is doing, and the consequences likely to follow from what he is doing, so that he could be said to have chosen the behaviour and its consequences. This correspondence – between the defendant's state of mind and the actions he took – forms the basis of the correspondence principle referred to above and means that there has been traditionally in the criminal law an emphasis on *mens rea* requirements necessitating subjective awareness by the defendant.[39] Andrew Ashworth says firmly: 'There should be recognition of the principle that no person should be liable to imprisonment without proof of sufficient fault'.[40]

Both the PHA, s2 and the PHA, s4 make it an offence to pursue a course of conduct that the offender knows '*or ought to know*' amounts to harassment. The inclusion of 'ought to know' introduces a negligence-based *mens rea* that is unusual; all other main offences against the person are based on intention or subjective recklessness.[41] Negligence as a term describes a behaviour pattern on the part of the defendant that falls below the standard that would be expected from a reasonable person in the defendant's position. A negligence-based *mens rea* allows a person to be found guilty of wrongdoing in circumstances where there is no proof that he "chose" to do wrong. In fact, there is no need to prove that the defendant was even aware of the consequences of his actions as long as a reasonable person in his situation would have been. Ashworth and Jeremy Horder state dryly with regard to the PHA that 'The combination of a negligence standard with a maximum penalty of five years is unfortunate'.[42] In fact, Parliament has recently increased the maximum sentence to ten years.[43]

Including a wholly objective *mens rea* as an option for the prosecution was a deliberate attempt by Parliament to circumvent some of the difficulties that were anticipated in the context of the prosecution of stalkers.[44] Howard explained to the House of Commons that 'The greatest difficulty that the police find in using existing legislation against stalkers is the need to prove the intention of the stalker'.[45] In any event, determining *mens rea* in the context of perpetrators who struggle with mental or personality disorders was felt to be too difficult. Parliament was persuaded that these are perpetrators who 'are so preoccupied with their obsession with the victims that they are unable to comprehend that their attentions may be unwelcome'.[46]

This view, that the PHA was passed with mentally ill defendants in mind, was certainly reflected in the early decisions of the courts. The Court of Appeal, for example, held in 2001 that:

> As is well known the Act was passed with the phenomenon of "stalking" particularly, although not exclusively, in mind. The conduct at which the Act is aimed, and from which it seeks to provide protection, is particularly likely to be conduct pursued by those of obsessive or otherwise unusual psychological make-up and very frequently by those suffering from an identifiable mental illness.[47]

More research is urgently needed into the issue of the extent to which perpetrators convicted under the PHA suffer from mental health or personality disorder-related issues which preclude them from understanding the significance of their conduct. Home Office early research on this subject concluded that 'The media portrayal of stalking is of repetitive, unwanted attention, communications or approaches from obsessive, psychotic strangers or fanatics'.[48] In fact, the Home Office report found that the kind of behaviour dealt with under the PHA was linked less with strangers or people with mental illnesses than with the unwanted attentions of ex-partners and harassment by neighbours.[49]

The Home Office findings are supported by research in the United States and the United Kingdom which concludes that while a minority of stalking cases involve the stalking of strangers by perpetrators with mental health issues, the majority of stalking has a domestic context – and 'perpetrators of this type of stalking generally are *not* suffering from any type of psychological disorder'.[50] Certainly the early constructions of stalking in the media referred to above relied heavily on the idea that there is an overlap between stalking and serious mental health issues. A proper examination of this issue is outside the scope of this book, but the question of the link between perpetrators of stalking and mental illness is likely to have a bearing not only on the appropriate *mens rea* for the PHA offences, but also on what *mens rea* standards should be included in laws criminalising coercive control.

It is not disputed that some perpetrators of harassment do have mental health conditions. In these cases, one unfortunate repercussion of the objective *mens rea* threshold is the inability to provide any resolution other than punishment for perpetrators who are in genuine need of help. In other words, there is no capacity-based exception. Ashworth and Horder, in their concluding remarks on the viability of negligence-based *mens rea* offences, make capacity-based exceptions a pre-condition.[51]

Some critics anticipated in 1997 that the lack of such an exception might be a problem: 'What of the mentally disturbed individual who simply does not see the distress their conduct is causing? Is this to be taken account of in the "reasonable person" test, and, if not, can this be just?'[52] These concerns are vindicated by cases such as *Colohan*, where the Court of Appeal upheld the conviction of a diagnosed schizophrenic who wrote threatening letters to his MP while in the grip of a delusional episode.[53] This was 'despite a finding that the defendant was compelled to act as he did due to suffering from schizophrenia and that he had no appreciation that his behaviour might engender a negative response'.[54] The Court of Appeal found that to do otherwise would weaken the protection available to stalking victims. This is a cause for concern.[55]

On the other hand, and while it is possible that Parliament was over-influenced by inaccurate media portrayals of stalking, it is important to remember that negligence liability is not strict liability. The English doctrinal tradition of restricting criminal liability to intention and recklessness alone fails to take into account that the risk of serious harm or injury can manifest greater culpability than some cases of so-called subjective recklessness, as even Ashworth and Horder acknowledge.[56] In other words, the negligence construct does not derail what Keating et al refer to as 'the central quest of identifying blameworthiness',[57] particularly because establishing the serious harm experienced by the victim is a constituent part of the offence. Any violation of the principle of contemporaneity is less of an issue in the context of stalking, where the timeframe of the criminal law has already been widened as a result of the nature of the criminal behaviour.

Furthermore, the principle of individual autonomy, while important, is not the only founding principle of the criminal law. The principle of welfare is described by Nicola Lacey as 'The fulfilment of certain basic interests such as maintaining one's personal safety, health and capacity to pursue one's chosen life plan'.[58] The principle of welfare recognises that citizens are entitled to protection, by the criminal law if necessary, to allow them to benefit from basic interests without being constrained by fellow citizens. The violations represented by the stalking offences targeted by the PHA affect the ability of the victim to pursue her basic interests. Ashworth concludes that 'Negligence may be an appropriate standard where there are well-known risks of serious harm'.[59] While the absence of a capacity-based exception is regrettable, my conclusion is that in principle the introduction of the objective *mens rea* in the context of the PHA can be justified.

Section 4 and the Fear of Violence

The wording of the section 4 offence unfortunately continues a preoccupation with violence that is physical. Section 4 does not encompass a textured understanding of the generalised anxiety dynamic generated by stalking. Instead, the focus is on a *specific* fear that violence will be used against the victim on at least *two* occasions. Lord Steyn considered the PHA in his judgment in the *Ireland* and *Burstow* appeals referred to above. He said:

> For the future there will be for consideration the provisions of section 1 and 2 of the Protection From Harassment Act 1997, not yet in force, which creates the offence of pursuing a course of conduct which amounts to harassment of another and which he knows or ought to know amounts to harassment of the other. The maximum custodial penalty is six months' imprisonment. This penalty may also be inadequate to deal with persistent offenders who cause serious psychiatric injury to victims. Section 4(1) of the Act of 1997 which creates the offence of putting people in fear of violence seems more appropriate. It provides a maximum custodial penalty upon conviction on indictment of five years' imprisonment. On the other hand section 4 only applies when as a result of a course of conduct the victim has cause to fear, on at least two occasions, that violence *will* be used against her. It may be difficult to secure a conviction in respect of a silent caller: the victim in such cases may have cause to fear that violence *may* be used against her but not more. In my view, therefore, the provisions of these two statutes are not ideally suited to deal with the significant problem which I have described.[60]

Lord Steyn's early criticism of the PHA – that the section 2 penalty is inadequate and that section 4 has an unhelpful focus on the *certain* expectation of physical violence – proved prescient.

In the previous chapter I suggested that, historically, the criminal law was based upon the assumption that victims are in need of protection from physical violence – and that there is in existence a laddering of harms that places physical violence, or the fear thereof, in some way at the top. The PHA, s 4 imports the old common assault emphasis on fear of physical violence into a piece of legislation that was introduced to help the criminal law take a new direction. It is an improvement on common assault in that the immediacy requirement is gone (section 4 necessitates a fear of violence but not a fear of *immediate* violence). Despite the broadening of the fear of violence component, however, section 4 retains a focus on physical violence that is curious in the context of what is understood about the behaviours that constitute stalking.

The section 4 physical violence requirement has been described as too "high" a threshold. It has been argued, for example, that 'In many stalking cases, the behaviour is too serious to merit section 2, but it falls short of meeting the very high threshold of section 4 which requires a fear that violence will be used on two occasions'.[61] Rather than being too "high", the section 4 threshold is simply inappropriate in the context of the offence of stalking. Emily Finch explains this:

> The wording of section 4 prioritises fear of physical harm over any other reaction to stalking, regardless of its severity or the impact on the life of the victim. This prioritisation of physical harm is indicative of the ongoing subordination of psychological harm that is evident elsewhere in the criminal law. It also represents a fundamental misunderstanding of the nature of stalking and the way in which victims react to being stalked. Research into the impact of stalking has indicated that there are a considerable range of responses to stalking victimisation. In particular, it is more common for victims to experience a heightened sense of generalised fearfulness - a fear of some innominate harm - rather than a specific fear that violence will be used against them. It is the fear of intrusion rather than the fear of a specific violation of one's physical person, that is anxiety provoking.[62]

The assumption that the threshold is too "high" rather than simply the wrong threshold invokes the "typical" victim of crime, who needs help safeguarding the physical boundaries of his person and his property from illegal transactional interference. It is still the case that generalised anxiety 'is viewed implicitly as being less serious than a fear of direct physical violence'.[63] Privileging the fear of physical violence in this way does not make sense in the context of stalking: which is ongoing, not transactional, and where it is the constant fear of intrusion (rather than violence) that it induces that is of a different, some would say more serious nature.

In fact, Lord Steyn's early observations on the likely limitations of both the PHA, s2 (too low a maximum sentence), and the PHA, s4 (unhelpful insistence that the victim must fear that violence *will* be used), proved to be correct. Attempts in the following decade to move section 4 away from an insistence on fear of the certainty of physical violence were not successful. This is not surprising in light of the clear wording of the section.

In 2000, for example, the victim in *Henley*[64] described a traumatic 'state of siege'[65] not dissimilar to that of the victim in *Burstow*. She ended her relationship with Henley, and he embarked on a campaign of terror. This campaign included continuous, abusive and frightening calls and breaking into her flat and causing damage. Henley was charged with the section 4 offence. The trial judge at first instance in her summing up directed the jury that 'to put (the victim) in fear of violence meant "to seriously frighten her as to what might happen"'. Being afraid 'of what might happen' is the 'fear of some innominate harm' articulated by

Finch,[66] or Susan Edwards' 'fear of future harm or being in fear',[67] and encapsulates the fear of intrusion that is the hallmark of stalking. In his appeal against conviction Pill LJ found that:

> When purporting to turn section 4(1) into English, the judge left out the word "violence" and said instead "to seriously frighten her as to what might happen"; that was confusing and did not necessarily bear the same meaning ... the direction so distorted the meaning of the section that the conviction could not be regarded as safe.[68]

Pill LJ was right in that the judge at first instance did "distort" the meaning of section 4 PHA, but perhaps wrong as to her motivation. Rather than trying to turn section 4(2) into English, she was possibly – like Lord Steyn before her in *Burstow* – struggling with the square peg of stalking and the round hole of section 4(2).

In any event, despite its limitations, the PHA came to be extremely useful to police, but not in ways that were anticipated by Parliament. The Home Office early evaluation of the PHA said that when the PHA was implemented, the government anticipated that it would be used relatively infrequently, perhaps around 200 cases a year.[69] In fact, in 1998 there were 4,300 section 2 charges and 1,500 section 4 charges.[70] By 2018 this number had dramatically increased; there were 11,922 charges brought in 2018 for harassment and stalking.[71] From 200 cases a year to 11,922 is a big jump: police interviewed for this project explained that the PHA has become increasingly central to their work. At the focus group I ran with senior police there was unanimous agreement that the PHA was used 'all the time. Daily. Bread and butter'.[72] Looking at how the PHA came to be used in this way, and why, is the focus of the rest of this chapter.

'An Unpleasant, Closed-Off World'[73]: Domestic Abuse and the Use of the Protection from Harassment Act 1997

In October 2012 TV comedian Justin Lee Collins was convicted at St Albans Crown Court of section 4 harassment (causing fear of violence) between January and July 2011. The case attracted an unprecedented amount of media attention, chiefly because of the bizarre demands he had made of his girlfriend, Anna Larke. BBC news coverage described the case as allowing the public access to something novel, dark and important, it was a court case that 'allows the general public to get an insight into *an unpleasant, closed-off world*'.[74] In fact, the behaviours exhibited by Collins (and demanded of Larke) will not be a surprise to anyone who has read this book. He controlled how she slept, where she slept (facing him) and when she slept (only after he had fallen asleep otherwise she was punished).[75] He demanded she shut down her Facebook page, and was not allowed an email account.[76] She was only allowed to look at inanimate objects (such as a tree, the ground, a bench) when they were out together (never another man).[77] Details of all of her previous sexual relationships were logged and used to belittle her.[78] So-called low-level physical violence occurred daily.[79] Collins was convicted and sentenced to 140 hours of community service.

The women's sector reacted angrily to the sentence, seeing it as wholly inadequate in the context of the 'state of siege'[80] in which Anna Larke had found herself trapped.[81] The sentence is undoubtedly too lenient. What is relevant here, however, is what this case demonstrates. *The most significant impact of the PHA lay in the use to which it was put.* The Home Office early report on the PHA took place three years after implementation, in 2000. It stated that 'The PHA is being used to deal with a variety of behaviour other than stalking, including domestic and inter-neighbour disputes, and *rarely for stalking itself*: the suspect and victim were known to each other in almost all cases'.[82] This reference to "stalking" is adopting the same non-relational connotations as was used by Parliament as it debated the Protection from Harassment Bill. In other words, the Home Office report makes the assumption that, where the 'suspect and victim were known to each other', this reflected behaviour other than stalking. The report goes on to observe that 'The most common reason for harassment was that the complainant had ended an intimate relationship with the suspect'.[83] What this early report was suggesting, in fact, is that the PHA was indeed being used to prosecute stalking: it was being used to prosecute *domestic* stalking.

The situation now is clear: the PHA is used most frequently in the context of domestic abuse,[84] but this gave the judiciary a problem. Finch noted in 2003 that, in the absence of a statutory definition, the parameters of the application of the PHA would have to be drawn by the courts. She observed that a 'line' was needed separating 'unpleasant conduct from actionable harassment' and that line, she said, 'will determine the parameters of acceptable conduct within society'.[85] She concluded: 'Where this line is to be is a question that is likely to occupy the courts in the future, as more harassment cases are heard'.[86] Finch was right, it did indeed fall to the courts to determine the boundaries of 'actionable harassment'. The extent to which the PHA could apply to domestic stalking was considered in three key Court of Appeal decisions *Hills*,[87] *Curtis*[88] and *Widdows*.[89]

Hills

Hills was decided first, in 2000. Gavin Hills was convicted at first instance of section 4 harassment. He was later charged with rape. The harassment consisted of two assaults that took place six months apart while he was still living with his victim. Otton LJ found that the assaults could not amount to a course of conduct for the purposes of the PHA. In the penultimate paragraph of the judgment, Otton LJ explains that he was influenced by his understanding of Parliament's intention for the PHA:

It is to be borne in mind that the state of affairs which was relied upon by the prosecution was miles away from the "stalking" type of offence for which the Act was intended. That is not to say that it is never appropriate so to charge a person who is making a nuisance of himself to his partner or wife when they have become estranged. However, in a situation such as this, when they were frequently coming back together and intercourse was taking place (apparently a video was taken of them having intercourse) it is unrealistic to think that this fell within the stalking category which either postulates a stranger or an estranged spouse.[90]

Otton LJ thus explains that there was a '"stalking" type of offence for which the Act was intended'. It is likely that here he is referring to the kind of non-relational stalking that was certainly the only kind of stalking referred to in the parliamentary debates. Otton LJ is prepared to extend the application of the PHA to include 'a person who is making a nuisance of himself to his partner or wife when they have become estranged'. He is prepared, in other words, to extend the PHA to cover domestic stalking, whether or not this was intended by Parliament, but only in cases of domestic stalking where the perpetrator is no longer in a relationship with his victim: a 'stranger or an estranged spouse'. He is not prepared to extend the application of the PHA to include domestic stalking where the partners are still in a relationship.

The difficulty for all those involved with the prosecution of domestic abuse is that while the non-relational "stranger" and even the domestic "estranged spouse" categories might seem relatively clear, the third, unnamed category in Otton LJ's analysis, the category into which he puts Gavin Hills and in respect of which he decided that the PHA does not apply, is not clear at all. Even as Otton LJ marks his boundary he recognises the instability of this category. He does not refer to Gavin Hills as "married" or as "in a relationship", for example, instead he refers to 'a situation like this ... when they were frequently coming back together and intercourse was taking place'.[91] The instability of the relationship between Gavin Hills and his partner is very typical of abusive relationships where a transactional moment of separation rarely exists.

It is understandable that Otton LJ felt the need to establish a boundary somewhere. The remit of the PHA *had* already been extended from that originally intended by Parliament. Parliament's intentions, however, were founded on a misunderstanding of what constitutes stalking, a misunderstanding that has become apparent only with the passage of time and by scrutinising the uses to which the PHA has been put. This decision has had significant consequences for the way in which domestic abuse is criminalised in England and Wales. This is because attempting to establish any boundary-dividing relationships that have ended from those that have not is fraught with difficulty. Giving the boundary legal significance was, in hindsight, a mistake.

Curtis

The facts of *Curtis*[92] and *Widdows*[93] are similar, and Pill LJ presided over both. *Curtis* was heard first, in January 2010. Daniel Curtis was convicted at first instance of section 4 harassment on the basis of six violent incidents that occurred while he was living with Donna Brand, his then partner and victim. Pill LJ considers what might amount to harassment. He reflects on both the definition of harassment and the type of victim that, in his view, should benefit from the protection of the PHA. In so doing, he draws on three separate sources: the House of Lords' judgment in *Majrowski*,[94] the Concise Oxford dictionary and Otton LJ's judgment in *Hills*.[95]

In *Majrowski*, the House of Lords considered the purpose of the PHA. Pill LJ draws on two paragraphs of Lord Nicholls' judgment: the first delineating the framework within which the PHA should be allowed to operate, and the second identifying the behaviour that the PHA should regulate. On the appropriate framework Pill LJ describes how Lord Nicholls states: 'The Act seeks to provide protection against stalkers, racial abusers, disruptive neighbours, bullying at work, and so forth'.[96] On where to draw the boundary between harassment and behaviour that could instead be classed as part of the 'irritations, annoyances, even a measure of upset' that 'arise at times in everybody's day-to-day dealings with other people', Lord Nicholls concludes: 'Courts are well able to recognise the boundary between conduct which is unattractive, even unreasonable, and conduct which is oppressive and unacceptable'.[97] Pill LJ goes on to use the Concise Oxford Dictionary definition to support Lord Nicholls' conclusions on the nature of harassment, before finishing with the comments of Otton LJ quoted at some length above on the type of victim to be protected: 'a stranger or an estranged spouse'.[98]

Pill LJ's concluding remarks are important. He states:

> In the present case, the jury would have been entitled, if they saw fit to conclude that, over the course of the relationship, the appellant's conduct was deplorable and worse than that of Donna. The incidents were far from trivial and significant force was on occasion used. However, we cannot conclude that, in this volatile relationship, the six incidents over a nine-month period amounted to a course of conduct amounting to harassment within the meaning for that statute. The spontaneous outbursts of ill-temper and bad behaviour, with aggression on both sides, which are the hallmarks of the present case, interspersed as those outbursts were with considerable periods of affectionate life, cannot be described as such a course of conduct. We do not exclude the possibility that harassment in section 1 may include harassment of a co-habitee but the appellant's conduct in this case could not properly be categorised as a course of conduct amounting to harassment within the meaning of the Act.[99]

These concluding remarks give an insight into the framework within which Pill LJ assesses Daniel Curtis' abusive behaviour. What is missing from the concluding remarks is a consideration of the power differential between Daniel Curtis and Donna Brand. To use the typologies of abuse that were explained in chapter 3, Pill

LJ is assuming (possibly) that the violence before him was the situationally specific "common couple violence" that can exist in the absence of control.[100] But was it?

Of the six incidents described in evidence, Daniel Curtis pushed Donna Brand (on three separate occasions, once so that she fell over and hit her head, once so that he bruised her chest), manhandled her, and put his hands around her neck (on two separate occasions). Donna Brand's only physical action was a punch made in self-defence (Daniel Curtis had his hands around her neck). On another occasion, she threw some beer over him, but only after he had been angry and was shouting at her. Even had Donna Brand been guilty of an equal amount of physical violence (which she was not) it is unlikely that acts of aggression between the two parties would have been "equivalent" as men are generally stronger than women. It has long been established in the research literature that this strength differential matters, in other words that 'meaning and context ... render men and women's violence fundamentally different'.[101]

At the beginning of his concluding paragraph, Pill LJ acknowledges that Daniel Curtis was more at fault than Donna Brand. He states that 'The jury would have been entitled to conclude that the appellant's conduct was deplorable and worse than that of Donna'.[102] He does not, however, explicitly consider whether the one-sided nature of the violence indicates the existence of a power imbalance between the parties in this case. Daniel Curtis was more at fault; it is more likely that he was a controlling perpetrator. Donna Brand was less at fault, her actions were mostly defensive. One possible reading of the facts that are set out in the judgment is that she was a victim of coercive control.

The fact that a consideration of the balance of power is often missing in legal analysis is regrettable:

> Concepts of coercive controlling violence are far less apparent in any legal analysis, which prefers to adopt an approach based on this assumed symmetry between violence inflicted by male and female partners as individual, physically aggressive responses to a relationship dispute. In doing so, it lacks full comprehension of the harm caused by the systematic process of oppressive behaviours highlighted by Stark, the long-term psychological damage caused to victims and their children and, most importantly, key indicators that risks may be escalating and indeed may be exacerbated by the legal response adopted.[103]

Unlike the judge in the Justin Lee Collins case, Pill LJ seems to view the violence before him in *Curtis* 'as individual, physically aggressive responses to a relationship dispute'.[104] At the end of his concluding paragraph Pill LJ states that 'The spontaneous outbursts of ill-temper and bad behaviour, with aggression on both sides, ... interspersed as those outbursts were with considerable periods of affectionate life, cannot be described as such a course of conduct'.[105] Pill LJ's use of the phrase 'on both sides', is suggestive of an *equal* balance of power between the parties, and that allowed him to find that what he framed as 'ill-temper' did not amount to a course of conduct.

It must be remembered that Pill LJ was reviewing an abusive intimate relationship with a view to deciding whether or not the defendant was guilty of
harassment. He was right to consider, as did Otton LJ ten years previously, that the
facts were not typical of the kinds of harassment anticipated by Parliament as they
debated the Protection from Harassment Bill in 1997. By the time of *Curtis* in
2010, however, it was becoming apparent that Parliament based its intentions for
the PHA on a misunderstanding of the nature of stalking. Rather than the non-
relational celebrity-type cases that were being reported in the press in the 1990s,
'The suspect and victim were known to each other in almost all cases'.[106]

It is well established that statutes are 'always speaking', which is to say they can
move, up to a point, with the times.[107] In this regard, 'The subjective intention of
the draftsman is immaterial'.[108] An example of this would be the decision in
Ireland, Burstow,[109] where viewing the OAPA as a 'living instrument' enabled the
House of Lords to find that psychiatric illness could amount to bodily harm. (It is
unlikely that the Victorians had this in mind. In 1861 psychiatry was in its infancy.)
Police and prosecutors were trying to be similarly creative with the PHA as they
were confronted with relational stalking.[110]

Widdows

The facts of *Widdows*[111] are similar to *Curtis.*[112] Pill LJ explains in his judgment
that David Widdows and his partner and victim Sarah Bunn: 'were involved in a
volatile relationship, and lived together'.[113] On a number of occasions during a
time-period of approximately 24 months David Widdows became violent with
Sarah Bunn, and on one occasion (according to Sarah Bunn's evidence) he raped
her twice. The section 4 harassment charge on the indictment was joined with two
counts of rape. The assaults were not charged separately but were relied upon as
creating the fear of further violence required by section 4.

David Widdows was acquitted of rape but convicted of section 4 harassment.
On appeal, Pill LJ decided that the section 4 conviction was unsound because the
judge, in summing up, did not:

> Have in mind the concept of harassment which is at the core of the 1997
> Act ... The section is not normally appropriate for use as a means of
> criminalising conduct, not charged as violence, during incidents in a long
> and predominantly affectionate relationship in which both parties persisted
> and wanted to continue.[114]

Just as in *Curtis,* Pill LJ was influenced by the fact that the relationship was 'long',
'predominantly affectionate' and by his finding that it was 'wanted' by both
parties. It was these facts that lead him to conclude that the PHA, s 4 was 'not ...
appropriate'.

There was certainly evidence of Sarah Bunn's affection for David Widdows
before Pill LJ. Referring to a holiday she had taken with David Widdows, for

example, Sarah Bunn said 'we had a really lovely time'.[115] There was also evidence before Pill LJ that, on occasions, having separated, Sarah Bunn 'invited him back'.[116] Pill LJ does not consider whether or not there was a power imbalance between David Widdows and Sarah Bunn that may have given a different context to the 'affectionate' nature of the relationship or its duration, or, even, to occasions when it looked like Sarah Bunn had 'invited him back'.[117] This is important: 'A period of affection may not necessarily signal a break in a course of conduct'.[118]

Responses to Hills, Curtis and Widdows

Much of the legal commentary on *Curtis* reflects a similar lack of consideration of the question of a power imbalance. For example:

> Spouses or cohabitees may put up with and even "enjoy" a volatile relationship. Often, there are constant arguments, rows, abusive language, threats, pushing, even striking; though basically the relationship is apparently close and affectionate. They make up with each other; peace is restored; and they are reconciled. Then trouble breaks out again: they make up again – ups and downs all the time. Eventually the female party goes to the police. Is this a case of harassment? The course of conduct and the alarm or distress will call for careful direction of the jury.[119]

Survivors spoken to as part of the empirical work conducted for this research project would agree that their abusive relationships were 'volatile'. None of them would refer to their abusive relationships as 'close' or 'affectionate'. That is not to say that they would deny ever feeling 'close' or 'affectionate' with their abusive partners. It is rather that once the moments of affection are seen as part of a controlling and manipulative strategy (on the part of the perpetrator) they take on a different significance.

Peace that is negotiated in this way is not 'restored', for example, it is carefully engineered by the survivor who "treads on eggshells" as the price for the survival of herself and her children. Karen, for example explained:

> Then obviously when the boys came along I just wanted everything to be OK so absolutely as you described it, treading on eggshells, and trying to make it OK. But it wasn't OK. And so it's like trying to paper the cracks, and there is only so many times that you can keep doing that before they start …[120]

In the same article, *Hills*[121] is cited as the authority for the principle that 'the odd nasty row between spouses or co-habitees does not suffice' as the course of conduct element for a PHA harassment charge.[122] The abuse in *Hills* included, (according to the particulars on the indictment), the fact that 'The appellant assaulted the complainant on a number of occasions by throwing a stool at her, hitting her, restricting her breathing by putting her hands over her mouth or around her throat and attempting to smother her with a pillow',[123] which is not how most of us would describe 'the odd nasty row'.[124]

More unfortunate wording can be found in legal commentary on *Curtis*:[125] 'Difficulties can, however, occur in on/off relationships where what would otherwise constitute a course of conduct, is often considered a routine aspect of a difficult relationship'.[126] Here, the suggestion is that what might, in other circumstances constitute harassment, is, in the context of a 'difficult' relationship considered 'routine'. Again, the consideration of the imbalance of power is missing. It is not just that such relationships are 'difficult'. Survivors do, tragically, learn to view the abuse they experience as 'routine'. Chapter 3 explained how Jessica described everyday physical violence as 'the usual'. She said, 'There was occasionally hitting and punching - the usual'.[127] Processing physical violence in this way as both inconsequential and not serious might be a protection mechanism for victims in a 'state of siege'[128] but from a normative perspective this should not be endorsed by the outside world.

Separation Issues

Without a consideration of coercive control, it is easy to make assumptions about what might be mistaken for the "decision" of the victims in "difficult" cases to "consent" to relationships with perpetrators. The expectation of the criminal justice system is that women who are abused should leave their abuser.[129] Underneath the assumption that the victim "chooses" to stay lie many others: for example that she had options,[130] or that employing those options would have kept her safe.[131] In other words: 'Law assumes - pretends - the autonomy of women, every legal case that discusses the question "why didn't she leave?" implies that the woman *could* have left'.[132] Or, put in another way: 'That individuals have choices is a basic legal assumption: that circumstances constrain choices is not'.[133] Unfortunately the victims of coercive control do not have free choices, the choices that they do have 'are subject to the arbitrary control of another'.[134] Not understanding this can lead to an unhelpful focus on a victim's responsibility for her own predicament.[135]

Separation is a particularly fraught issue. Distinguishing relationships that have been "left" by a victim from those that have not is not that simple for a number of reasons. Firstly, as has been noted: 'There is nothing simple about leaving'.[136] The assumption often made in legal circles, that separation is a one-off event, a 'binary concept' or a 'box that can be ticked' does not reflect the uncertainties and fluidities of leaving.[137] Leaving is a process; Sarah described the process as follows:

> Oh, God I tried so many times to get away from him, but I could never say "I'm leaving you". So it was a case that he would constantly threaten that this wasn't he wanted - and I would say - "I don't want to live with someone who doesn't want to live with me - let's separate". I even bought

my own house and moved back to (the countryside) with the two children. But he was coming down at weekends, for sex, you know - I could not get rid of him - and still my children have a father.[138]

Secondly, the control does not "end" with the relationship. As Sarah explained, 'I have never been more controlled by him than I am now'.[139] Karen spoke in some detail about the process of separating from her abusive partner. In particular she described the way the control that continued after separation as threatening and destabilising. She opened her interview with me by explaining that although she had – finally – separated from her abusive partner, the control continued: 'I am obviously still "in it", but obviously most people are anyway as it doesn't actually generally go away; that's the sad thing'.[140]

For Karen, the most difficult aspect of the post-separation control was the way in which it impacted on her son: 'But I'm living with my son, and with an order that is really unworkable – trying to co-parent with a perpetrator and a narcissist actually is really tricky'.[141] She also found the control and the fact that he could use their past intimacy against her intimidating and frightening. She was left with a nagging sensation that he might intrude at any time:

> And there were incidents at the house that were happening to make me feel scared, I couldn't prove it was him. I'd come home and there was a big footprint at the front door, it was like someone had kicked the door because it was like rubber. And in the middle of the night I've got a little dog, and he was barking, and I came downstairs and the back door was open. And things like my washing line - I really like hanging washing out, and he knew that, and the washing line had been cut.[142]

Her fear that he might intrude at any time was based on her knowledge of his capability (he had done so in the past) and his access (he knows where she lives, and also how to upset her, for example, he knows she likes to hang her washing). Thirdly, leaving *is* extremely dangerous.[143] The danger is linked to the fact that the control continues, but changes in emphasis. This is because separation often results in abusive perpetrators, 'changing the project from attempting to keep her within the relationship to destroying her for leaving it'.[144] Karen was right to fear what her abusive ex-partner might do: cutting her washing line (he had a knife) and the big footprint on the door (he has big feet, he is not afraid to use his physical advantage to inflict damage) are chilling reminders of how the violence might escalate. Another survivor, Kim explained how her abusive ex-partner 'wasn't violent until the end? And I think that's quite common in domestic violence? Until the end, when the relationship breaks down, I think that's the point where it can be incredibly dangerous and that was the case'.[145]

In *Hills*, Donna Brand was trying to leave Daniel Curtis. He was 'jealous' and 'possessive'.[146] She had 'wanted to separate' and was 'frightened of what the appellant would try to do'.[147] Her fear may have been well placed. The social science research on the dangers (to the victim) of separating from an abusive partner is extensive.[148] Exiting from an abusive relationship is extremely dangerous. Victims are at their most vulnerable once they *initiate* separation discussions with a controlling partner. It is then that they and their children are most at risk of serious violence or, tragically, homicide.[149]

In their recent study of risk factors for domestic homicides in the United Kingdom, Jane Monckton Smith et al. concluded that control was present in 92% of the domestic homicides reviewed, and that 'the key trigger appeared to be separation or its threat'.[150] As demonstrated by Kim, above, victims know and fear this. In fact, empirical research shows that even the *decision* to attempt to separate, if communicated, increases the risk of violence.[151] In these cases, where it is the communication of the intention to leave that has provoked abuse, rather than an actual separation, the fact of the communication is known only to the victim and her abuser. The communication might remain invisible even to friends and family, and certainly to police, prosecutors and the judiciary. Instead, women describe fear that can seem disproportionate to those on the outside. Interestingly, in *Widdows* Pill LJ says of the victim that: 'She was shaking with fear though he did not behave in a violent, aggressive or threatening way'.[152]

Anna Larke had separated from Justin Lee Collins by the time of his trial. Unfortunately, 'Women who stay occupy a morally ambiguous identity'.[153] The 'morally ambiguous identity' allocated to women who report yet remain – who are prepared to support a police investigation and court proceedings yet seem unable to leave their abusers – is apparent in the judgments of *Hills*,[154] *Widdows*[155] and *Curtis*.[156] It is perhaps not surprising that 'Where the case reveals an ongoing relationship between the alleged victim and perpetrator, there is judicial reluctance to acknowledge the existence of a course of conduct with the required qualities'.[157]

This 'judicial reluctance' can be seen, for example, in *Hills:* where despite evidence of disturbing ongoing domestic abuse Otton LJ was able to agree with the defence counsel's submissions that two proven incidents of abuse were unconnected:

> The complainant's most recent witness statement disclosed no evidence that the April incident was linked to the October incident. Harassment is a continuing offence. There was nothing to show that the April matter was more than an unconnected incident. *This was particularly so since the parties continued to live with each other during the relevant period* …[158]

The problem is that this takes no account of the significance of coercive control. Instead,

> The perception of victims as autonomous individuals who remain in or return to the relationship because they freely choose to do so means that judges find it difficult to understand a victim who reports the behaviour of her partner but remains in the relationship.[159]

Otton LJ, in other words, does not appear to consider that there may have been a power imbalance between Hills and his victim, and that the instability of the relationship, (which he specifically comments on as is discussed earlier), might therefore be a reflection of the victim's desire to escape from it.

The desire to distinguish and downplay domestic stalking that takes place while the relationship continues is an indication of the tendency that still exists to minimise the significance of abuse in the context of ongoing abusive relationships. Tuerkheimer explains:

> Violence within intimate relationships is justified as the product of choice on the part of its victims … . What would not be tolerated absent a relationship is quite acceptable for precisely this reason: the existence of an ongoing relationship becomes a proxy for a woman's consent to all that takes place within it (at least, to the point of physical assault).[160]

This is where a consideration of the question of power is essential. Once an imbalance of power has been identified, it is much harder to make 'the existence of an ongoing relationship' a '*proxy* for a woman's consent to all that takes place within it'.[161]

Whatever the reasoning behind *Hills*,[162] *Widdows*[163] and *Curtis*,[164] the effect of the judgments was that police and prosecutors had to draw a line between relationships that are over and those that were not. If the relationship was found to be over, the perpetrator's behaviour might constitute harassment (PHA), if the relationship was in fact on-going, since December 2015 he might be guilty of controlling or coercive behaviour (section 76). Originally, section 76 only applied if the parties were together; the PHA only applied if they were not.[165] Drawing that line was difficult: identifying separation as a moment in time is often impossible.[166] As Tuerkheimer explains:

> The paradigm of the transactional breakup – one that occurs at a distinct moment in time, upon mutual agreement by two parties hopelessly fails to capture the complexities that attend ending abusive relationships. In these relationships, separation is a process. Breaking up is often difficult, but the realities confronting battered women make separating from a partner distinctly dangerous, complicated, and protracted. For these women, there is typically no moment of breakup; rather, domestic violence victims "leave" relationships multiple times, in different ways, to varying degrees of success.[167]

Tuerkheimer's analysis of the false nature of the transactional breakup paradigm was supported by the experiences of the survivors interviewed for this project. As discussed in chapter 4 all of the survivors I interviewed had a difficult and complicated time leaving abusive partners.[168] There was usually a degree of tracking back and forth between "leaving" and "staying" (as described by Sarah, above), before any of the victims could be said to have escaped the relationship.[169]

This pattern is also visible in the caselaw. In *Widdows*, for example, Pill LJ reported that: 'They separated on many occasions during that period but reunited "after a few hours or days"'.[170] Police reports, for example, might record that the perpetrator has said that they are still together. A victim might point to her efforts to escape and say they are not. A suspect might say he is still living with a re- porting victim. The victim might say to the police that he is not welcome. Kim described this:

> And every time I made a 999 call they would then come, and it seemed like it was fruitless because he would just deny it. His defence would always be we were in a relationship, she wants me - she likes it. This kind of thing.[171]

This is a particular issue for the police, who did not, in those cases, know which crime had taken place; 'Legal preoccupation with a moment of departure does not comport with reality'.[172]

If identifying the moment of separation is difficult, it is also, from the survivor's perspective, not necessarily that significant. Analysis of the experiences of the survivors interviewed for this research clarifies that the perpetrator's controlling intent does not change with the end of the relationship.[173] As Sarah put it, 'I have never been more controlled by him than I am now'.[174] As Tuerkheimer said: 'Control is ratcheted up when women attempt to separate'.[175]

Post separation, the behaviour patterns manifested by the perpetrator might take a different form, but the malevolent strategic intent (that gives meaning to the patterns) continues in much the same way as they did before. What distinguishes him from all of the other people in her life is his desire to continue controlling her. In other words, the boundary between the period of her life when she is in an intimate relationship and the period when she could be finally said to have left it is not always a particularly conceptually significant one – *to the victim* – in the context of the coercive control exerted by him over her. Survivors such as Sarah explain that 'I would say that the coercive control is worse now, than it was before'.[176]

Conclusion

In the case of coercive control, there *is* no clear boundary between partners who are "estranged" and those that are not. Indeed, it is the lack of boundary that is part of the problem. Restricting the use of the PHA to Otton LJ's 'strangers' and 'estranged' partners did not make conceptual or empirical sense,[177] and it meant that further legislation was deemed necessary. In their later consultation document the government described the judgments in *Widdows* and *Curtis* as an 'unhelpful barrier'.[178] As Charlotte Bishop argues:

> Whether or not the 1997 Act was intended for use within the context of relationships involving violence and/or abuse, it could have been applied in this way ... that the legislation has not been interpreted in this way displays a

lack of judicial comprehension of the dynamics of domestic violence and/or abuse and has given rise to a legislative gap in this context.[179]

It was parliamentary recognition of a 'legislative gap' that paved the way for the introduction of section 76. This new offence, together with the Sexual Offences Act 2003 that came just over a decade before it, are two of the most important legislative developments in the twenty-first century for the survivors of coercive control. The Sexual Offences Act 2003 and section 76 are reviewed in the following two chapters.

Notes

1 Kathryn Westcott, 'Justin Lee Collins: Trial Highlights 'Invisible' Abuse' (9 October 2012) available at <https://www.bbc.co.uk/news/magazine-19783496> accessed 10 April 2022.

2 Deborah Tuerkheimer, 'Recognising and Remedying the Harm of Battering: A Call to Criminalize Domestic Violence' (2004) 94(4) Journal of Criminal Law and Criminology 959, 990.

3 Ibid.

4 'Call for Tighter Law as Victim Tells of Stalking Campaign' *The Times* (London 3 September 1996); 'Law Change after Stalking Case Acquittal' *The Guardian* (London 18 September 1996); 'Law in Urgent Need of Reform' *The Independent* (London 19 September 1996); 'Stopping Stalkers: How Would the Law Change?' *Daily Telegraph* (London 16 October 1996). For further examples and analysis see Emily Finch, *The Criminalisation of Stalking: Constructing the Problem and Evaluating the Solution* (Cavendish 2001) 111.

5 HC Deb 17 December 1996, Vol 287, Col 778.

6 Detective Constable James, Police Focus Group (30 November 2016) 7.

7 Finch, The Criminalisation of Stalking n4.

8 Tuerkheimer, Recognising and Remedying the Harm of Battering, n2 990.

9 HC Deb 6 March 1996, Vol 273, Col 370.

10 Home Office News Release, May 1996, as cited in Finch, The Criminalisation of Stalking n4 12.

11 HC Deb 17 December 1996, Vol 287, Cols 823–7 as cited in Finch, The Criminalisation of Stalking n4 10.

12 HC Deb 17 December 1996, Vol 287, Col 784.

13 HC Deb 17 December 1996, Vol 287, Col 789; Judith Garland, 'Comment: Protection from Harassment Act 1997: The 'New' Stalking Offences' (2013) 77 Journal of Criminal Law 387.

14 As inserted by the Protection of Freedoms Act 2012.

15 HC Deb 17 December 1996, Vol 287, Col 819.

16 Finch, The Criminalisation of Stalking n4 14.

17 Ibid. See also Garland, The "New" Stalking Offences n13 387.

18 HC Deb 17 December 1996, Vol 287, Col 782–4.

19 HC Deb 17 December 1996, Vol 287, Col 857.

20 HC Deb 17 December 1996, Vol 287, Cols 781–851.

21 *Hills* [2001] 1FLR 580; *Curtis* [2010] EWCA Crim 123; *Widdows* [2011] EWCA Crim 1500. This is discussed in some detail below.

22 The Police and Crime Act 2017 raises the maximum sentence for stalking and harassment from five years to ten, and from seven to 14 in the case of racially or religiously aggravated stalking and harassment.

23 Tuerkheimer, Recognizing and Remedying the Harm of Battering n2 990.

24 Andrew Ashworth and Jeremy Horder, *Principles of Criminal Law* (Oxford University Press 2009) 314.
25 The principle that there must be a coincidence in time of actus reus and mens rea has a degree of elasticity as demonstrated by cases such as *Thabo Meli* [1984] 1 All Eng 373 and *Church* [1966] 1 QB 59.
26 Tuerkheimer, Recognizing and Remedying the Harm of Battering n2 990.
27 Interview with Police Constable South (22 January 2018) 3.
28 Charlotte Bishop, 'Domestic Violence: The Limitations of a Legal Response' in Sarah Hilda and Vanessa Bettinson (eds), *Interdisciplinary Perspectives on Protection, Prevention and Intervention* (Palgrave Macmillan 2016) 68. For examples of judicial treatment of the "course of conduct" element of the offence see *Hills* n21, *Lau v DPP* [2000] Crim LR 580; *Qosja* [2016] EWCA Crim 1543; Tom Rees and David Ormerod, 'Case Comment Harassment: Separate Incidents Not Linked' [2001] Criminal Law Review 318, 319. See also Neil Addison and Timothy Lawson-Cruttenden, *Harassment Law and Practice* (Blackstone 1998) 30–2; Paul Infield and Graham Platford, *The Law of Harassment and Stalking* (Butterworths 2000) 10. On the nexus point see *Patel* [2004] EWCA Crim 3284.
29 *Hills* n21.
30 Ibid. [10].
31 Ibid. [9].
32 Ibid. [32].
33 Vanessa Bettinson and Charlotte Bishop, 'Is the Creation of a Discrete Offence of Coercive Control Necessary to Combat Domestic Violence' (2015) 66(2) Northern Ireland Legal Quarterly 179,188.
34 Emphasis added.
35 HC Deb 17 December 1996, Vol 287, Col 782.
36 Garland, The 'New' Stalking Offences n13.
37 Ibid.
38 Ashworth and Horder, Principles of Criminal Law n24 74.
39 Ibid. 16. Arguably this traditional focus on subjective mens rea is being challenged by a number of recent legislative developments – strict liability offences, for example – and also a number of offences that are reviewed in later chapters of this book, such as the Sexual Offences Act 2003 and the Serious Crime Act 2015, s 76.
40 Ibid. 168.
41 Kenneth Campbell, 'Stalking around the Main Issue' [1997/8] 8 Kings College Law Journal 128, 132.
42 Ibid. 328.
43 The Police and Crime Act 2017 raises the maximum sentence for stalking and harassment from five years to ten, and from seven to 14 in the case of racially or religiously aggravated stalking and harassment.
44 Finch, The Criminalisation of Stalking n4 22.
45 HC Deb 17 December 1996, Vol 287, Col 783.
46 Finch, The Criminalisation of Stalking n4 238.
47 *Colohan* [2001] EWCA Crim 1251 [18].
48 Jessica Harris, *An Evaluation of the Use and Effectiveness of the Protection from Harassment Act 1997* (Home Office Research Study 203, Home Office 2000) 9.
49 Ibid.
50 Laurie Salame, 'A National Survey of Stalking Laws: A Legislative Trend Comes to the Aid of Domestic Violence Victims and Others' (1993) 27 Suffolk University Law Review, 67 80. See also Jane Monkton-Smith et al, 'Exploring the Relationship between Stalking and Homicide' (Suzy Lamplugh Trust 2017).
51 Ashworth and Horder, Principles of Criminal Law n24 185.
52 Campbell, Stalking around the Main Issue n41 132.
53 *Colohan* [2001] EWCA Crim 1251.

54 Emily Finch, 'Stalking the Perfect Stalking Law' (2002) (Sep) Criminal Law Review 703, 710.

55 Garland, The 'New' Stalking Offences n13 392.

56 Ashworth and Horder, Principles of Criminal Law n24 183.

57 Heather Keating et al, *Clarkson and Keating: Criminal Law* (Sweet and Maxwell 2014) 146.

58 Nicola Lacey, *State Punishment: Political Principles and Community Values* (Routledge 1988) 104.

59 Ashworth and Horder, Principles of Criminal Law n24 184.

60 *Ireland, Burstow* 1997 UKHL 34 [153].

61 Garland, The 'New' Stalking Offences n13 393.

62 Finch, Stalking the Perfect Stalking Law n54 6.

63 Bishop, Domestic Violence n28 68.

64 *Henley* [2000] All ER 171 (CA).

65 Mary Ann Dutton, 'Understanding Women's Responses to Domestic Violence: A Redefinition of Battered Woman Syndrome' (1992) 21 Hofstra Law Review 1191, 1208.

66 Finch, Stalking the Perfect Stalking Law n54 6.

67 Susan Edwards, 'Recognising the Role of the Emotion of Fear in Offences and Defences' (2019) 83(6) Journal of Criminal Law 450, 461.

68 Henley n64 [582].

69 Harris, An Evaluation of the Protection from Harassment Act n48 vi.

70 David Povey and Julian Prime, *Recorded Crime Statistics England and Wales, April 1998–March 1999* (Home Office Research, Development and Statistics Directorate, Home Office 1999).

71 CPS, *Violence against Women and Girls Crime Report 2017–18*. Available at <https://www.cps.gov.uk/sites/default/files/documents/publications/cps-vawg-report-2018.pdf> accessed 31 April 2019.

72 Detective Constable James, Focus Group with Senior Police (30 November 2016).

73 Westcott, Justin Lee Collins n1.

74 Ibid.

75 Ibid. See also, for example, BBC News, 'Justin Lee Collins Found Guilty of Harrassing Anna Larke' (9 October 2012) available at <https://www.bbc.co.uk/news/uk-england-19869630> accessed 10 April 2022.

76 Ibid.

77 Ibid.

78 Ibid.

79 Ibid.

80 Dutton, Understanding Women's Responses n65 1208.

81 BBC News, Justin Lee Collins n75.

82 Harris, An Evaluation of the Protection from Harassment Act n48, vi, my emphasis.

83 Ibid. 17.

84 Of the 11,922 charges for harassment and stalking brought in 2018, nearly 75% had a domestic abuse context. See CPS, *Violence against Women and Girls Report* n71, 6.

85 Finch, The Criminalisation of Stalking n4 229.

86 Ibid. 230.

87 n21.

88 Ibid.

89 Ibid.

90 Ibid. [31].

91 Ibid. [31].

92 Ibid.

93 Ibid.

94 *Majrowski v Guy's and St Thomas's NHS Trust* [2007] 1AC 22.

95 n21.
96 *Curtis* ibid. [27].
97 Ibid [28].
98 Ibid [30].
99 Ibid. [32].
100 Michael Johnson, 'Patriarchal Terrorism and Common Couple Violence: Two Forms of Violence against Women' (1995) 57 Journal of Marriage and the Family 283.
101 Sarah MacQueen, 'Domestic Abuse, Crime Surveys and the Fallacy of Risk: Exploring Partner and Domestic Abuse Using the Scottish Crime and Justice Survey' [2016] Criminology and Criminal Justice 1, 2.
102 *Curtis* n21 [32].
103 Bishop, Domestic Violence n28 62.
104 Ibid. 62.
105 *Curtis*, n21 [32].
106 Harris, An Evaluation of the Protection from Harassment Act n48 9.
107 *Ireland, Burstow* [1998] AC 147, 158.
108 Ibid.
109 n60 [147].
110 Harris, An Evaluation of the Protection from Harassment Act n48.
111 n21.
112 Ibid.
113 *Widdows* ibid. [4] (my emphasis).
114 Ibid. [29].
115 Ibid. [9].
116 Ibid.
117 Ibid. [10].
118 Heather Douglas, 'Do We Need a Specific Domestic Violence Offence?' (2016) 39 Melbourne University Law Review 435, 440.
119 Alec Samuels, 'Harassment: Protection from Harassment Act 1997 (as amended)' (2013) (2–4) The Criminal Lawyer 216. See also Garland, The 'New' Stalking Offences n13 391.
120 Interview with Karen (24 November 2016) 5.
121 n21.
122 Samuels, Harassment n119 3.
123 *Hills* n21 [9].
124 Samuels, Harassment n119 3.
125 n21.
126 See Samuels, Harassment n119 3.
127 Interview with Jessica (26 May 2016) 10.
128 Dutton, Understanding Women's Responses n65, 1208.
129 Heather Douglas, *Women, Intimate Partner Violence and the Law* (Oxford University Press 2021) 216.
130 Victor Tadros, 'The Distinctiveness of Domestic Abuse: A Freedom Based Account' in Anthony Duff and Stuart Green (eds), *Defining Crimes Essays on the Special Part of the Criminal Law* (Oxford University Press 2005) 128.
131 Dutton, Understanding Women's Responses n65, 1226.
132 Martha Mahoney, 'Legal Images of Battered Women: Redefining the Issue of Separation' (1991) 90(1) Michigan Law Review 1, 164.
133 Barbara Hudson, 'Punishing the Poor: A Critique of the Dominance of Legal Reasoning in Penal Policy and Practice' in Duff et al (eds), *Penal Theory and Practice* (Manchester University Press 1994) 302.
134 Bishop, Domestic Violence n28 69.
135 Julia Tolmie, 'Coercive Control: To Criminalize or Not to Criminalize' (2018) 18(1) Criminology and Criminal Justice 8.

136 Tanya Palmer, 'Distinguishing Sex from Sexual Violation: Consent, Negotiation and Freedom to Negotiate' in Alan Reed et al (eds) *Consent: Domestic and Comparative Perspectives* (Routledge 2017) 8.

137 Douglas, Women, Intimate Partner Violence and the Law n129 236.

138 Interview with Sarah (29 June 2016) 8, brackets inserted to protect Sarah's anonymity.

139 Ibid.

140 Karen n120 1.

141 Ibid.

142 Ibid. 15.

143 Jane Campbell et al, 'Risk Factors for Femicide in Abusive Relationships: Results from a Multiple Case Control Study' (2003) 93 (7) American Journal of Public Health 1089; Holly Johnson and Tina Hotton, 'Losing Control: Homicide Risk in Estranged and Intact Abusive Relationships' (2003) 7(1) Homicide Studies 58; Maribeth Rezy, 'Separated Women's Risk for Intimate Partner Violence. A Multiyear Analysis Using the National Crime Victimization Survey' (2020) 33(5) Journal of Interpersonal Violence 1055.

144 Rebecca and Russell Dobash, *When Men Murder Women* (Oxford University Press 2015) 39.

145 Interview with Kim (6 October 2016) 1.

146 *Curtis* n21 [10].

147 Ibid. [13].

148 Clare Connelly, 'Institutional Failure, Social Entrapment and Post-Separation Abuse' [2010] Juridical Review 43, 43.

149 Dutton, Understanding Women's Responses n65; Salame, A National Survey n50; Cathy Humphreys and Ravi Thiara, 'Neither Justice nor Protection: Women's Experiences of Post-Separation Violence' (2003) 25(3) Journal of Social Welfare and Family Law 196; Evan Stark, *Coercive Control: How Men Entrap Women in Personal Life* (Oxford University Press 2007); Holly Johnson et al 'Intimate Femicide: The Role of Coercive Control' [2017] Feminist Criminology 1; Megan Bumb, 'Domestic Violence Law, Abusers' Intent, and Social Media: How Transaction-Bound Statutes Are the True Threats to Prosecuting Perpetrators of Gender-Based Violence' (2017) 82(2) Brooklyn Law Review 917.

150 Monkton-Smith et al, Exploring the Relationship between Stalking and Homicide n50 1; Jane Monkton-Smith, 'Intimate Partner Femicide: Using Foucauldian Analysis to Track and Eight Stage Progression to Homicide' (2020) 26(11) Violence against Women 1267. See also Alafair Burke, 'Domestic Violence as a Crime of Pattern and Intent: An Alternative Reconceptualization' (2007) 75 George Washington Law Review 558, 579.

151 Desmond Ellis, 'Post Separation Woman Abuse: The Contribution of Lawyers as "Barracudas", "Advocates," and "Counsellors"' (1978) 10 International Journal of Law and Psychiatry 403, 408.

152 n21 [13].

153 Jenny Davis and Tony Love, 'Women Who Stay: A Morality Work Perspective' (2018) 65(2) Social Problems 251, 251.

154 n21.

155 Ibid.

156 Ibid.

157 Bettinson and Bishop, Discrete Offence n33 188.

158 n21 [13], my emphasis.

159 Bettinson and Bishop, Discrete Offence n33 188.

160 Deborah Tuerkheimer, 'Breakups' (2013) 25 Yale Journal of Law and Feminism 51, 87.

161 Ibid, my emphasis.

162 n21.

163 Ibid.
164 Ibid.
165 This was amended by the Domestic Abuse Act 2021 as set out in detail in chapter 5.
166 June Keeling et al, 'A Qualitative Study Exploring Midlife Women's Stages of Change from Domestic Violence towards Freedom' [2016] Women's Health 1.
167 Tuerkheimer, Breakups n160 15.
168 See, for example Karen n120; Kim n145 3.
169 Ibid, see interview with Sarah (29 June 2016) 1.
170 n21 [2].
171 Kim n145 2.
172 Tuerkheimer, Breakups n160 15.
173 Sarah n169; Survivors Focus Group (8 September 2016).
174 Sarah n169 9.
175 Tuerkheimer, Breakups n160 84.
176 Sarah n169 8.
177 Hills n21 [31].
178 Home Office, 'Strengthening the Law on Domestic Abuse Consultation – Summary of Responses' (December 2014) 11 available at <https://assets.publishing.service.gov.uk/government/uploads/system/uploads/attachment_data/file/389002/StrengtheningLawDomesticAbuseResponses.pdf> accessed 30 April 2019.
179 Bishop, Discrete Offence n33 189.

Bibliography

Addison N and Lawson-Cruttenden T, *Harassment Law and Practice* (Blackstone 1998).

Ashworth A and Horder J, *Principles of Criminal Law* (Oxford University Press 2009).

BBC News, 'Justin Lee Collins Found Guilty of Harrassing Anna Larke' (9 October 2012) available at <https://www.bbc.co.uk/news/uk-england-19869630> accessed 10 April 2022.

Bettinson V and Bishop C, 'Is the Creation of a Discrete Offence of Coercive Control Necessary to Combat Domestic Violence' (2015) 66(2) Northern Ireland Legal Quarterly 179.

Bishop C, 'Domestic Violence: The Limitations of a Legal Response' in Sarah Hilda and Vanessa Bettinson (eds), *Interdisciplinary Perspectives on Protection, Prevention and Intervention* (Palgrave Macmillan 2016).

Bumb M, 'Domestic Violence Law, Abusers' Intent, and Social Media: How Transaction-Bound Statutes Are the True Threats to Prosecuting Perpetrators of Gender-Based Violence' (2017) 82(2) Brooklyn Law Review 917.

Burke A, 'Domestic Violence as a Crime of Pattern and Intent: An Alternative Reconceptualization' (2007) 75 George Washington Law Review 558.

'Call for Tighter Law as Victim Tells of Stalking Campaign' *The Times* (London 3 September 1996).

Campbell J, Webster D, Koziol-McLain J, Block C, Campbell D, Curry M and Laughon K, 'Risk Factors for Femicide in Abusive Relationships: Results from a Multiple Case Control Study' (2003) 93(7) American Journal of Public Health 1089.

Campbell K, 'Stalking around the Main Issue' (1997/8) 8 Kings College Law Journal 128.

Connelly C, 'Institutional Failure, Social Entrapment and Post-Separation Abuse' (2010) 122(1) Juridical Review 43.

CPS, *Violence against Women and Girls Report 2017–18*, 6, available at <https://www.cps.gov.uk/sites/default/files/documents/publications/cps-vawg-report-2018.pdf> accessed 31 April 2019.

Davis J and Love T, 'Women Who Stay: A Morality Work Perspective' (2018) 65(2) Social Problems 251.

Dobash R and R, *When Men Murder Women* (Oxford University Press 2015).

Douglas H, 'Do We Need a Specific Domestic Violence Offence?' (2016) 39 Melbourne University Law Review 435.

Douglas H, *Women, Intimate Partner Violence and the Law* (Oxford University Press 2021) 216.

Dutton M, 'Understanding Women's Responses to Domestic Violence: A Redefinition of Battered Woman Syndrome' (1992) 21 Hofstra Law Review 1191.

Edwards S, 'Recognising the Role of the Emotion of Fear in Offences and Defences' (2019) 83(6) Journal of Criminal Law 450.

Ellis D, 'Post Separation Woman Abuse: The Contribution of Lawyers as "Barracudas", "Advocates," and "Counsellors"' (1978) 10 International Journal of Law and Psychiatry 403.

Finch E, *The Criminalisation of Stalking: Constructing the Problem and Evaluating the Solution* (Cavendish 2001).

Finch E, 'Stalking the Perfect Stalking Law' (2002) (Sep) *Criminal Law Review* 703.

Garland J, 'Comment: Protection from Harassment Act 1997: The 'New' Stalking Offences' (2013) 77 Journal of Criminal Law 387.

Harris J, *An Evaluation of the Use and Effectiveness of the Protection from Harassment Act 1997* (Home Office Research Study 203, Home Office 2000).

HC Deb, 6 March 1996, Vol 273, Col 370.

HC Deb, 17 December 1996, Vol 287, Col 778.

HC Deb, 17 December 1996, Vol 287, Col 789.

HC Deb, 17 December 1996, Vol 287, Cols 781–851

HC Deb, 17 December 1996, Vol 287, Col 857.

Home Office, 'Strengthening the Law on Domestic Abuse Consultation – Summary of Responses' (December 2014) available at <https://assets.publishing.service.gov.uk/government/uploads/system/uploads/attachment_data/file/389002/StrengtheningLawDomesticAbuseResponses.pdf> accessed 30 April 2019.

Hudson B, 'Punishing the Poor: A Critique of the Dominance of Legal Reasoning in Penal Policy and Practice' in Duff R, Marshall S, Dobash R and Dobash R (eds), *Penal Theory and Practice* (Manchester University Press 1994).

Humphreys C and Thiara R, 'Neither Justice nor Protection: Women's Experiences of Post-Separation Violence' (2003) 25(3) Journal of Social Welfare and Family Law 196.

Infield P and Platford G, *The Law of Harassment and Stalking* (Butterworths 2000).

Johnson H and Hotton T, 'Losing Control: Homicide Risk in Estranged and Intact Abusive Relationships' (2003) 7(1) Homicide Studies 5.

Johnson H, Eriksson L, Mazerolle P and Wortley R 'Intimate Femicide: The Role of Coercive Control' (2017) 14(1) Feminist Criminology 1.

Johnson M, 'Patriarchal Terrorism and Common Couple Violence: Two Forms of Violence against Women' (1995) 57 Journal of Marriage and the Family 283.

Keating H, Kyd Cunningham C, Elliott S and Walters M, *Clarkson and Keating: Criminal Law* (Sweet & Maxwell 2014).

Keeling J, Smith D and Fisher C, 'A Qualitative Study Exploring Midlife Women's Stages of Change from Domestic Violence towards Freedom' (2016) Women's Health 1.

Lacey N, *State Punishment: Political Principles and Community Values* (Routledge 1988).

'Law Change after Stalking Case Acquittal' *The Guardian* (London 18 September 1996).

'Law in Urgent Need of Reform' *The Independent* (London 19 September 1996).

MacQueen S, 'Domestic Abuse, Crime Surveys and the Fallacy of Risk: Exploring Partner and Domestic Abuse Using the Scottish Crime and Justice Survey' (2016) 13 Criminology and Criminal Justice 1.

Mahoney M, 'Legal Images of Battered Women: Redefining the Issue of Separation' (1991) 90(1) Michigan Law Review 1.

Monkton-Smith J, 'Intimate Partner Femicide: Using Foucauldian Analysis to Track and Eight Stage Progression to Homicide' (2020) 26(11) Violence against Women 1267.

Monckton Smith J, Szymanska K and Haile S, *Exploring the Relationship between Stalking and Homicide* (Report by the Homicide Research Group, University of Gloucestershire, 2017) available at <http://eprints.glos.ac.uk/4553/> accessed 2 October 2017.

Palmer T, 'Distinguishing Sex from Sexual Violation: Consent, Negotiation and Freedom to Negotiate' in Reed A and Bohlander M (eds), *Consent: Domestic and Comparative Perspectives* (Routledge 2017).

Povey D and Prime J, *Recorded Crime Statistics England and Wales, April 1998–March 1999* (Home Office Research, Development and Statistics Directorate, Home Office 1999).

Rees T and Ormerod D, 'Case Comment Harassment: Separate Incidents Not Linked' (2001) Criminal Law Review 318.

Rezy M, 'Separated Women's Risk for Intimate Partner Violence. A Multiyear Analysis Using the National Crime Victimization Survey' (2020) 33(5) Journal of Interpersonal Violence 1055.

Salame L, 'A National Survey of Stalking Laws: A Legislative Trend Comes to the Aid of Domestic Violence Victims and Others' (1993) 27 Suffolk University Law Review 67.

Samuels A, 'Harassment: Protection from Harassment Act 1997 (as amended)' (2013) 216 The Criminal Lawyer 2.

Stark E, *Coercive Control: How Men Entrap Women in Personal Life* (Oxford University Press 2007).

'Stopping Stalkers: How Would the Law Change?' *Daily Telegraph* (London 16 October 1996).

Tadros V, 'The Distinctiveness of Domestic Abuse: A Freedom Based Account' in Anthony Duff and Stuart Green (eds), *Defining Crimes Essays on the Special Part of the Criminal Law* (Oxford University Press 2005).

Tolmie J, 'Coercive Control: To Criminalize or Not to Criminalize' (2018) 18(1) Criminology and Criminal Justice 8.

Tuerkheimer D, 'Recognising and Remedying the Harm of Battering: A Call to Criminalize Domestic Violence' (2004) 94(4) Journal of Criminal Law and Criminology 959.

Tuerkheimer D, 'Breakups' (2013) 25 Yale Journal of Law and Feminism 51.

Westcott K, 'Justin Lee Collins: Trial Highlights 'Invisible' Abuse' (9 October 2012) available at <https://www.bbc.co.uk/news/magazine-19783496> accessed 21 April 2021.

Cases

Hills [2001] 1FLR 580.
Church [1966] 1 QB 59.
Colohan [2001] EWCA Crim 1251
Curtis [2010] EWCA Crim 123.
Henley [2000] All ER 171 (CA).
Ireland, Burstow [1997] UKHL 34
Lau v DPP [2000] Crim LR 580.

Majrowski v Guy's and St Thomas's NHS Trust [2007] 1AC 22.
Qosja [2016] EWCA Crim 1543.
Patel [2004] EWCA Crim 3284.
Thabo Meli [1984] 1 All Eng 373.
Widdows [2011] EWCA Crim 1500.

Legislation

Offences against the Person Act 1861.
Sexual Offences Act 2003.
Serious Crime Act 2015.
Police and Crime Act 2017.
Protection of Freedoms Act 2012.
Protection from Harassment Act 1997.

4

FROM RELUCTANT SEX TO RAPE DOMESTIC SEXUAL ABUSE AND THE SEXUAL OFFENCES ACT 2003

Introduction

Sexual abuse is a key component of coercive control. In chapter 1, I introduced Tanya Palmer's conceptualisation of sexual abuse as either 'acute' or 'chronic'.[1] Palmer explains that when framing sexual violence as 'acute', she is drawing on

> Medical understandings of an acute illness, symptom, etc as being of rapid onset and short duration, an episode of crisis in which the patient is in serious and immediate danger, as well as more general uses of 'acute' to refer to a situation that is severe, intense and urgent.[2]

In essence she is referring to 'an identifiable event or encounter' which frames the violation of a person's sexual autonomy.[3] Palmer articulates 'chronic' sexual violation as taking place where a victim's autonomy is 'gradually eroded over a longer period of time'.[4] A perpetrator who is expressing dominance over, and control of, his victim via supposedly "low-level" sexual violence is, with behaviour that is at once menacing and strategic, inflicting violence that is chronic. In this case, the survivor might find it difficult to isolate any one of the seemingly "low-level" attacks, rather she articulates the abuse as an everyday backdrop, as part of the fabric of her life.

Palmer and I develop Stark's model of control in the specific context of sexual abuse in our article 'Telling the Wrong Stories'[5], and point out that sexual abuse experienced by survivors of coercive control can be both acute and chronic, and that this remains the area of domestic abuse that is the hardest to bring within the ambit of the criminal law. This knowledge is not new: research has suggested for some time that there are especially high attrition rates when it comes to the prosecution of domestic sexual offending.[6] The interviews that I conducted with

DOI: 10.4324/9780429201844-5

judges and police identified domestic rape as a particular problem for the justice system. Judge Little commented that:

> Stranger rapes are dead easy, and have the highest conviction rate therefore unsurprisingly. The people who meet at a party are very complex because often drink is involved and all the rest of it. But when you come to the context of "in a relationship", so a domestic setting ... it's the kind of thing that makes it very difficult.[7]

Judge Harwood said of the prosecution of sexual offences that, 'At the moment the conviction rate within intimate relationships from my experience is at such an all-time low', and that juries find it 'really hard to convict, [they] really struggle'.[8] Judge Wallace, when she was asked whether she thought that the application of the criminal law on rape in the context of an intimate relationship was problematic, was blunt in her response: 'I don't think it's the criminal law that's the problem, I think it's society's perception'.[9]

Interviews with police generated consistent findings. PC Hardie, for example, said that she felt that domestic rapes were particularly difficult at the moment, 'The overlap between rape and domestic abuse is really tough'.[10] PC Hardie went on to explain that she felt that convictions were prohibitively difficult to achieve. In her view, this is because juries are unable to convict due to their prejudicial views of what constitutes rape. She concluded:

> It's because rape conjures up images of people being dragged by their hair into the bushes, doesn't it, with a knife at their throat, it's just not – that's not how rapes usually happen, and the public don't realise that. The public perception is not as it should be.[11]

The idea that there is a "paradigmatic stranger-rape" that makes it difficult for juries to perceive acquaintance or domestic rape as rape was evident in many of my interviews with the judiciary and the police.

Jurors are, of course, bound by strict confidentiality requirements which means that they cannot discuss their deliberations outside the courtroom. The Contempt of Court Act 1981 prohibits research with real juries in England and Wales. While we therefore do not know for certain in any given case what jurors were thinking, contemporary research supports the idea that, generally speaking, the responses of jurors to rape cases involving acquaintances or intimates are complex. It is possible that people hold 'rape supportive beliefs' that influence how they assess sexual abuse that takes place between men and women who know each other.

In particular, work by Louise Ellison and Vanessa Munro using mock jury trials and reconstructions of acquaintance and also domestic rape suggests that jurors are not wedded to the paradigmatic stranger-rape scenario. Responses to surveys show mock jurors being receptive, in principle, to the idea that a woman could be raped by a man with whom she had had a relationship, for example.[12] Ellison and Munro found that juries do respond *differently* to rapes where the defendant and complainant are known to each other, however. While not being necessarily 'blinded by the "real rape" stereotype',[13] it is nevertheless fair to say that there are '*complexities at play* in framing jurors' responses' to these different scenarios.[14]

In this chapter I investigate three areas of complexity that affect the prosecution of domestic rape and sexual assault. First, I discuss the existence of resistance to the idea that forced sexual contact between intimate partners is rape or sexual assault. Second, I review the tendency to prioritise the importance of physical violence in the context of domestic rape and sexual assault, (and, furthermore, an insistence on the close proximity of the physical violence with the incident of domestic rape). Finally, I examine the confusion over the boundary in the domestic context between what is referred to as "submission" and the all-important construct of consent. All three of these issues are exacerbated by the failure of the current legislative regime to give enough, if any, guidance, in particular in the context of abuse that is chronic rather than acute. In this chapter I look at each of the three identified issues in turn in the context of the current regime, before concluding with a discussion of what research is needed to facilitate reform.

The Disavowal of Domestic Rape and Sexual Assault

The Survivor's Perspective

Resistance to the idea that forced sexual contact between intimate partners is rape or sexual assault is evident in survivors' stories. Abused women find it hard to articulate their experiences of sexual abuse in the language of the criminal law. Sarah, for example, when I asked her about the frequency of physical violence in her relationship, replied: 'It was frequent, but I didn't see it as violence because it was sexual violence … he would not take no for an answer for sex'.[15] At another point in the interview, she described being raped on her return from hospital (where she had just given birth via caesarean section):

> I discharged myself [from hospital] after six days. I was meant to be there for ten, because he kept saying - it was like a separation anxiety - so I went back because he was like a crying baby, you couldn't - you know - and sitting there having nursed Holly, massive lactating breasts and still had this metal suture, but he again forced sex - I hadn't even - but basically his view was that because I'd had a caesarean that area wasn't affected.[16]

When I asked her, 'Were his threats unspoken? In that did you know what would happen if you didn't comply?' she replied softly 'Yes, and I feared it'.[17] The Sexual Offences Act 2003 (the SOA) is discussed in detail below, but many of Sarah's experiences of marital sexual abuse come within the SOA, section 1 definition of rape. Nevertheless, Sarah preferred to talk about 'forced sex' rather than 'rape'. She explained:

> Rape is not something you can associate with … But I can remember the
> judge in the children's proceedings saying "Did he hit you? Did he rape
> you?", just like that. And I said no to both. But … [she trailed off].[18]

Jen, an Independent Domestic Violence Advisor (IDVA), said about a client,
Frankie, that 'Even when she reported the rape, on the tapes she says "I'm not
saying it is rape, I just didn't want to"'.[19]

The Historical Position

Resistance to the idea that forced sex between men and women who are married
is rape has deep legal roots. *Morgan*[20] is a landmark rape case of 1975 which is
remembered for its pronouncements on the need for subjective responsibility in
the context of the *mens rea* for rape; it is considered in more detail below. But what
is also interesting (and less talked about) in the context of *Morgan* is the lack of legal
attention given to its unquestioning sanction of the marital rape exemption. As
feminist legal commentator Ngaire Naffine has pointed out, *Morgan* 'is largely
invisible to the scholarly community as a marital rape case'.[21]

William Morgan and three of his junior sub-ordinates in the RAF spent the
evening drinking together in Wolverhampton. When they failed to find sex
workers in town, Morgan suggested to the others that they come back to his house
and have sex with his wife. Morgan told his friends to expect resistance from his
wife as she enjoyed feigning resistance to sex. Daphne Morgan shared a room with
her 11-year-old son, and when the four men returned home she was in bed,
asleep. Daphne Morgan was rudely awakened by the men, and frogmarched into
another room where there was a double bed. As she screamed for her life, the men
took it in turns to hold her down while each of them had sex with her. As Lord
Halisham explains in his extremely lucid judgement 'When each had finished and
had left the room, the appellant Morgan completed the series of incidents by
having intercourse with her himself'.[22] But, Lord Hailsham explains:

> The appellant Morgan, who also had connexion with his wife allegedly
> without her consent as part of the same series of events, was not charged with
> rape, the prosecution evidently accepting and applying the ancient common
> law doctrine that a husband cannot be guilty of raping his own wife.[23]

The 'ancient common law doctrine' referred to by Lord Hailsham is usually attributed to Lord Justice Hale, who wrote his Pleas of the Crown in the 1650s. His
stricture on marital rape is:

> The husband cannot be guilty of a rape committed by himself upon his
> lawful wife for by their mutual matrimonial consent and contract the wife
> hath given up herself in this kind unto her husband, which she cannot
> retract.[24]

There is nothing to indicate that this was anything more than Hale's personal view: unusually for him, he cited no other authority for the proposition.[25] The construct, which is of a kind of consent-for-all-time-which-cannot-be-retracted, is in complete opposition to the traditionally transactional focus of the criminal law (as discussed in previous chapters) and does not bear much legal scrutiny, either as a principle in contract[26] or in family law.[27] Nevertheless consent-for-all-time to sex within marriage was accepted as doctrine by the courts of England and Wales for over 300 years.

Lord Hailsham cannot, of course, be blamed for the prosecution's decision not to bring charges against William Morgan. But as Naffine points out, what is strange is the ensuing 'curious mix of attention and inattention' in the legal community to the Morgan case.[28] To say that none of the men in this story emerge in a good light would be an understatement. William Morgan, however, is the worst offender of the lot – he suggests the crime, organises it, and of the four of them is the one who *absolutely knew* his wife was not consenting. Yet such was/is the endorsement and acceptance of the marital immunity that even to this day William Morgan's pivotal role in setting up and partaking in the rapes goes remarkably unscrutinised. Despite the intense legal interest shown in *Morgan*, and its prominence in the analysis and the teaching of the criminal law, the fact of the non-prosecution of the principal rapist in the case hardly registered then and still does not today. Doctrinal scholars lined up, post Morgan, to assert their support for the thesis that the seriousness of the crime of rape meant that subjective responsibility was the only appropriate *mens rea*.[29] The non-application of the criminal law to the same serious crime when committed by the husband goes unremarked upon. The case is almost never spoken of as 'one which invoked the spousal immunity'.[30]

Ten years later, *Kowalski*[31] was one of the last cases to be heard by the Court of Appeal in the spousal immunity era. The victim and the defendant were married in January 1985. By September 1986 the marriage had failed, and they were living together in the same house but leading separate lives. The defendant raped the victim orally and vaginally at knifepoint. The details of the victim's ordeal are set out in the judgment as follows:

> On Sunday, 14 September 1986 the relevant events took place. The complainant returned to the house at about 6.15 p.m. She had occasion to go to the lavatory. While she was there, the appellant burst in, carrying a knife; he placed the point against her throat. He told her not to do anything foolish and then ordered her to take off all her clothing. This she did, including the tampon that she was wearing. He then forced her, still at knifepoint, to walk to the bedroom and there he made her undress him, again at knifepoint. In the middle of this process he remembered that she had an appointment elsewhere later that evening, so he took her to the telephone and made her telephone to say that she would be late. They returned to the bedroom; he had provided drinks for them both - a bottle of

rum and a plastic bottle of Pepsi Cola, which, because it could not be undone, he cut open with the knife. He compelled her to pour them each a drink. He said to her that she should take a drink in advance of what was going to happen. She took a few sips while she was kneeling in front of him.

He then began an act of oral intercourse with her. She objected, and took her hands away from his buttocks where she had had to place them. She took her hands away to wipe her mouth, and then she tried to put her hand between his body and hers. He said to her, angrily, that she must put her hands back on his buttocks. She did so, and he put his penis back in her mouth. While it was there he kept thrusting; because of the force of his thrusting she choked and began to, as she described it, "urge" - or, as one would suppose she meant, "retch". He asked her why she was doing that. She replied that he had "pushed it too far back". He continued with what he was doing, albeit not pushing as far back as he had been before. Throughout the whole of this episode the knife was at the nape of her neck.

He then stopped, withdrew his penis from her mouth and said, "Get on the bed". She lay on the bed. He told her to get on her front and instructed her to kneel, to put her head down and her hands behind her back. She obeyed. With her kneeling in that position he put his penis into her vagina. She could feel the knife in the region of her neck the whole while. He continued the act of sexual intercourse. She did not co-operate and he said to her, "You can do better than that. If you help me you will live, if you don't you will die; I am going to die tonight anyway." So she did something to appease him.

Although he was to continue the intercourse for some little time, that is a sufficient description of the events for the purposes of this case.

After setting out the facts of this ordeal, (which went on for two hours), Ian Kennedy J refers back to Lord Justice Hale:

> It is clear, well-settled and ancient law that a man cannot, as actor, be guilty of rape upon his wife. That exception, which traces its history back to *Hale's Pleas of the Crown*, is dependent upon the implied consent to sexual intercourse which arises from the married state, and which continues until that consent is put aside by decree nisi, by a separation order or, in certain circumstances, by a separation agreement. Self-evidently, none of those limitations in time arise in this case.[32]

Thus by a 'strange process of intellectual compartmentalisation',[33] domestic rape was not historically recognised as such at all. What Naffine has referred to as the 'vast legal status restriction on liability for rape'[34] gets little to no mainstream critical legal attention. The ordeal suffered by the victim in *Kowalski* and indeed by

Daphne Morgan in many aspects bore the hallmarks of the paradigmatic stranger attack referred to by DC Hardie in the introduction to this chapter. The victim in *Kowalski* was attempting to separate from her husband and was raped at knifepoint. Daphne Morgan was dragged screaming from her bed by her husband and gang raped by her husband and three strangers. Both victims were nevertheless correctly informed by the court that their abusive husbands could not be charged with rape.

Both Ian Kennedy J and Lord Hailsham did their best within the confines of the criminal law as it was then. Kennedy J found the defendant guilty of indecent assault as a result of the forced act of oral sex, which he was able to find was outside the marital exemption construct. Lord Hailsham made clear his views of William Morgan's cruelty and 'malignant character'.[35] Yet except in the limited circumstances referred to by Ian Kennedy J,[36] rape within marriage was not a criminal offence until *R v R* in 1992, as reinforced by the Criminal Justice and Public Order Act 1994, s 142.[37]

The committee set up in the aftermath of Morgan chaired by Mrs Justice Heilbron is the subject of a detailed focus below. Notably, it did not discuss the marital immunity that was at the heart of the Morgan debacle – it was 'simply taken as a given'.[38] In what Naffine refers to as 'the appropriately Orwellian year of 1984',[39] the Criminal Law Revision Committee of England and Wales published a report specifically addressing the question of whether a man should be allowed to rape his wife.[40] A majority decided against the full abolition of the immunity. The 17-member Committee decided in 1984, in other words, that a man's rape of his wife lacked the seriousness of a man's rape of any other woman. It is no surprise that the relatively recent entrenchment of the old regime casts a shadow over contemporary responses to domestic rape.[41]

The Sex Offences Review

Five years after Parliament had legislated to do away with the marital rape exemption, the Home Secretary set up the Sex Offences Review to re-examine the sexual offences regime. The Sex Offences Review published its findings in a green paper, *Setting the Boundaries*. That work culminated in the 2002 white paper, *Protecting the Public*, and finally in the Sexual Offences Act 2003, (the 'SOA'). Unfortunately, while the Sex Offences Review did consider some of the issues in relation to domestic sexual offending, (as discussed in more detail below), *Protecting the Public* and the SOA do not.

The Overview to *Protecting the Public* is instructive. Under the heading 'The Need to Reform the Law on Sexual Offences' there is a reference to changes in the way that sexual offences are understood:

> The conviction rate for rape is very low and has been falling in recent years. The number of persons found guilty of rape in comparison to the total number of offences reported has fallen from 25% in 1985 to 7% in 2000. Much of this is due to the change in the nature of the cases coming to trial, with many more instances of date or acquaintance rape being reported than before. These cases,

which often rely on one person's word against that of another, make the decision of juries much harder than in cases of stranger rape.[42]

Thus the Home Office in its report acknowledges 'date rape' and 'acquaintance rape' *but not "intimate" or "domestic" rape.* The Home Office had commissioned a report from its own directorate into the difficulties with prosecuting rape in the 1990s. *A Question of Evidence?* (referred to earlier in this chapter) was also published in 1999. The 'the most striking finding' of *A Question of Evidence?* was that:

> Rape committed by a person unknown to the victim ("stranger" rapes) formed only 12% of the sample, those committed by acquaintances or intimates accounted for 45% and 43% of cases respectively.[43]

The Home Office report includes family members in its definition of 'intimates'.[44] Adjusting this figure to subtract the family members that were included in the 43% leaves 36% of rapes that were committed by an abuser who had had a relationship with the victim. By 1999, then, it was known that over a third of rapes that are committed are identified as intimate partner rapes.

Three years later, a Home Office research study concluded that 'current partners' were responsible for 45% of the rapes reported to the survey.[45] What is unclear, is why was this not explicitly considered anywhere in *Protecting the Public* or, indeed, in the SOA? There have been considerable changes in the reporting of rape since 1999. It is now evident from the reported statistics that the *majority* of perpetrators of rape are not an acquaintance or a stranger: they are partners or ex-partners.[46] It is exactly this kind of "silence" in relation to the specific issues that relate to domestic sexual offending that are examined in this chapter that feeds into the rape-supportive belief that rape within an intimate relationship is not really rape.

Physical Violence and Rape

The Survivor Perspective

The second area of difficulty is the relationship between physical violence and domestic rape and sexual assault. As was explained in chapter 1, physical violence can, and often does, play a part in coercive controlling strategies but it need not. Evan Stark articulates domestic rape as 'rape as routine', which he says is 'perhaps the most common form of sexual exploitation, where women comply with their partner's sexual demands because of the "or else" proviso'.[47]

As I explained in chapter 1, the 'or else' can be explicit or implied. When Sarah, for example, spoke about her experiences of sexual abuse, some involved physical violence and some did not. When Sarah described the rape that took place after her return from hospital, for example, she confirmed that her abuser's threats were mostly unspoken.[48] Although Sarah was afraid, her abuser did not in that instant physically attack her. He did not need to – she knew he could if he so chose. Physical resistance in that context might have been extremely dangerous for Sarah, as she would have known. Yet for reasons that are explored below, it is likely that the absence of physical injuries in the context of domestic rape is a hurdle for the prosecution of domestic rape.

Physical Violence, Rape and the Criminal Law

Just as with the marital rape exemption, rape-supportive beliefs around violence and rape have their roots in legal history. The premise that physical violence is a component of rape was also historically legally accurate although with less clarity (than the marital rape exemption), and less recently. Historically, the common law on rape required that sexual intercourse occurred against the victim's will. In order for intercourse to have occurred against the victim's will, there had to be evidence of the use of 'force, fear or fraud'.[49] Force, fear or fraud included force or violence by the defendant, or the threat of immediate force or violence, and resistance by the victim.[50] It is thought that the abolition of the death penalty for rape in the early nineteenth century prompted judges to widen the scope of what might constitute rape.[51]

The leading case is *Camplin* in 1845,[52] where it was held that the use or threat of force is not an essential ingredient of the offence. However the caselaw post *Camplin* is confused – notwithstanding the finding in *Camplin* that force is not an essential ingredient, some judges continued to direct juries that force by the defendant and resistance by the complainant are essential ingredients of the offence of rape.[53] By the time of *Morgan*,[54] in 1975, the trial judge's restating of this (confused) common law position in his summing up to the jury attracted considerable criticism.[55]

Morgan has been discussed already in the context of the marital rape exemption. In fact, it was a controversial ruling chiefly for the impact it had on the development of the requisite *mens rea* of rape, but it also had an influence on the role of physical violence as part of the actus reus. The trial judge said:

> First of all, let me deal with the crime of rape. What are its ingredients? What have the prosecution to prove to your satisfaction before you can find a defendant guilty of rape? The crime of rape consists in having unlawful sexual intercourse with a woman without her consent and by force. By force. Those words mean exactly what they say. It does not mean there has to be a fight or blows have to be inflicted. It means that there has to be some violence used against the woman to overbear her will or that there has to be a threat of violence as a result of which her will is overborne.[56]

In the aftermath of *Morgan* the Government set up a committee chaired by a judge (Mrs Justice Heilbron) to conduct a review. The Heilbron committee expressed its disapproval of the judge's summing up as follows:

> It is wrong to assume that the woman must show signs of injury or that she must always physically resist before there can be a conviction for rape. We

have found this erroneous assumption held by some and therefore hope that our recommendations will go some way to dispel it.[57]

It recommended that:

> As rape is a crime which is still without statutory definition the lack of which has caused certain difficulties, we think that this legislation[58] should contain a comprehensive definition of the offence which would emphasise that lack of consent (and not violence) is the crux of the matter.[59]

The Sexual Offences Amendment Act 1976 was passed as a response. It does indeed emphasise that lack of consent and not violence is the 'crux of the matter' by section 1(1), which defines rape as sexual intercourse with a woman without her consent. The SOA confirms this position. The SOA, section 1 sets out the offence of rape, and states that a person commits rape if he intentionally penetrates the vagina, anus or mouth of another person with his penis, the victim does not consent to the penetration and the defendant does not reasonably believe that the victim consents. There is no reference in section 1 to physical violence; there is no need, in other words, to give evidence of physical violence on the part of the defendant, or resistance on the part of the victim, in order to show that the victim was not consenting.

The SOA is not entirely consistent in its approach to the relationship between physical violence and consent, however. The definition of consent is in section 74; sections 75–76 contain presumptions about consent. The three sections give the prosecution options, as it can use any of them to prove the absence of consent in relation to any given case. The SOA, section 76 sets out 'conclusive presumptions' about consent that, if proven, establish that no consent was given. As might be expected in light of a presumption that is 'conclusive' the presumptions are limited. They are based on the old common law provisions on deception and impersonation; they are not relevant here. Section 75 contains 'evidential presumptions' about consent that, if proved, must be rebutted by the defence. It is in this section that the old preoccupation with physical violence is most apparent. Finally, section 74 gives the general definition of consent and is used in all cases where the SOA, section 75 and 76 do not apply.

Section 75 was originally intended by the Sex Offences Review as an opportunity to give guidance: to dispel some of the unhelpful assumptions that still surrounded the prosecution of the sexual offences. In *Setting the Boundaries*, the Sex Offences Review explained that they wanted to adopt the approach used in a number of Australian States of setting out a list of examples of circumstances where consent was not present. The list would be a set of examples only, but it would 'help both practitioners and juries in coming to decisions in particular cases, and give broad guidelines for considering the issue'.[60] One of the recommended examples in the Sex Offences Review's list was where a person submits 'because of threats of fear of serious harm or serious detriment of any type to themselves or another person'.[61]

This wording had the potential to encompass a wide range of threats including the sorts of threats experienced by Sarah and other survivors of coercive control. Indeed, this was the Sex Offences Review's intention:

> These would cover the broad set of cases where there was force or coercion or threat to a person, their child etc. It could also cover situations where other threats were made – for example losing a job or killing the family pet. It would be for the court to consider in each case what the nature of the threat was and whether the victim would think that she or he would suffer serious harm. These could vary from case to case: the threat of loss of employment might be far more serious in a small community with few other opportunities, for example. The pressures in this section are all negative – there was a distinction between a threat and an inducement, and the distinction that consent was obtained by coercion.[62]

The references to the 'family pet' in this paragraph are an explicit, albeit indirect, reference to rape in the context of an abusive relationship. It is helpful – a threat to kill the family dog, for example, is an example of the kinds of coercive threats made by the perpetrators of coercive control. However, somewhere between the publication of the *Setting the Boundaries* in 2000 and the later *Protecting the Public* (2002) all references to domestic sexual abuse were forgotten.

By the time of the parliamentary debate in 2003, the Government took the view that the reference to 'serious detriment' was too wide, and that it would not be advisable to cover such a wide range of threats. It was also decided to make the list exhaustive rather than open. Lord Falconer, then Lord Chancellor, in resisting the suggestion that the exhaustive list should be more comprehensive, said 'The rebuttable presumptions should be limited sensibly. Something that might frighten someone in a particular condition might not frighten someone else'.[63] There was no reference to sexual abuse in a domestic setting.[64]

Six scenarios, (a)–(f), form the basis of section 75 of the SOA. The 'because of threats of fear of serious harm or serious detriment of any type to themselves or another person' from the Sexual Offences Review's list became scenarios (a) and (b). Section 75(a) reads as follows:

> Any person was, at the time of the relevant act or immediately before it began, using violence against the complainant or causing the complainant to fear that immediate violence would be used against him.

Scenario (b) mirrors scenario (a) except that it covers causing the victim to fear that immediate violence would be used against another. Thus, the reference to the Sex Offences Review's 'broad set of cases where there was force or coercion or threat to a person' has been narrowed down to become 'violence' and/or 'fear that immediate violence would be used'. This does not, of course, mean that it is necessary to provide evidence of violence in order to prove that consent was absent. But it does suggest that physical violence, or the fear of it, is considered to be more significant than other threats.

As I explain in chapter 1, the threats used by the perpetrators of coercive control are myriad and bespoke, they can include threats to exploit vulnerabilities, for example, or threats to expose secrets.[65] They do not necessarily involve threats of physical violence – but this does not mean that the victims of coercive control are less frightened, or more able to consent to sexual contact. Also difficult is the fact that the fear needs to be of *immediate* violence, the so-called immediacy requirement that was the subject of a detailed analysis in chapter 3. Including an immediacy requirement forces the prosecution on each occasion to prove a proximity that is out of step with the experiences of survivors like Sarah. It does not allow for any consideration of the interpersonal dynamic between the parties.

Criticism of the section 75(a) immediacy requirement was not confined to the feminist literature.[66] It also received criticism from criminal law textbooks. Rook and Ward, for example, observed that 'neither paragraph s75(2)(a) nor (b) deals with the situation where a complainant fears future violence, although in such circumstances the fear may well mean that the complainant does not consent. The justification for this omission is less than clear'.[67] The pre-2003 common law did not necessarily require the threat of force to be immediate, and section 75(a) is therefore unfortunately a step backwards in this context.[68]

As explained previously, the threats that Sarah reported in the context of sexual abuse were often implicit and unspoken. Sarah would therefore not benefit from the presumption in section 75(a) because, although she was afraid, her abuser did not in that instant make an explicit threat of immediate physical violence. He did not need to – he had access to her all of the time, so the threat could be *implicit*. Implicit threats are not necessarily transactional, they are not limited to a particular time and place, for example, but tend to be chronic – ongoing. An immediacy requirement makes more sense in the context of threats that are acute: explicit and transactional. An example of an acute threat is one that might be used by a stranger encountering his victim for the first time. The insistence on temporal proximity does not exclude an implicit threat but makes it more difficult for a survivor such as Sarah (who lived in fear) to prove a link between her fear and the incident of rape. It is an import from "stranger" type offences that misunderstands the nature of abusive relationships.

The Jurors Perspective

Ellison and Munro's work with mock jury trials supports the view that there may be especially unhelpful rape-supportive beliefs in the context of domestic rape. They certainly found that mock jurors have more rigid expectations about how a woman would react to an assault by someone with whom she is familiar. In a stranger rape context mock jurors were supportive of the idea that a woman might be so 'overcome by shock and fear of escalating violence that she would be unable to engage in physical, or even verbal resistance'.[69] In the context of acquaintance rape, however, 'Jurors were typically committed to the idea that a woman would do her utmost to avoid an assault by issuing strong verbal protests and fight back'.[70] There seemed to be an assumption that 'rape by a known assailant would provoke less fear'.[71]

In a later study, Munro and Ellison looked specifically at a domestic rape: a rape, in other words, where the trial parties had previously been involved in an intimate relationship. They found that:

> The onus was typically placed upon the complainant to correct any potential misreading of her behaviour by communicating her lack of consent unequivocally to the defendant ... for many jurors, this stretched to an expectation, and indeed a de facto requirement, that the complainant physically resist and/or use force where it was clear that her verbal protestations were not being taken on board by a defendant.[72]

While the mock jurors were prepared to accept that a woman could freeze during sexual abuse due to fear they only considered this response plausible in the context of the stranger rape scenario.[73] It should be noted that in the scenario in this later Ellison and Munro study, while the parties had previously been in a relationship they had separated and were no longer living together at the time of the alleged rape. There was also no suggestion of a history of abuse. Ellison and Munro report that some jurors suggested that a frightened freezing response might be more credible if there was such a history.[74]

As set out in chapter 1 my research suggests that the survivor response in this context is complicated. To assume that a woman experiencing coercive control can "choose" to resist her abusive partner's demands ignores the myriad ways in which coercive control curtails agency. This needs further investigation and research. In the absence of such research, however, it can be concluded that the existence of rape-supportive beliefs around physical resistance in the context of domestic rape is likely to be a problem for jurors who are not familiar with the dynamic of coercive control.

The Problem with Consent

Olugboja

As with the two previous problem areas reviewed in this chapter, the history of the reform of the law in the context of consent is instructive. *Olugboja*[75] was the leading authority on consent before the SOA, and was decided in 1981. Dunn LJ acknowledges that the issue of consent is difficult when the defendant threatens something other than violence.[76] He introduces the idea of a spectrum of responses, some of which collectively amount to consent and some of which do not. With regard to consent, he says that it 'covers a wide range of states of mind in the context of intercourse between a man and a woman, ranging from actual desire on the one hand to reluctant acquiescence on the other'.[77] However, there comes a point at which apparent "consent" ceases to be consent at all, and the victim's state of mind is such that it could more appropriately be associated with 'mere submission'. The identification of that point, that is the point at which reluctant acquiescence (no rape) becomes mere submission (rape), is up to the jury, to decide in any given case.[78]

This is a thoughtful and in many ways progressive decision whose exposition (of consent) is not necessarily out of step with the way in which survivors of domestic rape describe their experiences of sexual abuse. Sarah, when describing her experiences of domestic rape, did not use the words "consent" or "submission", but she was clear nevertheless that she was submitting to her husband's demand for sex and not consenting to it. What is missing from the later debate (it was not an issue in *Olugboja*) is an analysis of when the intersection between coercive control and domestic rape results in "submission" and not "consent". This is the discussion that is unfortunately mostly absent from the work of the Sexual Offences Review, and entirely absent from the later debates in Parliament on the Sexual Offences Bill. Commentators responding to the *Olugboja* judgment at the time,[79] and since,[80] have pointed out that the boundary between consent and submission is at once critical and unclear. The SOA does nothing to clarify this.

The Sexual Offences Act 2003 Definition of Consent: s 74

As stated above, the SOA, sections 74, 75 and 76 deal with consent. The shortcomings with regard to the section 75/76 presumptions have been reviewed above. The SOA, s 74 gives the general definition of consent, to be used when sections 75 and 76 of the SOA do not apply. Even without a consideration of survivors of domestic rape, it has been observed that 'Section 74 is not a model of tight drafting'.[81] The SOA, s 74 states that: 'A person consents if he agrees by choice, and has the freedom and capacity to make that choice'.[82] This is in many ways a progressive statement in that a specific reference to 'freedom' and 'capacity' points, it has been observed, to the need for a 'fuller exploration of the surrounding power dynamics and conditions within which (sexual) choices can meaningfully made'.[83]

While the definition of consent in section 74 of the SOA therefore has the *potential* to bring about a more progressive understanding of what constitutes sexual abuse, as it stands this terminology is challenging, and in need of explanation that is absent. It does not shed enough light on the distinction between submission and consent. Andrew Ashworth and Jennifer Temkin, for example, note that:

> It might be thought that "freedom" and "choice" are ideas which raise philosophical issues of such complexity as to be ill-suited to the needs of criminal justice - clearly those words do not refer to total freedom or choice,

so all the questions about how much liberty of action satisfies the "definition" remain at large.[84]

In other words, 'Freedom remains to be too loose a word to be useful in defining such a crucial element of such serious offences'.[85] Furthermore, it has been observed that the fact that 'freedom', 'choice' and 'capacity' are terms which everybody understands, does not mean that everybody understands them to mean the same thing, either generally, or in relation to specific incidents of rape.[86] Early work with mock juries suggested that the looseness of the terms caused juries considerable difficulties, and resulted in 'considerable leniency' towards the defendant.[87]

In the context of domestic sexual offending the boundary between consent and submission, even if clear to survivors, (and more research is needed on this point), appears to be especially difficult to communicate to jurors. Unexplained references to 'freedom' and 'choice' in this context are unhelpful. Criminal law textbooks suggest that 'choice' highlights that the victim had options from which to choose, and focus on whether or not sufficient information was conveyed so as to make that choice informed.[88] 'Capacity' supposedly covers cases where consent is negated by, for example, a mental disorder, youth, or intoxication.[89] 'Freedom' is said to rule out cases where it is negated by the immediate threat of physical force, or by fraud.[90]

None of these explanations would be of much help to Sarah. Sarah did not feel that she had options from which to choose, but for none of the reasons identified above. Sarah explained that she lived in chronic, constant fear of her partner. He could be extremely violent. On several occasions she feared for her life. The violence was not always immediate. The threats were usually unspoken. She was clear that, in this context of chronic fear and life-threatening danger, she often submitted to sex. This is not consent. IDVAs supported this view. One said to me,

> When you do it with someone who has been violent towards you, or who is, for want of a better word, a bully – and you are frightened of them – how easy is it for you to say no? So if you don't say no – where are we on the spectrum of consent there?[91]

The SOA, s 74, as it stands, does not assist with this important point, and neither do the s 75 presumptions as parameters on this question. To some extent these scenarios anchor the debate, they give an indication of the kinds of situations that Parliament was considering as it constructed the SOA, s 74. Scenarios (d)–(f) are a good example of where the anchor provided by the presumptions is unhelpful. (d)–(f) deal respectively with victims who are asleep or unconscious, physically disabled, or have been caused to take a substance capable of stupefaction without their consent. The fact that these are *rebuttable* presumptions implies that consent *can* be present – this 'does imply that consent can be present in highly coercive circumstances and thus undermines the definition of consent as "agreement by choice, [with] the freedom to make that choice"'.[92]

Furthermore, in this area the law has taken a step backwards. At common law, if a complainant was asleep or unconscious she was incapable of consenting.[93] Thus, section 75 of the SOA can still be said to be disappointing in the way that it operates to *undermine* the utility of section 74. It begs the question: 'Can freedom and capacity to make a choice really exist in any meaningful sense in this situation?'.[94]

Commentators at the time of the passage of the SOA expressed concern with regard to the then new framework on consent stating,

> The fact that responsibility for this interpretation is left, first, in the hands of the Judicial Studies Board and the judiciary, and then in the hands of jurors who will apply judicial guidance to the circumstances of each case, is also disconcerting.[95]

The use of judicial directions to guide juries in this area is the subject for further discussion below, but unfortunately, this concern has proved prescient. The central question for juries remains unclear: 'What degree of impairment should be taken to mean that any apparent consent was not free?'.[96] Or, 'What degree of coercion and/or abuse of position, power or authority has to be exercised upon a person's mind before he or she is not agreeing by choice with the freedom to make that choice?'[97]

The Mens Rea of Rape

Even if a survivor manages to explain to a jury that she was not consenting to sex, the prosecution case can still run into difficulties. This is because as well as proving that the victim did not consent, the prosecution has to prove the *mens rea* of rape further to the SOA, section 1. The SOA was reformist in its approach to *mens rea*.[98] As set out above, *Morgan*[99] – to widespread disapproval[100] – established the defence of honest but mistaken belief in consent. The SOA removes this by establishing a partly objective *mens rea* standard. The relevant question is whether or not the defendant reasonably believed that the complainant consented. An honest but unreasonable belief is no longer a defence. But section 1(2) qualifies the objective test by introducing the somewhat ambiguous requirement that: 'Whether a belief is reasonable is to be determined having regard to all the circumstances, including any steps A has taken to ascertain whether B consents'.[101]

Commentators have observed that the section 1(2) qualification muddies the objective standard in an unhelpful manner, invites jurors to use the complainant's behaviour to determine whether it could have induced a reasonable belief in consent, and 'is confusing for jurors who find themselves left to interpret the level of objectivity or subjectivity required by the test'.[102] In particular, early work with mock juries suggested that the invitation to consider all the circumstances encouraged jurors to focus on the victim and allowed jurors to deduce the defendant's reasonable belief in consent from other, unrelated events.[103]

This is especially problematic in the context of an ongoing abusive relationship. The invitation to consider all the circumstances introduces unhelpful assumptions about sexual access, and communication of that access. Jurors rely on inferences extrapolated from views on "appropriate" socio-sexual interaction that they impute to the defendant and use these assumptions to attribute to the defendant a reasonable belief in consent.[104] As explained earlier in this chapter, the scenario under review by these particular mock jurors involved a complainant and a defendant who had been in a relationship that had ended two months prior to the incident in question. It is possible that the ways in which conduct on the part of the complainant may be held to signal sexual interest is even more complex in a scenario where the relationship is continuing.

Data from my interviews with the judiciary suggest that determining whether or not the complainant had signalled sexual interest is particularly an issue in prosecutions of domestic rape where the relationship is ongoing. In cases where there is a continuing intimate relationship between the parties, judges observed that the defence often used evidence of previous (and post) consensual sex to cast doubt in the juries' minds as to whether the complainant had done enough to communicate a lack of consent. Judge Little said:

> Because rape is two parts, it's not simply that she wasn't consenting, but that the defendant knew she wasn't consenting. And clearly if he is hurting her at the time then it's much easier to say, "well of course he would have known she wasn't consenting". But when it's an assault that happened two months ago, or even just two weeks ago … and, of course, very often in the context of those relationships, as well, the witness will be saying, "I have had sex with him in the interim and it was fine, but it's just this occasion, and I said no, and he got very angry, and so I didn't like to kind of … " It's that kind of thing that makes it very difficult … If the witness is saying "I was not consenting and he would have known I was not consenting because … " from a jury's point of view it's that, "it's my belief that it is that", that causes them the concern.[105]

Judge Little observes that the prosecution faces a number of hurdles as it attempts to persuade the jury that the defendant has the appropriate *mens rea* for rape in an ongoing intimate relationship. The absence of physical violence, the passage of time, and the presence of interim consensual sex, in her opinion, all lead the jury to doubt whether or not the defendant would have known that the complainant was not consenting to sex.

From the survivors' perspective, it is the backdrop to the relationship, the strategy of domination that constitutes coercive control, that explains why "He would have known that I was not consenting". For jurors, rape-supportive beliefs that legitimise assumptions on the part of the defendant about sexual access in the context of an ongoing relationship get in the way. IDVAs agreed with this. Jen, for example, said,

But when you are trying to prove consent, particularly in a domestic abuse relationship, it's very difficult because you will have moments where it all looks to the CJS or the public that she is - you know - how could she have been raped when she is, you know, texting him that she loves him the next day.[106]

In other words, even if the difference between submission and consent is clear to a victim, and even if she manages to explain this to a jury, the 'spectre of sexual miscommunication loom(s) large' in the context of the *mens rea* requirement of the SOA, section 1.[107] Juries still need to be sure that there was clarity (from the defendant's perspective) in the complainant's communication to the defendant. In the context of a previous, and even post, consensual sexual relationship this can be an extremely difficult hurdle to overcome.

Judicial Directions

In *Doody*[108] in 2008 the Court of Appeal said that balanced directions could, in certain circumstances in rape cases, be given to the jury. Balanced directions can be given where they are necessary to ensure fairness to the complainant, where there is a danger, in other words, of the jury jumping to conclusions in the absence of an appropriate warning. Any such comment must be uncontroversial – that is to say it must be general in nature. Since 2008, judicial comment has become a routine feature in cases involving rape and sexual assault, although it is not compulsory. There is a question mark over its value. This is because there is a risk a direction will entrench rather than overcome any rape-supportive beliefs held by jurors.[109]

It was not possible within the confines of this research project to put detailed questions to the judiciary on the question of judicial comment in the context of domestic sexual offending. Readings of the Crown Court Compendium in 2016, and then again in December 2019, suggest that while there have been improvements in the way that the judges are advised to direct juries, some concerns remain. There is still a risk, in other words, that the recommended directions will have the opposite effect to that intended.

The suggested wording for a specific direction on consent for judges in the context of domestic sexual offending is set out at section 20–21, under the heading of 'Non-consensual activity within or immediately after a long-term relationship'. It reads:

It is agreed that D and W have had a long-term sexual relationship. This is relevant to the question of whether or not W consented to D (specify act) on this occasion. That is because the situation between two people who have/have had such a long-term sexual relationship is quite different from a situation in which two people are strangers or have met one another only a few times. When two people have/have had such a relationship, there is likely to be some give and take between them in relation to any number of things, including their sexual relationship. And sometimes a partner who is not feeling enthusiastic may nevertheless reluctantly give consent to sex.[110]

This part of the direction, (which has not changed substantially since 2016), puts the idea that the victim's evidence may be construed as reluctant acquiescence, in light of the long-term sexual relationship that she and her partner have had, at the forefront of the jury's mind. Reluctant acquiescence, ('Sometimes a partner who is not feeling enthusiastic may nevertheless reluctantly give consent'), is not offset by an example of where, when two people have an abusive relationship, consent might become submission. In other words, there is no consideration given to the possibility of a power imbalance, just as was the case with the pre-Serious Crime Act, section 76 case law on harassment that I reviewed in the previous chapter.[111]

The next section of the advice has been improved. In 2016, it continued 'This is not to say however that when two people are/have been in such a relationship it must follow that both of them will consent to any sexual activity that takes place'.[112] This set a benchmark in the wrong place and therefore contained strong echoes of the *rape within a relationship isn't really rape* belief which was unfortunate as the intention of the direction was to dispel such unhelpful rape-supportive beliefs.

The direction now reads: 'When two people are/have been in a long-term sexual relationship it is not the case that both of them will consent to any sexual activity that takes place'. This wording is more neutral and is to be preferred. The direction finishes in much the same way as it did in 2016:

> One party is fully entitled to say "no" to the other regardless of their relationship. What you must decide in this case is whether W consented freely and by choice, even if reluctantly, to what took place or whether W did not consent but submitted to it. You must also decide whether D may have reasonably believed that W was consenting, taking into account all the evidence including the nature of the [previous] relationship between W and D.[113]

Both parts of this section could have the opposite effect to that intended. The first part deals with the actus reus: was she consenting? It contains a reference to a type of choice that may look like submission but is nevertheless a choice ('consented freely and by choice, even if reluctantly'), but contains no reference to a submission that may look like a choice, but is nevertheless submission (submission in the context of control).

The second part of this section deals with the *mens rea*: did he reasonably believe she was consenting? It asks the jury to consider whether, in light of the previous relationship, D may have reasonably believed her to be consenting but does not ask the jury to consider whether, in light of the previous relationship, D must have known that she was not consenting, (as in Sarah's situation, for example). In other words, as has been noted with regard to other well-meaning judicial directions, 'Quite unintentionally, the direction would appear to be ideally formulated to ensure that the false claim it highlights becomes more rather than less influential'.[114]

I accept that judges giving directions are in an awkward position. They have to safeguard the defendant's position even as they try to counter any unhelpful stereotypical beliefs. This balance is a delicate and difficult one to strike.[115] It is possible however that the recommended judicial direction 'What you must decide in this case is (a) whether V consented freely and by choice, albeit reluctantly, to what took place or whether she did not consent but submitted to it' gives little assistance. It merely brings the idea of reluctant acquiescence to the forefront of juries' minds without giving any guidance on the critical point of the distinction between reluctant sex and submission.

Juries need to consider the context – is there an imbalance of power between the defendant and the victim? Juries could be asked, for example, to consider the state of mind of the victim. Was she very afraid, terrified even, of the defendant? Did she have any reason to be afraid? Would the defendant have known that she was afraid? In the absence of physical evidence, and the presence of prior and/or subsequent consensual sex between the parties, some understanding of what an abusive power differential looks like is essential. In the absence of that understanding, it is not surprising that juries find it difficult to be sure that the defendant knew that the victim was not consenting.

Suggestions for Further Work and Reform

It has been suggested that the pervasiveness of rape-supportive beliefs is part of a more general prejudicial belief system centred around discriminatory views on gender/sex roles.[116] Temkin identifies factors that have been found to be associated with what she frames as 'rape myth acceptance' as: 'sex role stereotyping, adversarial sexual beliefs and the acceptance of interpersonal violence, [and] hostile attitudes towards women'.[117]

Many of the abusers discussed in chapter 1 displayed behavioural traits that could be attributed to these factors. Sarah, for example, described the sex role she was ascribed; Karen explained that she was a 'tart' for dressing the way that she did. The acceptance of interpersonal violence was present in all but one of the women's stories. Hostile attitudes to the survivors were certainly present in all of the stories, hostile attitudes to women in general was not a focus of the interviews but it would be interesting to see if this kind of generalised hostility was also present. Analysis of the data from this research project suggests a high correlation between the factors that Temkin identifies as associated with 'rape myth acceptance' and the perpetrators of coercive control.

Stark suggests that domestic rape would be better framed as part of coercive control.[118] He argues that 'stranger rape and IPSV [intimate partner sexual violence] have little in common'.[119] He states:

The perpetrators and victims have different psychological and behavioural profiles and demographic characteristics. Stranger rape and IPSV occur in different settings; derive from different notices; incur different experiences of violation; and involve different risks of repeat, injurious, and/or fatal physical/sexual violence.[120]

The logical conclusion of Stark's line of reasoning would be the inclusion of domestic rape within a domestic abuse offence. Judge Little was resistant to this idea. She said:

> I do think that controlling and coercive behaviour and rape are different things. I think one of the ways that people control and coerce people can be by the use of rape, but I do think it's important to keep the distinction between them, because rape is a very serious offence, and should never - to my mind it would be downgrading it to say, "Well, it was part of the controlling and coercive behaviour, so it just all gets dealt with as one" - I think controlling and coercive behaviour and rapes should be dealt with separately. The minute we start to downgrade rape we are taking a backward step. And I think even in the context of a domestic relationship rape should always be seen for the offence that it is, not as part and parcel of the way somebody was being treated in their relationship. That should be one offence, the rape should be another. I think that it is very important that it is still seen - because it is the ultimate act of power over a woman and it should in my view never be watered down or lessened, and therefore there should never be a sense of, "well, it's just a domestic rape".[121]

For Judge Little, the seriousness of rape means that it needs to be kept separate. Any attempt to incorporate the crime of rape into a more general domestic abuse offence would inevitably downgrade it.

Judge Harwood took a more pragmatic view. She said, (on the question of incorporating rape into a domestic abuse offence):

> It does have the potential of almost dumbing it down. But at the moment the conviction rate within intimate relationships from my experience is at such an all-time low, that isn't it better that you create the right framework for juries to be able to understand what is going on in that relationship? Rather than worry about the title. I think that as long as the sentencing guidelines reflected that it wasn't seen as a lesser offence ...[122]

This is an extremely difficult question and one that goes to the heart of the issues that are being discussed in this book. Is a separate domestic abuse offence, one that puts the power imbalance at the centre, and includes all of the different manifestations of that power imbalance – sexual abuse, physical abuse, psychological abuse – to be recommended? As Stark argues, 'the "rape is rape" approach throws the normative nature of IPSV and its typical context into the shadows'.[123] By this, Stark means that if you abstract rape from the intimate partner sexual violence ('IPSV') context, you lose much of what makes sexual abuse within an abusive relationship a wrong like no other.

It is possible to argue, however, that some manifestations of control have the potential to be so discrete as wrongs that they become a separate offence. It is clear that domestic homicide, for example, is the most serious manifestation of control. Nevertheless, the taking of someone's life is so serious, so qualitatively different as a wrong both in terms of the culpability of the defendant and the harm done to the victim that it *has* to be dealt with as a separate offence. Arguably the same could be said for the crime of rape. It is such an extreme manifestation of control that it needs to be identified and labelled as such.

Furthermore, cases such as *Kowalski*, and the history of resistance to the recognition of domestic rape outlined in detail earlier in this chapter shows that this area of law is historically sensitive. In the past, domestic rape was treated differently to rape that was not domestic in a way that was extremely prejudicial. Long and insistent campaigning by women's groups eventually brought change. Bringing domestic rape within a domestic abuse statute would not be downgrading it. Sentencing guidelines could make clear that this was the case. Nevertheless, it would be reform that insisted on the *different* treatment of domestic rape and to the women's sector and survivors' groups this might appear insensitive.

An alternative to the inclusion of domestic rape within a domestic abuse statute might be to adopt the kind of compromise position taken by the Domestic Abuse (Scotland) Act 2018 (the 'DASA'), which I refer to in more detail in the following chapter. Section 1 of the DASA makes it an offence for a person to engage in a course of behaviour that is abusive towards a partner or an ex-partner. Section 2 defines abusive behaviour and includes behaviour that is 'violent'. Subsection 2(4) makes it clear that the reference to physical violence includes 'sexual violence'. 'Sexual violence' is not defined further in the Act, but the Guidance Notes are clear that non-violent sexually abusive behaviour comes within section 2(4).[124] Technically, rape is a legitimate constituent part of a section one offence.[125] The Crown Office and Procurator Fiscal Service has made it clear that while domestic rape will always be charged separately, domestic sexual abuse that does not amount to rape can be charged as part of the DASA, section 1 offence.[126]

This approach would fit with Temkin's idea of reform to create offences that are graduated. Temkin writes:

> Juries may not be willing to convict of rape men who obtain agreement to sex by the use of trivial threats, even though these threats were serious to the complainant ... [a lesser offence] could be retained to give the prosecutor choices.[127]

'Trivial' does not seem the correct adjective in the context of experiences such as Sarah's, but it would be interesting to know what Sarah might think about the proposition. She might, for example, feel comfortable charging some of the acute incidents that she recounted as rape. The incident that she referred to as 'rape' when she was 'manhandled' down onto the bed, and the incident post-caesarean that she referred to as 'forced sex' might be two examples of acute incidents that could be charged as rape. In addition to the rape charges, a charge under DASA, s 1 would allow the chronic sexual abuse that occurred outside of these incidents to be particularised as part of the pattern of coercive control. Sarah was the only survivor interviewed for this project who spoke in any depth about her experiences of domestic sexual abuse. More research is needed firstly into how survivors experience chronic and/or acute sexual abuse in the context of coercive control, and secondly how they would view reform of the criminal law in this difficult area.

Conclusion

In 2006, Emily Finch and Munro concluded their then early assessment of the SOA with the observation that, 'It is abundantly clear that the 2003 Act does not and cannot represent the end of the line for rape reform'.[128] This is still the case today. It is not possible to come to a conclusion on the future of sexual offences reform in this chapter, but the chief hurdles – the ambiguity of the wording of the SOA, the lack of guidance, (that is needed to balance the existence of rape-supportive beliefs in the context of intimate sexual abuse), and the resulting difficulties with the communication of the boundaries between consent and submission – need to be addressed.

Framing sexual domestic abuse as part of a chronic pattern of coercive control might help with some of the issues identified, but because of the extreme nature of the offence and the historical sensitivities explored in this chapter, it is my view that domestic rape will always need to be prosecuted separately as rape. This is an area where further research is urgently needed: in the first instance, the way in which survivors experience and articulate domestic sexual assault in the context of coercive control needs to be better understood. Secondly, existing work with mock jury trials could be built on to have a specific coercive control focus. How the 'pre-existing evaluative schema' that jurors bring to a courtroom affects the way that they respond to domestic rape in the presence of coercive control, and how to improve the guidance that is given to them, for example, needs consideration.

Recent studies confirm that defendants' barristers still use the rape-supportive beliefs that exist about rape to undermine victims' assertions about consent.[129] Judicial direction, as recommended in the Crown Court Bench Book in the context of domestic rape, is unlikely to do enough to combat this. It is important to remember that 'Feminists have been urged not to write off legislation dealing with sexual assault where its failures are evident, but to recognise that success and failure exist side by side when it comes to inevitably controversial reforms of this kind'.[130] But recent tabloid newspaper headlines suggest there is significant public unease at the fall in number of successful prosecutions of rape cases.[131] The

Government finally published its long-awaited 'End-to-End' Rape review in the summer of 2021.[132] The findings are stark: only 1.6% of rapes that get reported end in a charge, for example.[133] Victims felt 'unable to pursue the case' in 57% of all adult rape cases.[134] In what commentator David Ormerod described as 'an unusual step'[135] the Government declared that it is 'deeply ashamed of the findings', and that 'Victims of rape are being failed. Thousands of victims have gone without justice'.[136] Further research along the lines proposed in this chapter would help progress in understanding of why this is the case.

Notes

1 Tanya Palmer, 'Failing to See the Wood for the Trees: Chronic Sexual Violation and the Criminal Law' 2020 84(6) The Journal of Criminal Law 573, 573.
2 Ibid. 574.
3 Ibid. 575.
4 Ibid. 573.
5 Tanya Palmer and Cassandra Wiener, 'Telling the Wrong Stories: Rough Sex, Coercive Control and the Criminal Law' [2021] Child and Family Law Quarterly 331.
6 The Home Office Study, 'A Question of Evidence', (discussed in more detail later in this chapter) found in 1999 that cases of sexual offending involving intimate partners were most likely to be discontinued by police and/or the Crown Prosecution Service. Jessica Harris and Sharon Grace, *A Question of Evidence? Investigating and Prosecuting Rape in the 1990s* (Home Office Research Study, Home Office 1999). See also Jeanne Gregory and Sue Lees, 'Attrition in Rape and Sexual Assault Cases' (1996) 36(1) The British Journal of Criminology 1 and Liz Kelly, Jo Lovett and Linda Regan, *A Gap or a Chasm? Attrition in Reported Rape Cases* (Home Office 2005).
7 Interview with Judge Little (20 March 2018) 3.
8 Interview with Judge Harwood (21 May 2018) 6.
9 Interview with Judge Wallace (13 March 2018) 6.
10 Interview with PC Hardie (15 January 2018) 1.
11 Ibid. 2.
12 Lousie Ellison and Vanessa Munro, 'Better the Devil You Know? "Real Rape" Stereotypes and the Relevance of a Previous Relationship in (Mock) Juror Deliberations' (2013) 17 The International Journal of Evidence & Proof 299.
13 Ibid. 321.
14 Ibid. 303 (my italics).
15 Interview with Sarah (29 June 2016) 6 (brackets inserted).
16 Ibid.
17 Sarah n15 6.
18 Sarah n15 10.
19 Interview with Jen (15 January 2016) 2.
20 DPP v Morgan [1975] UKHL 6.
21 Nagaire Naffine, *Criminal Law and the Man Problem* (Hart 2019) 7.
22 *Morgan* n20 205.
23 Ibid.
24 1 Hale 269 as cited in Peter Rook and Robert Ward, *Rook and Ward on Sexual Offences* (Sweet and Maxwell 2016) 70.
25 Richard Brooks, 'Marital Consent in Rape' [1989] Criminal Law Review 877, 878.
26 For an example of a contractual analysis see Lalenya Siegal, 'The Marital Rape Exemption: Evolution to Extinction' (1995) 43 Cleveland State Law Review 351.
27 Michael Freeman, 'But if You Can't Rape Your Wife, Who Can You Rape: the Marital Rape Exemption Re-examined' (1981) 15 Family Law Quarterly 1, 14.

28 Naffine, Criminal Law and the Man Problem n21 16.
29 Glanville Williams, Tony Honore, J C Smith and Brian Hogan are just some of the distinguished men of the law who wrote in support of the importance of subjectivism in the context of rape law – see for example Naffine, Criminal Law and the Man Problem n21 12–16.
30 Naffine, Criminal Law and the Man Problem n21 19.
31 [1988] 1FLR 447.
32 Ibid. 449.
33 Jennifer Temkin, *Rape and the Legal Process* (Oxford University Press 2002) 72.
34 Naffine, Criminal Law and the Man Problem n21 23.
35 Ibid.
36 If a separation order existed or, in certain limited circumstances, a separation agreement.
37 *R v R* [1992] 1AC 599 HL. For an account of the resistance to the repeal of the marital exemption see Adrian Williamson, 'The Law and Politics of Marital Rape in England, 1945–1994' (2016) 26(3) Women's History Review 1.
38 Naffine, Criminal Law and the Man Problem n21 114.
39 Ibid.
40 Criminal Law Revision Committee, 'Sexual Offences' (15th report) (HMSO 1984).
41 Candice Monson and Jennifer Langhinrichsen-Rohling, 'Does "No" Really Mean "No" after You Say "Yes"? Attributions about Date and Marital Rape' (2000) 15(11) Journal of Interpersonal Violence 1156.
42 Home Office, *Protecting the Public Strengthening Protection against Sex Offenders and Reforming the Law on Sexual Offences* (CM 5668, 2002) para 10.
43 Harris and Grace, A Question of Evidence n6 iv.
44 Ibid. 6.
45 Andy Myhill and Jonathan Allen, *Rape and Sexual Assault of Women: The Extent and Nature of the Problem* (Home Office Research Study 237, Home Office 2002).
46 John Flatley, 'Sexual Offences in England and Wales Year Ending 20 March 2017' (Office for National Statistics Bulletin 2018).
47 Evan Stark, 'Forward' in Louise McOrmond-Plummer et al (eds), *Perpetrators of Intimate Partner Sexual Violence: A Multidisciplinary Approach to Prevention, Recognition and Intervention* (Routledge 2016) xxvii.
48 Sarah n15 6.
49 Rook and Ward, Sexual Offences n24 6.
50 Ibid.
51 Ibid.
52 (1845) 1 Cox CC 220.
53 *Camplin* ibid; *Morgan* n22.
54 Ibid.
55 Temkin, Rape and the Legal Process n33.
56 Morgan n22 356.
57 Home Office, *Report of the Advisory Group on the Law of Rape* (Cm 6352, 1975) 21.
58 This is a reference to what became the Sexual Offences Act 1978, which was being considered by Mrs Justice Heilbron as part of her review.
59 Home Office, Report of the Advisory Group 1975 n57 84.
60 Home Office, *Setting the Boundaries: Reforming the Law on Sex Offences* (2000) para 2.10.6.
61 Ibid. para 2:10:9.
62 Ibid. para 2.10.8.
63 Hansard HL Deb 2 June 2003, vol 648, col 1082.
64 Ibid.
65 Sarah n15.
66 See Temkin, Rape and the Legal Process n33 for an example of the feminist critique.

67 Rook and Ward, Sexual Offences n24 130.
68 Temkin, Rape and the Legal Process n33 130; Also see Jennifer Temkin and Andrew Ashworth, 'The Sexual Offences Act 2003: (1) Rape, Sexual Assaults and the Problems of Consent' [2004] The Criminal Law Review 328, 339.
69 Louise Ellison and Vaness Munro, 'A Stranger in the Bushes, or an Elephant in the Room? Critical Reflections upon Received Rape Myth Wisdom in the Context of a Mock Jury Study' (2010) 13 New Criminal Law Review 781, 790.
70 Ibid.
71 Ibid.
72 Ellison and Munro, Better the Devil You Know n12 314.
73 Ibid.
74 Ibid. 315.
75 [1982] QB [321].
76 Ibid. 448–9.
77 Ibid. [331].
78 Ibid.
79 Glanville Williams, *Textbook of Criminal Law* (Stevens and Sons 1983) 551.
80 David Ormerod and Karl Laird, *Smith and Hogan's Criminal Law* (Oxford University Press 2015) 822.
81 Rook and Ward, Sexual Offences n24 79.
82 Sexual Offences Act 2003, s 74.
83 Vanessa Munro, 'Shifting Sands? Consent, Context and Vulnerability in Contemporary Sexual Offences Policy in England and Wales' (2017) 26(4) Social and Legal Studies 417, 418.
84 Temkin and Ashworth, Rape, Sexual Assaults and the Problems of Consent n68 336.
85 Bethany Simpson, 'Why Has the Concept of Consent Proven So Difficult to Clarify?' (2016) 80(2) The Journal of Criminal Law 97, 100. See also Vanessa Munro, 'An Unholy Trinity? Non-consent, Coercion and Exploitation in Contemporary Responses to Sexual Violence in England and Wales' (2010) 63 (1) Current Legal Problems 45.
86 Emily Finch and Vanessa Munro, 'Breaking Boundaries? Sexual Consent in the Jury Room' (2006) 26(3) Legal Studies 303.
87 Ibid. 317.
88 See, for example Heather Keating et al, *Clarkson and Keating: Criminal Law* (Sweet and Maxwell 2014) 647–58; Simpson, Concept of Consent n85.
89 Keating, Clarkson and Keating n88 647–58.
90 Ibid.
91 Interview with Jen n19 6. See also interview with Anita (6 June 2015) 9; and the comments of Shirin and Maya at the Survivors Focus Group (8 September 2016) 7.
92 Tanya Palmer, *Contested Concepts: Sex and Sexual Violation in the Criminal Law* (PhD Thesis, University of Bristol 2011) 73–4.
93 Rook and Ward, Sexual Offences n24 131.
94 Temkin and Ashworth, Rape, Sexual Assaults and the Problems of Consent n68 337.
95 Finch and Munro, 'Breaking Boundaries n86 307.
96 Andrew Ashworth and Jeremy Horder, *Principles of Criminal Law* (Oxford University Press 2009) 352.
97 Rook and Ward, Sexual Offences n24 81.
98 Ibid. 4.
99 1976 AC 182.
100 See, for example, Temkin, Rape and the Legal Process n33 119.
101 Sexual Offences Act 2003, s 1(2).
102 Finch and Munro, Breaking Boundaries n86 317; Temkin and Ashworth, Rape, Sexual Assaults and the Problems of Consent n68.
103 Finch and Munro, Breaking Boundaries n86.

104 Finch and Munro, Breaking Boundaries n86.

105 Judge Little n7 3.

106 Jen n19 7.

107 Ellison and Munro, Better the Devil You Know n12 314.

108 [2008] EWCA Crim 2557.

109 Jennifer Temkin, '"And Always Keep A-Hold of Nurse for Fear of Finding Something Worse": Challenging Rape Myths in the Courtroom' (2010) 13(4) New Criminal Review 710, 725.

110 Courts and Tribunals Judiciary, 'Crown Court Compendium Part One' (section 20–21, 2019) available at <https://www.judiciary.uk/publications/crown-court-bench-book-directing-the-jury-2/> accessed 15 May 2020.

111 This direction is drawn from the judgment of Pill L (as he was then) in *Mohammed Zafar* (No. 92/2762/W2) unreported 18 June 1993 CA. Pill LJ is the judge who decided both of the leading pre Serious Crime Act 2015, s 76 cases on harassment that are discussed in chapter three: *Widdows* and *Curtis*.

112 Courts and Tribunals Judiciary, 'Crown Court Compendium' (2016) available at <https://www.judiciary.uk/publications/crown-court-bench-book-directing-the-jury-2/> accessed 15 November 2018.

113 Crown Court Compendium 2019 n110, brackets in original text.

114 Temkin, Always Keep A-Hold of Nurse n109 727.

115 Louise Ellison and Vanessa Munro, 'Turning Mirrors into Windows? Assessing the Impact of (Mock) Juror Education in Rape Trials' (2009) 49 British Journal of Criminology 363.

116 Jennifer Temkin, Jaqueline Gray and Justine Barrett, 'Different Functions of Rape Myth Use in Court: Findings from a Trial Observation Study' (2018) 13(2) Feminist Criminology 205, 17; Evan Stark, *Coercive Control: How Men Entrap Women in Personal Life* (Oxford University Press 2007).

117 Temkin et al, Different Functions ibid. 17.

118 Evan Stark and Marianne Hester, 'Coercive Control: Update and Review' (2019) 25(1) Violence against Women 81.

119 Stark, Forward n47 3.

120 Ibid.

121 Judge Little n7 9.

122 Judge Harwood n8 6.

123 Stark, Forward n46 xxvii.

124 Domestic Abuse (Scotland) Act 2018 Explanatory Notes <http://www.legislation.gov.uk/asp/2018/5/notes> accessed 30 April 2019.

125 Emma Forbes, 'The Domestic Abuse (Scotland) Act 2018: The Whole Story?' (2018) 22 Edinburgh Law Review 406, 409.

126 Interview with Crown Office and Procurator Fiscal Service (Edinburgh 23 October 2019).

127 Temkin, Rape and the Legal Process n33 102.

128 Finch and Munro, Breaking Boundaries n86 320.

129 Oliva Smith and Tina Skinner 'How Rape Myths Are Used and Challenged in Rape and Sexual Assault Trials' (2017) 26(4) Social and Legal Studies 441; Temkin et al Different Functions n99; Jennifer Gray and Miranda Horvath, 'Rape Myths in the Criminal Justice System' in Emma Milne et al (eds), *Women and the Criminal Justice System* (Palgrave 2018).

130 Temkin and Ashworth, Rape, Sexual Assaults and the Problems of Consent n68 346.

131 Owen Bowcott and Caelainn Barr, 'Just 1.5% of All Rape Cases Lead to Charge or Summons, Data Reveals' *The Guardian* (London 26 July 2019) available at <https://www.theguardian.com/law/2019/jul/26/rape-cases-charge-summons-prosecutions-victims-england-wales> accessed 16 May 2020; Lizzie Dearden, 'Only 1.7% of Reported Rapes Prosecuted in England and Wales, New Figures Show' *The*

Independent (London 25 April 2019) available at <https://www.independent.co.uk/news/uk/crime/rape-prosecution-england-wales-victims-court-cps-police-a8885961.html> accessed 16 May 2020.

132 Ministry of Justice, 'End-to-End Rape Review' (18 June 2021) available at <https://www.gov.uk/government/publications/end-to-end-rape-review-report-on-findings-and-actions> accessed 9 May 2022.

133 Ibid. iii.

134 Ibid. para 9.

135 David Ormerod, 'The End-to-End Rape Review' (2021) 9 The Criminal Law Review 723, 724.

136 Ministry of Justice, 'Ministerial Forward' in Ministry of Justice, End-to-End Rape Review n132.

Bibliography

Ashworth A and Horder J, *Principles of Criminal Law* (Oxford University Press 2009).

Bowcott O and Barr C, 'Just 1.5% of All Rape Cases Lead to Charge or Summons, Data Reveals' *The Guardian* (London 26 July 2019) available at <https://www.theguardian.com/law/2019/jul/26/rape-cases-charge-summons-prosecutions-victims-england-wales> accessed 16 May 2020.

Brooks R, 'Marital Consent in Rape' (1989) Criminal Law Review 877.

Courts and Tribunals Judiciary, 'Crown Court Compendium (2016)' available at <https://www.judiciary.uk/publications/crown-court-bench-book-directing-the-jury-2/> accessed 15 November 2018.

Courts and Tribunals Judiciary, 'Crown Court Compendium Part One (2019)' available at <https://www.judiciary.uk/publications/crown-court-bench-book-directing-the-jury-2/> accessed 15 May 2020.

Criminal Law Revision Committee, 'Sexual Offences' (15th report) (HMSO 1984).

Dearden L, 'Only 1.7% of Reported Rapes Prosecuted in England and Wales, New Figures Show' *The Independent* (London 25 April 2019) available at <https://www.independent.co.uk/news/uk/crime/rape-prosecution-england-wales-victims-court-cps-police-a8885961.html> accessed 16 May 2020.

'Domestic Abuse (Scotland) Act 2018 Explanatory Notes' available at <http://www.legislation.gov.uk/asp/2018/5/notes> accessed 30 April 2019.

Ellison L and Munro V, 'Turning Mirrors into Windows? Assessing the Impact of (Mock) Juror Education in Rape Trials' (2009) 49 British Journal of Criminology 363.

Ellison L and Munro V, 'A Stranger in the Bushes, or an Elephant in the Room? Critical Reflections upon Received Rape Myth Wisdom in the Context of a Mock Jury Study' (2010) 13 New Criminal Law Review 781.

Ellison L and Munro V, 'Better the Devil You Know? "Real Rape" Stereotypes and the Relevance of a Previous Relationship in (Mock) Juror Deliberations' (2013) 17 The International Journal of Evidence & Proof 299.

Finch E and Munro V, 'Breaking Boundaries? Sexual Consent in the Jury Room' (2006) 26(3) Legal Studies 303.

Flatley J, 'Sexual Offences in England and Wales Year Ending 20 March 2017' (Office for National Statistics Bulletin 2018).

Forbes E, 'The Domestic Abuse (Scotland) Act 2018: The Whole Story?' (2018) 22 Edinburgh Law Review 406.

Freeman M, 'But if You Can't Rape Your Wife, Who Can You Rape: The Marital Rape Exemption Re-examined' (1981) 15 Family Law Quarterly 1.

Gray J and Horvath M, 'Rape Myths in the Criminal Justice System' in Milne E, Brennan K, South N and Turton J (eds), *Women and the Criminal Justice System* (Palgrave 2018).

Gregory J and Lees S, 'Attrition in Rape and Sexual Assault Cases' (1996) 36(1) The British Journal of Criminology 1.

Hansard HL Deb 2 June 2003, vol 648, col 1082.

Harris J and Grace S, *A Question of Evidence? Investigating and Prosecuting Rape in the 1990s* (Home Office Research Study, Home Office 1999).

Home Office, *Report of the Advisory Group on the Law of Rape* (Cm 6352, 1975).

Home Office, *Setting the Boundaries: Reforming the Law on Sex Offences* (2000).

Home Office, *Protecting the Public Strengthening Protection against Sex Offenders and Reforming the Law on Sexual Offences* (CM 5668, 2002).

Keating H, Kyd Cunningham C, Elliott S and Walters M, *Clarkson and Keating: Criminal Law* (Sweet & Maxwell 2014).

Kelly L, Lovett J and Regan L, *A Gap or a Chasm? Attrition in Reported Rape Cases* (Home Office 2005).

Ministry of Justice, 'End-to-End Rape Review Report' (18 June 2021) available at <https://www.gov.uk/government/publications/end-to-end-rape-review-report-on-findings-and-actions> accessed 9 May 2022.

Monson C and Langhinrichsen-Rohling J, 'Does "No" Really Mean "No" after You Say "Yes"? Attributions About Date and Marital Rape' (2000) 15(11) Journal of Interpersonal Violence 1156.

Munro V, 'An Unholy Trinity? Non-consent, Coercion and Exploitation in Contemporary Responses to Sexual Violence in England and Wales' (2010) 63(1) Current Legal Problems 45.

Munro V, 'Shifting Sands? Consent, Context and Vulnerability in Contemporary Sexual Offences Policy in England and Wales' (2017) 26(4) Social and Legal Studies 417.

Myhill A and Allen J, *Rape and Sexual Assault of Women: The Extent and Nature of the Problem* (Home Office Research Study 237, Home Office 2002).

Naffine N, *Criminal Law and the Man Problem* (Hart 2019).

Ormerod D, 'The End-to-End Rape Review' (2021) 9 The Criminal Law Review 723.

Ormerod D and Laird K, *Smith and Hogan's Criminal Law* (Oxford University Press 2015).

Palmer T, *Contested Concepts: Sex and Sexual Violation in the Criminal Law* (PhD Thesis, University of Bristol 2011).

Palmer T, 'Failing to See the Wood for the Trees: Chronic Sexual Violation and the Criminal Law' (2020) 84(6) Journal of Criminal Law 573.

Palmer T and Wiener C, 'Telling the Wrong Stories: Rough Sex, Coercive Control and the Criminal Law' (2021) Child and Family Law Quarterly 331.

Rook P and Ward R, *Rook and Ward on Sexual Offences* (Sweet and Maxwell 2016).

Siegal L, 'The Marital Rape Exemption: Evolution to Extinction' (1995) 43 Cleveland State Law Review 351.

Simpson B, 'Why Has the Concept of Consent Proven So Difficult to Clarify?' (2016) 80(2) The Journal of Criminal Law 97.

Smith O and Skinner T, 'How Rape Myths Are Used and Challenged in Rape and Sexual Assault Trials' (2017) 26(4) Social and Legal Studies 441.

Stark E, *Coercive Control: How Men Entrap Women in Personal Life* (Oxford University Press 2007).

Stark E, 'Forward' in Louise McOrmond-Plummer et al (eds), *Perpetrators of Intimate Partner Sexual Violence: A Multidisciplinary Approach to Prevention, Recognitio, and Intervention* (Routledge 2016).

Stark E and Hester M, 'Coercive Control: Update and Review' (2019) 25(1) Violence against Women 81.

Temkin J, *Rape and the Legal Process* (Oxford University Press 2002).

Temkin J '"And Always Keep A-Hold of Nurse for Fear of Finding Something Worse": Challenging Rape Myths in the Courtroom' (2010) 13(4) New Criminal Review 710.

Temkin J and Ashworth A, 'The Sexual Offences Act 2003: (1) Rape, Sexual Assaults and the Problems of Consent' (2004) The Criminal Law Review 328.

Temkin J, Gray J and Barrett J, 'Different Functions of Rape Myth Use in Court: Findings from a Trial Observation Study' (2018) 13(2) Feminist Criminology 205.

Williams G, *Textbook of Criminal Law* (Stevens and Sons 1983).

Williamson A, 'The Law and Politics of Marital Rape in England, 1945–1994' (2016) 26(3) Women's History Review 1.

Cases

Camplin (1845) 1 Cox CC 220.

Curtis [2010] EWCA Crim 123.

Doody [2008] EWCA Crim 2557.

DPP v Morgan [1976] AC182 HL.

Kowalski [1988] 1FLR 447.

Mohammed Zafar (No. 92/2762/W2) unreported 18 June 1993 CA.

Olugjuba [1982] QB 321.

R [1992] 1AC 599 HL.

Widdows [2011] EWCA Crim 1500.

Statutes

Contempt of Court Act 1961.

Criminal Justice and Public Order Act 1994.

Domestic Abuse (Scotland) Act 2018.

Serious Crime Act 2015.

Sexual Offences Act 1978.

Sexual Offences Act 2003.

5

THE CONTROLLING OR COERCIVE BEHAVIOUR CONSTRUCT: SERIOUS CRIME ACT 2015, S 76

Introduction

In the last chapter I focused on the first legislative development to take place this century that is particularly relevant to the survivors of domestic abuse and coercive control: the Sexual Offences Act 2003. This chapter continues with a review of later legislative developments that lie at the heart of this book. Firstly, I take up the story of the development of the criminal law where chapter 3 left off. I explain the review of the Protection from Harassment Act 1997, (the 'PHA') that resulted in considerable amendments. I also review other developments in 2012–2015 that led to the introduction of the Serious Crime Act 2015, s 76 (section 76). Secondly, I review Parliament's intentions for section 76 via an analysis of the relevant parliamentary debates and finally, I go on to assess section 76 itself. The Domestic Abuse Act 2021 (the 'DAA') received Royal Assent on 29 April 2021, and I conclude the chapter with a discussion of this Act, and suggestions for further work and reform.

Before the introduction of section 76, domestic abuse was prosecuted via statutes that were reviewed in the previous three chapters, as an offence against the person, harassment and as a sexual offence. None of these crimes account properly for the strategic patterns of control outlined in chapter 1 of this book, either in terms of the behaviour of the perpetrator or the harm experienced by the victim. Section 76 was an opportunity to put this right. Recognising coercive control as a crime does represent significant progress. Unfortunately, Parliament did not give enough consideration to the behaviour (coercive control) that it was trying to regulate. As a result, while section 76 is innovative up to a point, it reflects mistaken assumptions as to the nature of coercive control. The 'controlling or coercive behaviour' construct set out in section 76 does not properly capture the phenomenon of coercive control as set out in this book. For the avoidance of

DOI: 10.4324/9780429201844-6

doubt, and as explained in chapter 1, I use the label 'coercive control' in this book to describe the empirical phenomenon articulated originally by Evan Stark.[1] When I use the label 'controlling or coercive behaviour' I am referring to the construct set out in section 76, which is the subject of this chapter. The fact that these two constructs, 'coercive control' and 'controlling or coercive behaviour' are not the same thing goes to the root of the problems that persist with the criminalisation of domestic abuse in England and Wales.

There are three mistaken assumptions that I focus on in this chapter. One of these mistaken assumptions has, thankfully, been put right by the DAA. This is the assumption that there is a transactional moment of separation for a victim that is a useful legal boundary. The two mistakes that still stand are: first, that coercive control is "psychological" abuse, a bullet point in a list of behaviour types that make up domestic abuse, and second that focusing on the victim's response to coercive control is an appropriate way to define the offence. As a result of these mistakes, Deborah Tuerkheimer's mismatch between 'life' and 'law'[2] referred to in chapter 3 remains, as do many of the issues identified in the context of the old regime.

Developments since 2015 show how this could be improved upon: the Domestic Abuse (Scotland) Act 2018 (the 'DASA') deals with both of the outstanding issues raised above and is an example of what Evan Stark has referred to as a 'gold standard' for domestic abuse and coercive control legislation.[3] It could point the way for further reform in England and Wales. In the absence of that reform, I conclude that, while section 76 and the amendments put in place by the DAA represent progress, the criminal law still does not allow for the proper recognition of the wrong of coercive control.

The Road to the Serious Crime Act 2015, s 76

I reviewed the PHA in detail in chapter 4. The first significant development in the time period 2012–2015 took the form of substantial amendments to the PHA, one of which provided the template for the later section 76. Secondly, a new working definition (the 'Working Definition') of domestic abuse was introduced in 2012 which fed into the third development – Theresa May's governmental consultation of 2014–15 on the criminalisation of 'controlling or coercive behaviour'. These developments will be looked at in turn.

The Protection of Freedoms Act 2012

In February 2012, the Justice Unions' Parliamentary Group conducted an extensive review into the PHA. Their concluding report referred to Home Office research that suggested that the police chose to press charges under the lesser PHA, s 2 'harassment' offence over the more serious PHA, s 4 offence 'causing fear of violence'. This, it was reported, true even where the nature of the offending in question meant that the PHA, s 4 was available.[4] This is because the section 2 offence was perceived to be 'easier to run with'.[5]

My empirical work with police supports this finding. Detective Constable Shell, for example, confirmed that he does not tend to use the PHA, s 4 charge 'technically, just because it is a definition of section 4, it does not mean that we will charge it'.[6] By this he meant that, just because he comes across behaviour that fits the definition of a section 4 offence, it does not mean that the defendant will end up being charged with a section 4 offence. He went on to explain, 'if you charge a lesser offence, they might plead guilty, or you might get an early magistrates'.[7] An earlier trial, a guilty plea, a trial in a lower court, all of these points made by Detective Constable Shell in favour of the lesser charge are examples of the section 2 charge being 'easier to run with'. This meant that the PHA, s 4 was 'rarely used'[8] and that the maximum sentence available under the PHA, s 2 (six months' imprisonment) was out of step with the more serious offences which were being prosecuted. As a result of the difficulties with the PHA, s 4 and the limitations of the PHA s 2, the PHA was declared no longer fit for purpose in the context of stalking.

The enactment of the PHA followed an extensive parliamentary debate around the decision of whether or not to define stalking. This was reviewed in chapter 3. The so-called list approach recommended by the then opposition party was abandoned because it was not thought necessary or helpful to attempt to define stalking in law. The Justice Unions' Report concluded that this had been a mistake: 'many believed that the chief shortcoming of the 1997 iteration of the PHA was its failure to name "stalking" in law'.[9] The report argued that 'behaviours' were 'being hidden and missed as they are recorded under different crime categories such as malicious communications, common assault, harassment and so on'.[10] The report concluded that 'the victim's perspective was missing' and that 'many incidents were not recorded as crimes and that stalking behaviour was therefore hidden'.[11]

I explained how Tuerkheimer describes 'cloaking' in chapter 2. Cloaking occurs when there is a failure to recognise aspects of offending behaviour and/or harm in the criminal law.[12] Cloaking is the resulting exclusion of the crime, or part of the crime, from the criminal law meaning that harm experienced by the victim goes unrecognised and unacknowledged. Emily Finch uses the term 'fragmentation' to describe the process by which the sum of parts of behaviours recorded under different crime categories amounts to less than a recognition of the behaviour as a whole.[13] It is interesting that the Justice Unions' Report appears to support Tuerkheimer and Finch, as it finds that the failure to properly define the stalking behaviour being criminalised leads to it being 'hidden' (cloaked) and 'recorded under different crime categories' (fragmented). This, concludes the Report, leads to behaviours being 'missed'.

Parliament addressed these concerns with the Protection of Freedoms Act 2012, which inserts two offences, sections 2A and 4A, into the PHA.[14] Section 2A introduces an offence of stalking by replicating the old section 2 but with a reference to 'stalking'. The PHA, s 2A states that a person is guilty of an offence where he commits an offence under the existing section 2 offence *and* his course of conduct includes actions or omissions 'associated with stalking'.

Examples of actions or omissions 'associated with stalking' are given in exactly the list approach that was rejected by the government 15 years previously. Examples include following, contacting, publishing any statement, monitoring the use by a person of the internet, email, loitering, interfering with any property, watching or spying. There is no new *mens rea* requirement. The possibility that the offence can be committed with an objective *mens rea* is included with the wording 'knows *or ought to know*':[15] the same as for the existing PHA, s 2.

The new section 4A offence is entitled 'stalking involving fear of violence or serious alarm or distress' and has two limbs. The first limb, section 4A(1)(b)(i), states that a person whose course of conduct amounts to stalking and who causes another to fear, on at least two occasions, that violence will be used against them, is guilty of an offence. This is the old section 4 base offence (harassment involving fear of violence) but amended to include a specific reference to stalking. The second limb, section 4A(1)(b)(ii), states that conduct that amounts to stalking and causes the victim serious alarm or distress that has a substantial adverse effect on their day-to-day activities is an offence.

This second limb of section 4A is thus the only significant insertion made by the Protection of Freedoms Act 2012 to the PHA in that it constitutes a brand-new offence.[16] The "new" section 2A, and section 4A(1)(b)(i) (the so-called first limb of s. 4A), simply add emphasis to the old section 2 and section 4 of the PHA. The potential to prosecute stalking always existed under the old section 2 and section 4 offences. The Protection of Freedoms Act simply clarifies that this is so.

The second limb of section 4A creates a significant new offence which was hailed at the time as having the potential to 'fill an important gap in the protection offered to victims of stalking'.[17] It is this new offence that was used as a template for the construction of the later section 76. The new offence is especially innovative in that it does, finally, abandon the old 'fear of violence' paradigm. It also has less of an incident-specific focus. This is because it moves further away from the necessity of temporal specificity with the wording 'substantial adverse effect'. It does not require the identification of any particular incident as 'especially alarming or serious'.[18] Instead, it looks at the overall effect on the victim's life. This is important because 'looking at the cumulative effect of stalking and indeed all harassment is what is important, rather than getting bogged down in the effect and nature of individual incidents'.[19] By defining the crime in terms of an ongoing 'substantial adverse effect' rather than an incident-based fear of something specific, the statute is moving towards a more contextual, less transactional approach that is helpful in the context of stalking.

As is to be expected, it is apparent from the guidance notes that were issued by the Home Office to accompany the amendments that the 'substantial adverse effect' was considered by the government in terms of the harms that result from stalking. This is relevant because the same wording is used in the later section 76, (which is attempting to capture the harms that result from coercive control, not from stalking). The guidance notes state that:

The second arm of the offence prohibits a course of conduct which causes "serious alarm or distress" which has a "substantial adverse effect on the day-to-day activities of the victim". It is designed to recognise the serious impact that stalking may have on victims, even where an explicit fear of violence is not created by each incident of stalking behaviour.[20]

The guidance goes on to give examples of what might constitute 'substantial adverse effect on day-to-day activities' as follows:

> The Home Office considers that evidence of a substantial adverse effect when caused by the stalker may include: the victim changing their routes to work, work patterns, or employment, the victim arranging for friends or family to pick up children from school (to avoid contact with the stalker), the victim putting in place additional security measures in their home, the victim moving home, physical or mental ill-health, the victim's deterioration in performance at work due to stress, the victim stopping/or changing the way they socialise.[21]

Changing work patterns, moving house etc are all indications of behaviour designed to minimise contact with a stalker, who is therefore conceived of as a stranger, or an ex-partner, but not as someone who is still in a relationship with the victim. As explained above this becomes important in the context of the later section 76 which I review later on in this chapter.

The Working Definition of Domestic Abuse

Two further developments with regard to definitions of domestic abuse since 2012 need consideration. The first was the introduction of the Working Definition of domestic abuse which I will set out here. Secondly, and more importantly, a legal definition of domestic abuse has been introduced for the first time into law by the DAA, which replaces the Working Definition. I will come back to this development when I discuss the DAA at the end of this chapter.

Previously, on 14 December 2011, the government launched a consultation on whether or not to change the cross-governmental working definition of 'domestic violence' (as it was then).[22] The government first introduced a single working definition of domestic violence in 2004, for use across government and the public sector. The definition was not given statutory footing but was used by government departments to inform policy development and by agencies such as the police, the Crown Prosecution Service and health services to help with the identification of domestic abuse. The 2004 definition was as follows:

> Any incident of threatening behaviour, violence or abuse (psychological, physical, sexual, financial or emotional) between adults who are or have been intimate partners or family members, regardless of gender or sexuality.[23]

As part of the consultation, participants were asked whether they thought that coercive control should form part of the definition of domestic abuse. The vast majority of respondents (85%) indicated that it should.[24]

Feedback from consultees indicated that the incident-specific nature of the 2004 definition was unsatisfactory, as it 'equates domestic violence with discrete incidents of threats or assaults', which 'seriously distorts the nature of abuse experienced by the vast majority of abuse victims'.[25] Furthermore, 'The current (2004) definition fails to identify coercive control, the most common class of abuse cases in which victims seek outside assistance'.[26] As a result of the consultation, the Working Definition, which also had no legislative status (and therefore received little or no attention in the legal literature), was published in September 2012:

> Any incident or pattern of incidents of controlling, coercive or threatening behaviour, violence or abuse between those aged 16 or over who are or have been intimate partners or family members regardless of gender or sexuality. This can encompass but is not limited to the following types of abuse:
>
> - psychological
> - physical
> - sexual
> - financial
> - emotional
>
> Controlling behaviour is: a range of acts designed to make a person subordinate and/or dependent by isolating them from sources of support, exploiting their resources and capacities for personal gain, depriving them of the means needed for independence, resistance and escape and regulating their everyday behaviour.
>
> Coercive behaviour is: an act or a pattern of acts of assault, threats, humiliation and intimidation or other abuse that is used to harm, punish, or frighten their victim.[27]

This is in many ways a helpful definition that accurately defines and portrays both the "wrong" and the "harm" of domestic abuse. In part, this definition is helpful because it begins from the behaviour being defined, (what domestic abuse really looks like), rather than the existing criminal law legislative infrastructure, (how fragments of domestic abuse are currently prosecuted). It uses coercive control as a wrapper within which to locate its constituent parts, by stating that any pattern of incidents of coercive control *encompasses* various examples of abusive behaviour.

The reference to 'family members' is in my view unfortunate,[28] but apart from that, this definition reflects the interconnected nature of the different physical and non-physical behaviour patterns that constitute coercive control. It also recognises the perpetrator's strategic intent. Most importantly, the definition correctly puts 'controlling, coercive or threatening behaviour' at the heart of the definition. Much of the wording for the definition was in fact taken from the response to the consultation drafted by Davina James-Hamman and Evan Stark.[29] In particular, the definitions of 'controlling behaviour' and 'coercive behaviour' were drafted by Stark.[30] Unfortunately, the new definition introduced by the DAA reverts to a bullet point list approach. This is a step backwards, as I explain at the end of this chapter.

One side effect of the Working Definition with its paradigm-shift style focus on coercive control is that it served to highlight that the existing criminal infrastructure was inadequate. The central component of the Working Definition – the controlling/coercive behaviour – was not captured by the criminal law. Furthermore the Working Definition had no legal status and did nothing to resolve the main issue created by *Hills*, *Curtis* and *Widdows*. Thanks to those judgments, which the Government later referred to as an 'unhelpful barrier',[31] the ability of police to take action in a situation where a victim was still in an intimate relationship with her partner was limited. In August 2014 the government launched a consultation to investigate exactly this issue.[32] It is this consultation that led directly to the passage of section 76.

The Government Consultation of 2014–15

The Home Office was clear from the start about the remit of the consultation: its scope was extremely narrow. This was a mistake. Parliament's intentions for section 76 can be understood partly as a response to this consultation, and the eight weeks that it was given (the consultation ran from 20 August to 15 October 2014), puts it in the camp of 'single-stage, executive controlled' legislation, which, it has been pointed out, 'tends to be fast and driven by Cabinet with limited or no opportunity for consultation or independent input'.[33] The equivalent consultation in Scotland (prior to the DASA) was much more extensive.[34] The English/Welsh consultation description states:

> This consultation is specifically focused on whether we should create a specific offence that captures patterns of coercive and controlling behaviour in intimate relationships, in line with the Government's non-statutory definition of domestic abuse.[35]

Many important issues were overlooked. There is no attempt to unpick or define 'patterns of coercive and controlling behaviour in intimate relationships'. Theresa May was clear: in her mind coercive control *is* non-violent behaviour. She explains: 'The consultation asks whether reinforcing the law to capture patterns of *non-violent behaviour* within intimate relationships will offer better protection'.[36] This assumption – that coercive control is non-violent behaviour – is not interrogated.

Moving on to the legal position, there is no suggestion that it might be appropriate to consider how, or to what extent, the existing legal infrastructure was capturing the behaviour patterns that constitute domestic abuse in general and coercive control in particular. The fact that a core part of the government's own definition of domestic abuse, (the strategic intent), was not captured by the existing infrastructure might have suggested that a review of the regime was in order, not unlike the review of the sexual offences regime that took place before the introduction of the Sexual Offences Act 2003 that was the subject of the last chapter.

Around 85% of respondents to the consultation felt that the law as it stood did not adequately protect the victims of coercive control.[37] The government's conclusions at the end of the consultation period are summarised as follows:

> On balance, we are persuaded that there is a gap in the current legal framework around patterns of coercive and controlling behaviour, particularly where that behaviour takes place in an ongoing intimate partner or inter-familial relationship. Non-violent coercive behaviour, which is a long-term campaign of abuse, falls outside common assault, which requires the victim to fear the immediate application of unlawful violence.[38]

The Home Office makes a number of problematic assertions in this extract that I will review in turn. First: the conclusion begins with the reference to a 'gap in the current legal framework'. It has been pointed out that 'one of the most powerful tropes in criminalisation debates is the identification of the alleged "gap" that needs to be "filled"'.[39] One of the pitfalls of identifying a "gap" in this way is that it cements the surrounding legislative infrastructure.

The second part of the first sentence locates coercive and controlling behaviour in two contexts: 'an ongoing intimate partner' context, and an 'inter-familial relationship' context. 'Inter-familial relationship' is not defined, but presumably the Home Office is referring to relationships within a family but not between intimate partners. The empirical research to date has focused on coercive control between intimate partners. More research is needed before it can be decided whether other relationships (between siblings, for example, or between parents and children) are affected by coercive control.[40]

The second sentence refers to 'non-violent coercive behaviour', and comments that this kind of behaviour falls outside the law on common assault. This is the "gap" referred to in the preceding sentence. This is a good example of where assuming 'a simple lacuna into which a new offence can be inserted to "fill" … has the capacity to obfuscate the well documented problematic operation of current criminal laws'.[41] It is correct to state that non-violent coercive behaviour falls outside common assault. But what about violent coercive behaviour? The implication seems to be that it is already covered by common assault. This is not entirely correct. Violent behaviour per se falls within the law on assault. The Offences against the Person Act 1861, however, as I explained in chapter 2, is transactional, incident-specific, and does not take either a controlling perpetrator's strategic intent or the full extent of the harm he inflicts into account. Violent *coercive* behaviour is only partially captured by the law on common assault.

The other false implication is the one already touched upon above, that 'controlling or coercive behaviour' can be described as 'non-violent coercive behaviour'. The government Working Definition states that, 'Incidents of coercive, controlling or threatening behaviour' can encompass psychological *and* physical types of abuse.[42] Vanessa Bettinson and Charlotte Bishop, commenting on the Serious Crime Bill as it was in the summer of 2015, highlight this confusion as an obstacle. They argue that

> Such a concept of coercive control is difficult to criminalise while … this separation of physical and non-physical forms of domestic violence and/or abuse does not reflect … the complex way that both physical and non-physical forms of behaviour often co-exist.[43]

Stark is clear. He writes:

> Some have contrasted coercive control as a "psychological" crime to the "physical crime" of domestic violence. This is a mistake. Coercive control often includes psychological abuse. But it is not primarily a psychological or a physical process but a course of deliberate conduct.[44]

My empirical work supports this. In chapter 1, I explained how the survivors I spoke to described a combination of violent and non-violent tactics. It is possible for coercive behaviour to exist in the absence of physical violence, but it is unusual.

The government continues:

> The law on stalking and harassment does not explicitly apply to coercive and controlling behaviour in intimate relationships. Indeed, as some respondents to our consultation pointed out, the law on stalking and harassment is not designed to capture the dynamic of sinister exploitation of an intimate relationship to control another, particularly where a relationship is ongoing. The element of control is not such a feature of stalking or harassment, which is generally intended to intimidate or cause fear. Domestic abuse adds an extra layer to such intimidation, with perpetrators operating under the guise of a close relation or partner to conceal their abuse, and safe in the presumption that the victim is likely to want to continue a relationship despite the abuse. For these reasons, domestic abuse may be said to be more subversive than stalking.[45]

These observations are the most interesting of all, in light of the legislation that followed (section 76). The government correctly identifies that coercive control is not the same thing as stalking. As stated in chapter 3, while there is no doubt that stalking and coercive control are highly correlated in that they are often simultaneously present,[46] stalking forms *part* of the controlling or coercive behavioural repertoire of a perpetrator. The government therefore recognises that, as different phenomena, coercive control and stalking require a different legislative approach. Despite this, the law that was designed to capture coercive control used the PHA (stalking law) as a template, as is discussed in more detail below.

Serious Crime Act 2015, s 76

Parliamentary Debate

Then Attorney General Robert Buckland introduced a new clause on 'controlling or coercive behaviour' into the Serious Crime Bill in January 2015, which was the government's major crime bill of 2014–2015. This clause is quietly tucked away in Part V of the Act under the heading 'Protection of Children and Others'. This seems unfortunate, in light of the Attorney General's rousing introduction to the committee:

> Abuse is hidden behind the closed doors of far too many families. We must bring domestic abuse out into the open if we are to end it. The first step is to call it what it is: a crime of the worst kind.[47]

'Protection of Children and Others' seems a far cry from 'call it what it is'. With regard to coercive control and stalking, Buckland comments:

> I am sure that the Committee would agree that a person who causes someone to live in constant fear through a campaign of intimidations should face justice for their actions. If such a person is unknown to their victim or is known but unrelated they would be called a stalker … We must create a new offence that makes it crystal clear that a pattern of coercion is as serious within a relationship as it is outside one.[48]

Buckland would appear to be making the assumption that coercive control and stalking are much the same thing. Controlling or coercive behaviour is constructed as a kind of stalking within a relationship. The purpose of the new law on controlling or coercive behaviour is simply to overcome the barrier put into place by the Court of Appeal and the House of Lords – in other words, to criminalise 'stalking within a relationship' in the same way that the PHA criminalises 'stalking outside a relationship'. This shows a misunderstanding of both coercive control and stalking as empirical phenomena; it also assumes that this boundary is a useful marker around which to delineate behaviour that is coercive and controlling from that which is not.

Secondly, on the question of coercive control and physical violence Buckland says:

> In the consultation we identified a gap in the law - behaviour that we would regard as abuse that did not amount to violence. Violent behaviour already

captured by the criminal law is outside the scope of the offence. Within the range of existing criminal offences a number of tools are at the disposal of the police and prosecution, which are used day in and day out. We do not want duplication or confusion; we want an extra element that closes a loophole.[49]

He thus adopts the assumption made previously by the Home Office that coercive control, like stalking, is behaviour that by definition does not involve physical violence. This is, as has been stated, empirically incorrect. Perhaps the thread that connects all of the above is his last sentence: 'we want an extra element that closes a loophole'.[50] It is possible that in his desire for an 'extra element' he is over-influenced by the 'loophole'.

In other words, the Attorney General appears to construct his understanding of controlling or coercive behaviour around a legal lacuna that he has previously identified, and not the other way around. It would have made more sense to reverse that process, to begin with an understanding of coercive control, and then conduct a review of legislation. By approaching the project in terms of a legislative gap rather than as a (relatively) newly recognised form of behaviour in need of a fresh approach, Buckland reified much of what was unhelpful about the old regime. The reporting of the new offence in the legal press at the time confirmed this impression, for example:

> Section 76 of the Serious Crime Act 2015 ... creates an offence of controlling or coercive behaviour in an intimate or family relationship. The new offence is designed to close a gap in the law surrounding patterns of controlling or coercive behaviour in ongoing intimate or family relationships.[51]

In any event, the clause on controlling or coercive behaviour generated significant cross-party agreement and was adopted as the Serious Crime Act 2015, s 76:

Controlling or coercive behaviour in an intimate or family relationship

1. A person (A) commits an offence if –

   a. A repeatedly or continuously engages in behaviour towards another person (B) that is controlling or coercive,
   b. At the time of the behaviour, A and B are personally connected,
   c. The behaviour has a serious effect on B.

I use the rest of this chapter to reflect on the constituent parts of section 76. Throughout, I report on how section 76 has been interpreted by the courts so far, drawing on my interviews with some of the judges and police who have been involved with these early cases, and the sentencing decisions that have been reported to date. The last part of the chapter concludes with a summary of the relevant (to this chapter), changes brought in by the DAA and some suggestions for further reform.

Section 76(1)(a) The Conduct Element of the Offence

Repeatedly or Continuously

Section 76(1)(a) deals with the criminal conduct itself. The first innovative step is the abandonment of any reference to a "course of conduct". The original intention was to use the PHA course of conduct model, or to define the conduct element around a single "incident" of controlling or coercive behaviour.[52] The inadequacy of the course of conduct model, and the tendency of some judges and legal academics to 'lapse back'[53] into incident-specific analysis, was highlighted in chapter 3. Instead, section 76(1)(a) states that A commits an offence if A 'repeatedly or continuously' engages in controlling or coercive behaviour. This aroused suspicion in the legal literature, with the meaning of repeatedly or continuously causing questions from concerned commentators such as: 'how consistent does D's controlling or coercive behaviour have to be in order for it to be repeated or continuous?'.[54]

In fact, repeatedly and continuously appear to be given their ordinary meanings and this marks significant progress. It allows the victim to move away from dates/times of "incidents" of control, and instead take a more contextual approach, which is more in line with the 'chronic'[55] nature of coercive control as explained in chapter 1. This conclusion, (that the move away from an incident-specific focus is workable and working), is supported by a review of the first 107 section 76 cases which concluded: 'None of the reported cases in our research suggests that there have been any noticeable issues in relation to the prosecution needing to establish particulars such as dates, times and locations for alleged behaviours'.[56]

Judge Little, who has presided over three section 76 trials, agreed that juries understand and like the wording 'repeatedly or continuously'. She felt that it was appropriate to move away from the course of conduct approach taken by the PHA: 'Harassment is a different thing – there has to be that – minimum number before it can be considered to be harassment, but coercive and controlling behaviour is a different thing'.[57] It is possible that the new wording successfully allows for a move away from the tendency for judges to 'lapse back'[58] into an incident-specific focus.

Lack of a Definition of 'Controlling or Coercive Behaviour'

An 'interesting anomaly'[59] with the conduct element, however, is the lack of a definition of controlling or coercive behaviour. The phrase 'controlling or coercive' in 1(a) is given no further explanation. Even the construct of 'controlling or coercive' is awkward, with the use of the conjunction 'or' potentially suggestive of a further fragmentation of meaning. In fact, 'or' as a conjunction can be used to connect possibilities as well as alternatives, and thankfully there has been no suggestion to date in either the academic or the policy-based literature that the government's intention is to fragment coercive control into 'controlling' and 'coercive' behaviour as alternatives from a legislative/crime category perspective.

The statutory guidance issued by the Home Office further to section 77, (the 'Statutory Guidance'), does define 'controlling' behaviour and 'coercive' behaviour separately, but there is no indication that there is an expectation that the one will exist without the other, rather that they work together to encompass a behaviour that is criminal via its manifestation of both. Stark himself, while he describes the different aspects of coercive control separately in his book does not intend the reader to assume that the 'coercion' and the 'control' that make up coercive control can exist in isolation.[60] Certainly the possibility of "controlling behaviour" existing as a separate phenomenon to "coercive behaviour" was not raised by any of the survivors, Independent Domestic Violence Advisers ('IDVAs'), police or judiciary that I spoke to while researching this book. It is also not raised by the Court of Appeal in any of the first thirty or so reported cases on section 76.

A clumsy construction notwithstanding, early research into the implementation of the new offence suggests that the lack of definitional clarity is a problem, because it means that services do not understand controlling or coercive behaviour and are not prepared to report, prevent or prosecute it as a result.[61] The Attorney General explained the decision not to include a definition of controlling or coercive behaviour as follows:

> The Government's new clause has no reference to domestic violence or domestic abuse. That is deliberate. We are dealing with specific behaviour that can be characterised as coercive or controlling, but that should not be the subject of over-prescriptive statutory definition, which would do a disservice to victims … we did not fall into that trap when it came to the law on stalking and harassment. We should not fall into it now with the law on coercive and controlling behaviour within the context of domestic abuse.[62]

In fact, the issue of how to define harassment and/or stalking caused Parliament considerable difficulty in the context of the PHA, as was explained in chapter 3. The decision not to define stalking was eventually reversed, (as explained above), by the Protection of Freedoms Act 2012. A definition of stalking was inserted into the PHA precisely because it was recognised that stalking consists of interlinking and complicated behaviour patterns and therefore is especially in need of clear labelling. There was a realisation that the PHA as it stood, without a definition, missed an opportunity to fulfil the educative function of the criminal law. It is thus odd that the Attorney General states, 'We did not fall into that trap when it came to the law on stalking and harassment'. If indeed there was a trap, it was not to define stalking and harassment, a misstep that was corrected with the "list" approach introduced by the Protection of Freedoms Act 2012.

The final reason that a lack of a definition was a mistake relates to the confusion over what controlling or coercive behaviour *is*. Does it incorporate physical abuse? As stated above Stark is absolutely clear on this: it does.[63] Michael Johnson, also a prominent academic commentator on coercive control, (whose work is reviewed in detail in chapter 1), is also clear that coercive control usually includes physical and non-physical behaviours.[64] My empirical work with survivors and IDVAs supports Stark and Johnson on this.

The tension between the Statutory Guidance, and the new definition of domestic abuse that is set out in the DAA, suggests that there is ambiguity at a Home Office level as to what behaviours should be charged further to section 76, and what should be charged separately.[65] The definition set out in the Statutory Guidance is clear: controlling or coercive behaviour includes behaviours that are physically violent as well as behaviours that are psychologically and/or emotionally abusive. Furthermore, on the following page, under the heading 'Types of Behaviour', the Statutory Guidance helpfully lists behaviours that may be associated with controlling or coercive behaviour. It explains that the types of behaviours listed 'may or may not constitute a criminal offence in their own right'. Both physical and sexual violence are included in the list.

As I explain below, however, the new definition of domestic abuse in the DAA lists 'controlling or coercive behaviour' as a bullet point alongside physical and sexual violence, suggesting that it is being constructed as something separate to physical and sexual violence. Certainly, the approach taken to date by the Crown Prosecution Service and the courts is inconsistent. A review of early sentencing decisions confirms this inconsistency. In *Barratt*,[66] for example, the Court of Appeal observes that:

> In our judgment, a sentence of 30 months' imprisonment before a reduction for the guilty plea for the offence in this case of controlling and coercive behaviour is appropriate and is not manifestly excessive, given the conduct involved. The offence involves a sustained period of abuse and violent and controlling conduct by the appellant towards his former partner. There was prolonged and serious aggression and violence.

The Court of Appeal in *Barratt*, in other words, seems to be making the assumption that controlling or coercive behaviour incorporates violent behaviour. The "conduct" which comprises the section 76 offence includes violent conduct. In *Conlon*, however, the Court of Appeal took a different approach. It said: 'The new offence targets psychological abuse in which one partner to a relationship coerces or controls the life of the other without necessarily or frequently using threats or violence'.[67] Thus in *Conlon* although the Court of Appeal leaves open the possibility that violence can be used (whether this is alongside, or as part of, the controlling or coercive behaviour is not entirely clear), the main purpose of the offence is to target psychological (non-violent) abuse.

Challen[68] is also interesting on this point. *Challen* is not a sentencing decision, but a review of a murder conviction. Sally Challen killed her husband Richard in 2010, and the Court of Appeal was asked to consider whether the criminalisation of coercive control constituted new evidence in that it encouraged a legitimisation, from a criminal law perspective, of Sally's experiences of coercive control and her resulting mental state at the time of the homicide. The Court of Appeal, therefore, was being asked to consider the impact of the introduction of the section 76 offence, and the high profile nature of the judgment makes it potentially influential and therefore important. At paragraph [35] Hallet LJ explains that:

> Parliament enacted s. 76 of the Serious Crime Act 2015 to make it a criminal offence to exercise coercive control over one's partner. S. 76 criminalises a pattern of abusive behaviour, the individual elements of which are not necessarily unlawful in themselves.

As violence is unlawful in itself, this suggests that Hallet LJ leaning towards constructing controlling or coercive behaviour as non-violent abuse. The use of the word 'necessarily' implies a degree of ambiguity, so it could be said that Hallet LJ is not ruling out the inclusion of violent offending.

Sentencing is the subject of a full discussion later in this chapter, but present in many of the sentencing decisions is evidence of the difficulty caused by the lack of clarity with regards to what, exactly, constitutes controlling or coercive behaviour. In *Conlon,* for example, there is evidence of violence which is constructed as separate to controlling or coercive behaviour and which goes uncharged as a result. Robert Conlon was charged separately with one assault occasioning actual bodily harm, but there are numerous references throughout the judgment to his *frequently* violent behaviour to the victim. For example, paragraph 4 of the judgment states:

> While on police bail, on 8th November 2015 the appellant jumped on top of the complainant when she was in bed, she screamed and to stop her screaming the appellant put his fingers in the complainant's mouth. The neighbours again contacted the police and the appellant was arrested. On that occasion the complainant told the police the appellant controlled every aspect of her life.[69]

Paragraph 8 refers to the fact that 'On occasions the complainant reported that the defendant had been violent to her, pinning her to the wall and shouting at her'.[70] In paragraph 13 there is a reference to the defendant punching the victim in the right breast. Paragraph 18 of the judgment reports: 'In anger he repeatedly punched the complainant to the head and face, kicked her to the back and pulled her by the hair to prevent her from leaving'.[71]

None of the references to violence in paragraphs 8, 13 or 18 are charged separately (the assault occasioning actual bodily harm charge relates to yet another violent episode). The violence exhibited by Conlon in this case is very typical of the violence in coercive control that I have described in previous chapters, and, indeed of behaviours evident in other section 76 reported cases.[72] This is a good example of a continuing mismatch between 'life' and 'law' in the area of coercive control.[73] In other words, if an offence of "psychological abuse" as something separate to "physical violence" is constructed then this has the potential to mean that a significant amount of violence goes uncharged.

This point was made by the Court of Appeal in *Berenger*.[74] Joshua Berenger was charged with one count of controlling or coercive behaviour and one count of assault occasioning actual bodily harm contrary to the Offences against the Person Act 1861, s47. The Court of Appeal observed that:

> That controlling behaviour took a number of forms of an essentially non-violent, but nevertheless, coercive kind. However, in addition he had also been violent towards her on a number of occasions … he had on occasions pulled her hair, ripped her clothing, punched her to the face, threatened her with a knife, spat in her face, stamped on her, thrown a drink on her, elbowed her to the face and head butted her.[75]

This use of 'in addition' in the second sentence suggests that the controlling or coercive behaviour is being constructed as separate to physical violence. The Court of Appeal recognises that this is problematic:

> For reasons which we have not had to investigate, these serious offences of violence were charged as coercive or controlling behaviour which is a new offence designed to capture conduct of that description specifically when it does not involve some other more serious substantive offence.[76]

The "solution" proposed by the Court of Appeal in this case is that violence should be properly charged separately.[77] Especially in relation to the apparently "low-level" violence that is so typical of coercive control, this is a step backwards. As is explained in some detail in chapter 2, the incident-specific nature of the Offences against the Person Act 1861 is inconsistent with victims' experiences of physical abuse that are 'chronic'[78] – that is consistent and ongoing.

If it is not always possible to charge low-level violence separately, the same cannot be said, perhaps, about one-off serious incidents of violence that amount to inflicting grievous bodily harm. For the same reasons that were put forward in the preceding chapter in the context of rape, there is an argument to suggest that serious violence that amounts to grievous bodily harm could – or even should – be charged separately. Survivors that were interviewed for this research tended to remember specific incidents of serious violence in a way that is more compatible with an incident-specific focus. Is the infliction of grievous bodily harm so discrete as a wrong that it becomes a separate offence? I argued in the previous chapter that the taking of someone's life is an example of a wrong that is so serious, so qualitatively different as a wrong both in terms of the culpability of the defendant and the harm done to the victim that it *has* to be dealt with as a separate offence. I said that arguably the same could be said for the crime of rape. Could the same be said for the infliction of grievous bodily harm? I come back to this point with the discussion of the DASA in the following chapter.

To conclude, if the physical and psychological aspects of coercive control are separated this makes it more difficult to prosecute both fragments of coercive control. If the physical abuse is prosecuted separately further to the Offences against the Person Act 1861, survivors will still have to pinpoint ongoing abuse to specific dates on which particular assaults took place. This is difficult in the context of supposedly "low-level" physical abuse that is 'chronic',[79] that is ongoing. Coercive control is harder to understand in the absence of the physical abuse that often underpins it. In other words, 'the binary juxtaposition of physical and psychological/emotional abuse fails to capture the embodied physicality and brutality of coercive control'.[80] As explained in chapter 1, the victim obeys the perpetrator because she has reason to be frightened of him. The physical assaults are often (not always) the reason.

Early research into media reports of the first cases suggests that police and CPS are struggling to be consistent on the question of how to charge section 76. Should "incidents" of violence be charged separately? Should "on-going" violence be simply 'part of the factual matrix constituting the course of controlling or coercive conduct'?[81] Or can supposedly "low-level" day-to-day violence be ignored altogether?

The authors of this early research conclude that 'Given this apparent conflict between the sociological and legislative conceptualisations of coercive control, it is perhaps unsurprising that the various police forces in England and Wales have taken what seem to be quite disparate approaches to charging alleged offences'.[82] Some forces charge violence separately.[83] Some put it forward as evidence of the controlling or coercive behaviour.[84] In some cases there is no mention of physical or sexual violence,[85] which could mean that there was not any, or could mean that the relevant force has decided to leave it out altogether.

Statistics published by the Ministry of Justice show that in 2018, half the defendants who were prosecuted for coercive or controlling behaviour were also prosecuted for common assault and battery.[86] The Home Office, in its early review of section 76, concludes that there is 'insufficient evidence to confidently assess what is driving the current practice'.[87] It surmises that it could be that it is easier to prosecute 'controlling or coercive behaviour' when it is charged alongside other offences that are perceived as less difficult to prosecute. Another explanation for the charging practices put forward by the Home Office review is the low maximum sentence tariff of the section 76 offence,[88] (which I come back to in more detail below). Finally, it could be 'a lack of understanding among the CJS that these other crimes could be charged and prosecuted as part of coercive or controlling behaviour'.[89]

Earlier, in the same review, the Home Office captures this ambiguity perfectly. It states:

While CCB (coercive and controlling behaviour) (sic) often includes both physical and non-physical forms of abuse, a key aim of the creation of the offence was to provide a clearer legal framework to capture patterns of non-physical domestic abuse, where were not prosecutable under alternative offences in the same way that forms of physical abuse might be.[90]

The Home Office is contrasting in one sentence the reality of the behaviour (physical and non-physical) with the fragmentation effect of section 76, as it only captures, or only tries to capture 'patterns of non-physical domestic abuse'. In my view, it is not surprising that there is a 'lack of understanding' in the Criminal Justice System as to how and what to charge.

In this respect there may be lessons to learn from Scotland, who have taken a different approach. The DASA received Royal Assent on 9 March 2018. Referred to as, 'One of the most radical attempts yet to align the criminal justice response with contemporary (feminist) conceptual understandings of domestic abuse as a form of coercive control'[91] newspapers reported on its novel approach – i.e. that a central feature of this new Scottish law is that, 'The legislation will cover not only physical abuse but psychological abuse and controlling behaviour'.[92] In fact, extensive research was conducted by the Scottish Parliament Justice Committee over a ten-year period prior to the drafting of the Bill, which I return to and examine in the following chapter.[93]

Section 76(1)(b) The Circumstances Element of the Offence

Section 76(1)(b) originally dealt with the necessary circumstances of the offence. At the time of the behaviour, defendant and victim must be 'personally connected'. As originally drafted, subsection 76(4) stated that two people were personally connected if they were in an intimate personal relationship (but not necessarily living together); or, if they lived together and were members of the same family; or, if they lived together and had previously been in an intimate personal relationship. This was at once too narrow and too wide. It was too narrow because the so-called residency requirement meant that section 76 was not always available to protect a victim who was trying to separate from her abusive partner. The partner who has ended her relationship and who is no longer living with the perpetrator did not come within section 76(4). It was too wide because it included family relationships other than intimate partnerships, and it is not clear that broader family relationships are relevant in the context of coercive control.

The difficulties with using the moment of separation as a legal boundary were explored in some detail in Chapter 3. Firstly, separation rarely exists as a transactional moment.[94] Secondly, if identifying the moment of separation is difficult, it is also, from the survivor's perspective, not necessarily that significant. This is because the perpetrator's controlling intent does not change with the end of the relationship.[95] Karen comments: 'I am obviously still "in it", but obviously most people are anyway as it doesn't actually generally go away, that's the sad thing'.[96]

Finally, leaving a relationship is dangerous. This is because the controlling behaviours often intensify once a perpetrator fears that his relationship with his victim is over, and separation is a well-established homicide trigger.[97] It is not a good time to be withdrawing protection and support.

Judge Harwood became aware of this section 76 limitation – that it does not apply where a couple has separated and is no longer living together – for the first time in her interview with me. She commented:

> Well that is definitely a change that needs to happen. As you will know from your research, and I know from my limited experience, very often the controlling and coercive behaviour is ongoing ... If you have had the strength to leave - we are suddenly not supporting those people? They have got the legislation wrong, haven't they as they are probably missing about 50 or 60% of the people who need to be protected? Those that manage that to escape but are still being controlled? That has got to be wrong. We have to change the law.[98]

Early research into the first media reports of cases concluded that limiting the application of section 76 to current partners in this way caused police and the Crown Prosecution Service considerable confusion. In some cases, behaviour which post-dated the relationship appeared to be included in the evidence put forward in court of the section 76 charge.[99] This had potentially serious implications for the validity of the criminal sanction.

I used these findings to assist leading domestic abuse charity, Surviving Economic Abuse, with its excellent campaign to use the Domestic Abuse Bill 2021 to change the faulty definition of 'connected persons' in section 76. We were not successful at the Commons stage of the debate in June 2020. This was partly, to be fair because the Public Bill Committee wanted to wait for the Home Office review into the section 76 offence that was, at that time, about to be published. It was also partly because the Justice Minister Alex Chalk MP was under the misapprehension that the stalking offences provided adequate protection for the victims of coercive control post-separation. We organised a coalition of supportive peers who rallied behind us during the parliamentary debates. At the Second Reading of the Domestic Abuse Bill, in the House of Lords, Baroness Hayman said:

> Cassandra Wiener ... has pointed out that the residency requirement for protection under Section 76 of the Serious Crime Act means that an abused partner is not protected under the Act when the couple stop living together. Yet there is mounting evidence that violence, the danger of injury and even death, actually increase at the point when an abused partner leaves the shared home. While some continuing abuse can be pursued by police through legislation on harassment and stalking, not all forms of abuse are covered, as was pointed out earlier in the debate, particularly in relation, for example, to financial abuse and coercive control around childcare arrangements.[100]

On 22 February 2021, we asked the Domestic Abuse Commissioner, Nicole Jacobs, to host an online (mid-pandemic) round table. Nicola Sharp Jeffs (CEO, Surviving Economic Abuse) and I presented to ten peers, together with representatives from the Home Office and the Ministry of Justice. Using the story of an expert by experience, Nicola and I were able to demonstrate how the existing definition of 'connected persons' in section 76 hampered police efforts to protect women when they were at their most vulnerable. On Monday 1 March, the Home Office announced that it was adding a new clause to the Domestic Abuse Bill which would extend the definition of 'connected persons' in section 76 to include ex-partners no longer living with victims. Clause 69 of the Domestic Abuse Bill 2021 duly replaces the faulty section 76(1)(b) with the improved section 76(6). In other words, clause 69 of the Domestic Abuse Bill 2021 amends section 76 by removing the residency requirement so that ex-partners no longer living together are 'personally connected' for the purposes of the controlling or coercive behaviour offence. This is welcome progress.

Another difficulty with the old subsection 76(1)(b) that has not been improved is the way it defines 'members of the same family' for the purposes of section 76(4). This is the part of the definition that is unnecessarily wide. The defendant and victim were held to be members of the same family, and therefore personally connected, if they were 'relatives' and lived together (section 76(6)(c)). The new clause 69 of the Domestic Abuse Bill 2021 extends this further – the removal of the residency requirement means that in the future, defendant and victim will be personally connected if they are related, whether or not they live together. There is, as yet, not enough research on the important question of the extent to which coercive control might apply to family relationships. It is likely that coercive control is perpetrated almost always by men who are, or who have been, in an intimate relationship with their victims. Certainly data from the early convictions suggests that the majority of defendants (between 97% and 99%) are overwhelmingly male and are partners, or ex-partners, of the victim.[101] From the clear labelling perspective it is therefore detrimental to draft the offence so widely that it could include, for example, an overbearing parent or a controlling sibling. Some police expressed confusion on this point at the interview.[102]

There have been prosecutions of cases involving non-partners in England and Wales, some of which have been reported in the media. Often in these cases the perpetrator was convicted of extracting money from his parents/ adopted parents. Many of the indicators of coercive control as set out in chapter 1 (the coercive intent, for example, or the desire to control victim behaviour) appear to be absent.[103] My concern is that if we are unnecessarily extending the legislation to include other family relationships, we could be diluting and therefore diminishing our response to coercive control. I come back to this point when I review the approach taken by the Scottish government in the next chapter.[104]

Section 76 (1)(c) The Result Element of the Offence

Section 76(1)(c) is the result element of the crime and is defined in terms of the effect that the perpetrator's behaviour has on his victim. Section 76(1)(c) states that the controlling or coercive behaviour is an offence only where it has a 'serious effect' on the victim. 'Serious effect' is defined in subsection (4): if it causes the victim to fear, on at least two occasions, that violence will be used against the victim or if it causes the victim serious alarm and distress which has a substantial adverse effect on her usual day-to-day activities. This mirrors the wording of the new PHA, s 4A (as inserted by the Protection of Freedoms Act 2012) that was discussed above. Using this construct thus has the advantage that it is familiar, which has the potential to be helpful for police and prosecutors.

Familiarity is only helpful, however, if the harm experienced by the victims of coercive control is properly captured by section 76(1)(c). The case law on the offences against the person regime that I referred to in chapter 2 limited the re-cognition of emotional distress to diagnosed clinical disorders. It was suggested that the PHA was in part a political response to Parliament's perception (guided by the media) of the inadequacy of the old offences against the person regime to deal with such emotional distress. Social science analysis of the victim's response to coercive control indicates that it is complicated: such responses incorporate cognitive, emotional, behavioural and physiological reactions.[105]

While the definition of 'adverse effect' does not incorporate all of this com-plexity, it should be remembered that criminal justice recognition of purely psy-chological harm is still recent. It would be unrealistic to expect section 76 to incorporate all of the nuances of the extensive harms suffered by victims. Emotional harm is, as has been pointed out, difficult to operationalise.[106] As I explained in Chapter 2, the only psychological harm recognised in an Offences against the Person Act 1861 prosecution is harm that constitutes a clinical mental illness. To the extent that section 76(1)(c) does go some way towards addressing the 'cloaking'[107] of any emotional response that is not a clinical condition, it is progress.

However, the wording of the two limbs of the result element of section 76 seems a better description of the harm experienced by victims of the stranger stalking type offences for which they were originally intended, than for the harm experienced by victims of coercive control. The first limb, if it causes the victim to fear that violence will be used against her on two occasions, brings with it the incident-specific focus reviewed in chapter 3 with all of its attendant problems.[108] The generalised fear induced by coercive control cannot always be located to a singular threat or violent event. The fear experienced by the victim is not always (although often can be) of violence. She might fear disgrace. Or shame. Her fear is most likely to be generalised, in response to the 'state of siege'[109] described by survivors in chapter 1.

The second limb, 'if it causes the victim serious alarm or distress that has a substantial adverse effect on her day-to-day activities' has more potential. Even this wording, however, focuses on the state of mind of the victim, her 'alarm or distress'. This runs the risk of necessitating medical and psychological evidence as to depression or anxiety, for example.[110] It is also too imprecise.

Specialist police interviewed for this project found the second limb too broad. Detective Constable Canford, for example, a specialist domestic abuse officer, explained that 'The wording is too broad. I think that it is far too broad ... debatable and poorly defined'. When I questioned him as what he meant by this, Detective Constable Canford explained that 'The issue is less about the serious adverse effect, and more about the evidence of control and the nature of the control'.[111] In other words, Detective Constable Canford felt from an investigative perspective that the behaviour of the perpetrator is more relevant than the mindset of the victim.

Stark conceptualises the harm experienced by victims of coercive control as political: 'A deprivation of rights and resources that are critical to personhood and citizenship'.[112] Alafair Burke, who has written extensively about domestic abuse legislation in the US, argues for a doctrinal conceptualisation of the harm experienced as 'restricting the victim's "freedom of action".[113] Jennifer Youngs and Charlotte Bishop both advocate this approach, Bishop arguing that the 'freedom of action' construct 'is a useful and preferred approach that focuses less on the mental capacity of the victim and her reactions to the offending behaviour. It more adequately reflects the nature of coercive control as a liberty crime'.[114]

I agree with Bishop and Youngs. Survivors who took part in the focus group expressed the harms they experience in terms of what they felt they had lost, (their freedom), rather than in terms of an impact on day-to-day activities. A statute could capture this by, for example, listing examples of ways in which a victim's freedom might be constrained, such as the dependence she might have on her abuser, the isolation she might be experiencing, the economic abuse she might be experiencing. The DASA, s 2 defines abusive behaviour in exactly this way. Subsection 3 lists the 'relevant effects' on the victim's behaviour both in terms of restrictions on her liberty (isolation, dependence, being punished) *and* emotional distress (being afraid).

Finally, the resilient survivor is the survivor who, against the odds, manages to continue with her roles at work and/or in the home without displaying visible signs of distress. This has, in fact, proved to be a thorny issue. Judge Harwood, when asked about the result element, commented:

> I think that this is unnecessary for this offence. Yes, yes so if you are someone who is able to cope with it, and it hasn't affected your daily life. You are still able to go to work, and see friends. The fact that you're living in coercive or controlling relationship, the court will say this hasn't had enough of an effect on you yet, terribly sorry, we are not going to be supporting a prosecution. That can't be right.[115]

Recent media reports seem to support Judge Harwood's concern. Paul Measor subjected his partner Lauren Smith to horrific abuse, teaching their toddler son to tell her to "fuck off" and spitting in her face. Nevertheless, District Judge Helen

Cousins acquitted him, (in my view, from the limited amount of information I have gleaned from the media, correctly), of a section 76 offence. District Judge Cousins ruled that while Paul Measor's actions were 'disgraceful', they did not have a 'serious effect' on Lauren's life. District Judge Cousins said:

> I have to be satisfied the behaviour was controlling, coercive and had a serious effect on the victim. There's no doubt the victim is a strong and capable woman. It is to her credit that I cannot find his behaviour had a serious effect on her in the context of the guidelines.[116]

The women's sector responded angrily with Women's Aid calling for judges to be 'sent for training on the Serious Crime Act 2015'.[117] Suzanne Jacob, Chief Executive of SafeLives, argued immediately after the ruling that 'Yes, you can be strong and still be a victim of coercive control'.[118] All of the points Jacob makes in her article – that there is a link between assault and coercive control, that leaving your abusive partner shouldn't be a justification for not holding that partner liable for his crimes, and that 'This analysis of Lauren's strength is entirely subjective and plays into the narrative of what a "perfect victim" should look like'[119] – are entirely accurate. But the problem lies with the wording of the offence, and not in District Judge Cousins' application of the law.

Irrespective of how the harm is defined, therefore, there is a second question that is more fundamental. Is the prominent role that harm plays in the construction of s.76 appropriate? The Home Office reported in its review that 'The requirement for proof of the "serious effect" that the controlling or coercive behaviours have had on the victim likely creates further difficulties in gathering and providing the necessary evidence for the CCB (controlling or coercive behaviour) offence'.[120] Or is a focus on the response of the victim, rather than the actions of the perpetrator, in the context of coercive control unhelpful? One of the concerns expressed by commentators researching the likely legal implications of the criminalisation of coercive control is that:

> People who do not understand how entrapment operates - because they have not personally lived the manner in which coercive control can inhibit resistance and who have life experiences that have led them to expect personal safety at all times and for whom calling the police will always be an effective means of achieving this - can be vehement and entrenched in their judgments of victims.[121]

Many of the judges interviewed for this research project showed, in fact, an impressive understanding of how entrapment operates. No judge was 'vehement' in his or her judgment of victims. Nevertheless, it is fair to say that their appreciation of how difficult it might be for the victim to portray her experience of harm in the courtroom was, as is to be expected, more limited than that of other criminal justice agents such as IDVAs or police.

Police spend time with survivor-witnesses on an almost daily basis in the run-up to a trial. Judges do not speak to witnesses outside the courtroom, and the judicial perspective is necessarily detached. While judges interviewed for this project tried to be sympathetic, they admitted frustration at what they perceived to be the victim's inadequacies as a witness. In other words they expressed frustration that the victim-witness is frequently unable to deliver what is needed in order to persuade a jury of the defendant's guilt. Judge Little, for example emphasised that, 'I am not unsympathetic as I know the reasons that very often women are unwilling [to give evidence] because they have been rather ground down by the situation in which they've been'.[122] At the same time Judge Little expressed frustration with what she called 'woolly witnesses'.[123] She explained:

> From a judge's point of view the difficulties are often in getting women to come to court and to speak fully and openly and honestly about their experiences - probably the most frustrating thing … They come to court, and they are a bit wishy washy and they are trying to water it down because they still love him and so trials can be very frustrating.[124]

Judge Little's perception that victim/witnesses are 'woolly' or 'a bit wishy washy', and that they 'water it down because they still love him' might be entirely fair, but it must be remembered that an abusive partner who is not in custody, or on bail with no-contact conditions, may still have access. That a victim-witness finds it difficult to testify against an abusive and controlling partner who still has access to her might be because she is afraid.[125] It could also be that it is particularly complicated to portray the effect of the perpetrator's behaviour in an adversarial court of law. Adversarial justice, it has been pointed out, is not sensitive generally to the needs of victims experiencing trauma.[126] Coercive control involves the repetition of stress for the victim in a way that has a direct impact on the memory function.[127] Complications arising from the interplay between trauma, the giving of testimony and the requirements of adversarial justice process are particularly acute in the case of the victim of coercive control.

The process of cross-examination is a good example of the "catch-22" situation experienced by the coercive control victim in court. There is much empirical evidence that suggests that the way in which a witness gives evidence affects jurors' perception of their credibility.[128] Furthermore, giving cross-examination is highly stressful. In fact, the experience is challenging 'even for professional witnesses (eg police officers and experts)'.[129]

The first hurdle, therefore, is for the coercive control victim to 'maintain her perspective under cross-examination'.[130] If she cannot hold her ground she, like all victims of crime whose trauma interferes with their ability to produce evidence under pressure, will have failed in her role as prosecution witness.[131] But the victim of coercive control has an additional evidential hurdle to surmount. This is because, if she *can* hold her own, it may 'undercut her claim to have been the victim of coercive control'.[132] Even where a victim is able to give evidence 'it is difficult ... to present a complex account of women as both oppressed and struggling'.[133] What Stark refers to as the 'victimisation narrative' allows us, as he puts it, a 'personal buffer'. 'Picturing battered women as pathetic, tragic and helpless allows us to act sympathetically, while remaining at a safe distance'.[134] If a woman is too competent and articulate as a witness, the court will inevitably ask 'why the victim didn't leave if the effect of the behaviour was so bad'?[135] Jen, a criminal justice IDVA who supports survivors through the trial process, put it this way: 'Fundamentally, the bottom line is judges think that she is somewhat complicit or it is her fault'.[136]

My empirical work shed some light on the issues facing victims. In the focus group that I ran with survivors I asked expressly for survivors' thoughts on their experiences of the criminal justice process. No two survivors had an identical experience, but the difficulties that they encountered included a lack of support, a lack of legal aid, and a feeling of being "bullied" all over again by police and prosecutors.[137] Underpinning all of their experiences was fear for their safety, and that of their children in the face of what they knew about perpetrator capability and the inadequacy (to their minds) of the safeguarding capabilities of the police.[138]

Judge Fern agreed that domestic abuse trials are incredibly frustrating from the judicial perspective. He said:

> Oh yes, they are a nightmare. They are a total nightmare to prosecute. Because as we know the problem with the controlling coercive relationship is that the victims of that behaviour inevitably are persuadable by the individual. I mean that is the old problem. So, what ends up happening is that we have a compete nightmare - or the prosecution which is more to the point have a complete nightmare - trying to get the witness, the complainant at that stage - to court. It's very - you end up with: do you issue witness summonses? To somebody who has clearly suffered a great deal? Is that the best way to deal with it? Often they just won't co-operate. Withdraw statements, and so it goes on, and we lose a lot of cases that cannot be prosecuted because witnesses are, for whatever reason - you don't always get to the bottom of it - persuaded not to give evidence. Whether they persuade themselves or they are persuaded.[139]

Judge Fern thus exhibits a similar mix of sympathy and frustration as that expressed by Judge Little. He recognises that victims have 'clearly suffered a great deal', but is frustrated by the 'nightmare' of trying to get victims to testify in court. Intermixed with the sympathy and frustration is, perhaps, a lack of understanding of the complexity of the survivor's situation.

Judge Fern says, for example, that the victims of coercive control are 'persuadable'. He says 'Witnesses are, for whatever reason – you don't always get to the bottom of it – persuaded not to give evidence. Whether they persuade themselves or they are persuaded'. Survivors encountered for this research project were bullied and terrorised, rather than persuaded. In fact, Judge Fern recognises that he does not understand the victim's behaviour, 'you don't always get to the bottom of it', and this only adds to his frustration.

Specific research into the behavioural response of abused women has shown that victims are resourceful and strategic in what amounts to impossibly complex life situations.[140] Stark and others have vividly described how a victim will try to at once conform to the perpetrator's demands while remaining in a permanent state of hyper-vigilance to keep herself and her children safe.[141] Being responsibilised as a witness entails testifying in court against her abuser, and is a difficult and potentially dangerous experience. The impact of trauma, and the way that it can cause dis-orientation and confusion, can undermine perceptions of credibility still further.[142]

Thus, a focus on the victim's response is unhelpful in the context of coercive control legislation because of the pressure that it puts on the victim to disclose intimate details about her emotional state when under cross-examination, and possibly while living with her abusive and controlling partner. As has been pointed out, offences that are 'heavily reliant on the victim's testimony' are unhelpful when, 'frequently victims are in dangerous and/or compromised positions when it comes to giving that testimony'.[143] Certainly the data from my interviews with judges and the police show that the requirement for the survivor to play the dual role of victim and chief witness for the prosecution creates pressure points right the way through the criminal justice system.

Mens Rea

The last aspect of section 76 to be considered in this chapter is the *mens rea*. The *mens rea* is set out in s. 76 (1) (d) as follows:

1. A person (A) commits an offence if – ...

   d. A knows or ought to know that the behaviour will have a serious effect on B.

Section 76(1)(d) thus states that the *mens rea* can be satisfied both subjectively, in terms of what the perpetrator actually knew, or objectively, in terms of what the reasonable person would have known. As with the PHA, section 76(5) states that the reasonable person for these purposes is in possession of the same information as the perpetrator. Including the possibility of a wholly objective *mens rea* as a route to conviction was justified in the context of the PHA in that it was thought necessary to make sure that stalkers whose mental illness precluded them from appreciating the impact of their behaviour were not excluded from the scope of the legislation.[144]

Chapter 3 argued, in addition, that the negligence construct did not derail 'the central quest of identifying blameworthiness'[145] in the context of the PHA in part because establishing the serious harm experienced by the victim is a constituent part of the offence. As far as section 76 is concerned, however, it could be argued that including the possibility of an objective *mens rea* is harder to justify. More research is needed to investigate the issue of whether or not perpetrators of coercive control are mentally ill. If a correlation was found between perpetrators and mental ill-health this would introduce a new factor into the debate: perpetrators should not be subject to a *mens rea* standard that they cannot meet. The reasonable person, it could be argued, is not an appropriate culpability standard in these circumstances.

Another potential negative consequence relates to what an objective *mens rea* says about the crime of coercive control. In the introduction, I highlighted that the correct labelling of a crime is one of the most important functions of the criminal law. Research shows that, 'An abuser's intent is now a crucial and engrained portion of our modern understanding of intimate partner violence'.[146] From the perspective of the survivor of coercive control, the malevolence of the strategic campaign of domination is *the* central (and most harmful) feature of the abuse. If crimes must be defined in a way that 'reflects what makes the conduct of defendants who are convicted under them publicly wrongful',[147] then is ostracising the motive of the defendant counterproductive? In other words, the perpetrator's strategic intent is a key part of what makes him culpable. Does the criminal law need to reflect this if it is to fulfil its educative and normative function?

Arguments as to the inclusion of an intention requirement in a domestic abuse statute are more developed in the US literature. Tuerkheimer and Burke disagree on the relative merits of subjective/objective *mens rea* in the context of coercive control.[148] Burke supports the arguments set out above in relation to the result element of the crime, and argues that a 'discursive shift' away from the victim focus is necessary. She sees a *mens rea* of intent as a necessary part of this 'shift'. She argues that:

> By grounding a specialized domestic violence statute in the requirement of intent, this Article's proposal would bring an important discursive shift in the criminal law's treatment of domestic violence by turning the focus away from the claimed effects of domestic violence on a victim's autonomy and instead toward the coercive motivations of the batterer.[149]

I agree with Burke that the discursive shift away from the victim focus is necessary and desirable, but I do not agree that a requirement of intent is necessary to achieve this. I consider this in more detail in the following chapter, but the DASA achieves a shift away from the victim without a *mens rea* of intent.

Finally, it is possible for reasons that have been put forward in the literature and that are supported by my empirical work with judges, that a *mens rea* of intent would create as many problems as it would solve. Tuerkheimer, herself a former prosecutor, argues that a *mens rea* of intent would place too great a burden on the prosecution. She says:

Prosecutors would understandably balk at a requirement that intentional mens rea be proven with respect to the exercise of power and control. The difficulty of convincing jurors beyond a reasonable doubt that a batterer *consciously* intended to dominate his victim may be practically insurmountable.[150]

Bishop and Bettinson also point out that, just as with the PHA, the behaviour could appear innocuous.[151] They argue that:

The defendant could simply claim that they just wanted their partner to be at home for a particular reason or did not realise that preventing their partner from leaving the house on occasions would have that effect upon her, whereas, the harm to the victim is the same regardless of the intention of the perpetrator.[152]

Bishop and Bettinson conclude by agreeing with Tuerkheimer that, 'The objective standard is to be welcomed as providing the best possible means of securing a conviction given the present limitations to legal and societal understandings of coercive control'.[153] I agree with Tuerkheimer, Bettinson and Bishop that the objective standard is necessary in the context of what is currently understood about the mindset of perpetrators of coercive control.

Data from my interviews with judges support this conclusion. Judge Little emphasised that, for her, a mens rea of intent 'would change it completely'. She said 'I think actually it would make it far more difficult to get convictions, I feel that very strongly'.[154] She gave as an example a defendant in one of the cases she had presided over, Robert Clint.[155] In Judge Little's view, Robert Clint was 'your typical kind of offender'. 'But', she went on to explain, while 'He intended to control her', 'he had no concept that what he was doing was wrong'.[156]

Judge Little thought that this would be difficult for a jury because, 'For a jury an intent is a very specific *mens rea*, so it has to be something somebody has thought about, the consequence of their action'. Judge Little used assault occasioning grievous bodily harm as an example to illustrate her point. She said:

If you intend to do GBH, you intend to do somebody really grievous bodily harm, if you intend to control somebody, it seems to me you can only intend to effectively diminish the quality of their life - Robert Clint actually I don't believe intended to diminish the quality of her life. There may well have come a point when he did.'[157]

Judge Little thus identified a difference between the intention to dominate and the intention to cause harm. This difference, for Judge Little, allows for a disconnect in the minds of defendants between the two constructs. Despite the presence of the intention to dominate, there is a simultaneous absence of the intention to cause harm that makes a *mens rea* of intent inappropriate. While Judge Little conceded that Robert Clint had a specific intention to dominate, she felt that if there was a *mens rea* of intent, then the fact that he *did not intend to cause harm* would cause problems for a jury. It would remain open to Clint to escape liability by claiming that he did not know that his behaviour would have a harmful effect on the victim, despite his intention to dominate.

Judge Little thus raises an important issue. I agree that, while a defendant's strategic intent to control his partner might be clear, his conviction that that intent (his desire to control her) is benign, and not intended to cause her harm, might indeed cause problems for a jury. There is no doubt that the perpetrator's strategic intent is a key part of what makes him culpable, but it is possible that the perpetrator might confuse a jury by convincing them of his lack of intention to cause harm. My empirical work did not include interviews with perpetrators, and more research is urgently needed on this point. In the meantime, it would appear that including the possibility of an objective *mens rea* is appropriate in the context of the section 76 offence.

Sentencing

The sentencing difficulties experienced by judges in the context of a section 76 conviction are the practical repercussion of what this chapter has found is the fundamental (and unhelpful) confusion generated by the controlling or coercive behaviour construct. Whether or not so-called low-level physical violence is charged alongside section 76, the low maximum sentence of imprisonment for section 76 (five years), makes sentencing an especially delicate exercise.

The most common accompanying counts on a section 76 indictment are, as is to be expected, offences against the person and sexual offences. The difficulty for the sentencing judge is how to separate out the different strands of the offending behaviour while avoiding the possibility of double counting. Judge Little referred specifically to this dilemma. She said:

> Because where we have to be a bit careful, and the reason I gave (the defendant) four years with the plea, was the two offences of violence I said effectively were aggravating features of the overall behaviour, and this is one of the difficulties, because the CPS do put the violence where they have got specific incidents they can point to ...

In the sentencing decision Judge Little is referring to (which has been upheld by the Court of Appeal) the other counts on the indictment are assault occasioning actual bodily harm (one count) and perverting the course of justice (two counts). There is a significant amount of additional violence detailed in the Court of Appeal judgment that is not charged separately.[158] Judge Little decided to use the section 76 offence as the principal offence to reflect the totality of the offending for the sentence on that count, and to make the sentencing for the aggravated assault charge concurrent. The Court of Appeal confirmed that it is happy with this approach. If there had been an even more serious charge on the indictment then it would have been open to Judge Little to use that charge (for example rape, or inflicting grievous bodily harm) as the principal offence and to make the sentencing of the section 76 offence concurrent.[159]

Difficulties remain, however. I did not ask Judge Little the extent to which she felt able to take into account (for sentencing purposes) the additional violence that was not charged separately, and this is an important question. The risk is that if controlling or coercive behaviour is constructed as 'psychological' or 'non-violent' abuse (as suggested by the judgments in *Challen*, *Conlon* and *Beringer* referred to above) then a significant amount of low-level violence continues to go unpunished.

Furthermore, even where serious violence is charged separately, the approach that has been taken by the courts, (to make the serious violence the principal offence and to punish the controlling or coercive behaviour with a concurrent sentence), means that the distinct harm of coercive control potentially does not get enough recognition. *Parkin*[160] is a good example of the pitfalls of this approach. Parkin was convicted of three counts of rape (counts one to three) for which he received a total of seven years imprisonment. He was also convicted of controlling or coercive behaviour (count four), for which he received two years imprisonment concurrent. Application for leave was made by the Attorney General to refer the sentence on the basis that it was too lenient. The application was granted, with the Court of Appeal explaining:

> There was effectively no sentence passed in respect of count 4, which was quite separate coercive behaviour. We do not agree that that offence could properly be simply absorbed into the overall low sentence that he was already going to pass for the three other offences. The controlling behaviour was a quite separate offence requiring to be reflected either in a separate consecutive sentence or by an uplift of the principal sentence.[161]

The Court of Appeal is therefore suggesting that the judge could properly have sentenced the controlling behaviour separately, or by using the totality principal to "uplift" the principal sentence. Neither approach is ideal. Sentencing separately raises the issues of double counting highlighted by Judge Little above. And using the violence as the 'principal sentence' means we are still left with the hierarchy of harms that places physical violence at the top, which is not the way that survivors articulate their experiences of abuse. The 'mismatch' between life and law, in other words, continues.

Unfortunately, the low maximum sentence of imprisonment for controlling or coercive behaviour, (five years), adds to the perception of a hierarchy of harms.[162] Judges interviewed for this project agreed that this is too low.[163] The low sentencing threshold contributes to a perception of a hierarchy of harm that places physical violence at the top, which is not how survivors articulate the harms they have experienced. Furthermore, it does not reflect the severity of coercive control. The DASA deals with this issue by incorporating the violent and non-violent behaviours into a single offence with a maximum penalty on conviction on indictment of 14 years imprisonment.[164]

Domestic Abuse Act 2021

The DAA received Royal Assent on 29 April 2021. Hailed as a once in a lifetime opportunity to improve the lot of men and women experiencing domestic abuse, its torturous journey through Parliament began in 2017 when it was introduced by Theresa May as one of her government's flagship reform initiatives. While the DAA is not as radical or reformist as many in academia and the women's sector had hoped, it does include some helpful procedural and doctrinal improvements for survivors of abuse. I have already set out the reform introduced by section 68 of the DAA, which amends the definition of 'connected persons' in section 76 to include ex partners. The other important innovation for this chapter is the new statutory definition of domestic abuse for all agencies with safeguarding obligations, which is introduced by section 1.[165]

As I mentioned earlier, the problem with the DAA, s1 definition (which replaces the Working Definition) is that it uses a bullet point approach which emphasises the fragmentation of domestic abuse into constituent parts, and moves away from Stark's conception of coercive control. In the Working Definition I explained that the five behaviour types listed (psychological, physical, sexual, financial and emotional abuse) are given correctly as constituent *parts* of coercive control. The DAA s 1 definition, on the other hand, lists 'controlling or coercive behaviour' as one of five different examples of what constitutes "abusive" behaviour:

1(2). Behaviour of a person ("A") towards another person ("B") is "domestic abuse" if –

a. A and B are each aged 16 or over and are personally connected to each other, and
b. The behaviour is abusive.

1(3). Behaviour is "abusive" if it consists of any of the following –

a. Physical or sexual abuse;
b. Violent or threatening behaviour;
c. Controlling or coercive behaviour;
d. Economic abuse (see subsection (4));
e. Psychological, emotional or other abuse;

and it does not matter whether the behaviour consists of a single incident or a course of conduct.

Rather than using the coercive control paradigm as the wrapper for what constitutes domestic abuse, the DAA, s 1 definition follows the fragmentation approach of the existing criminal law legislative infrastructure. 'Controlling or coercive behaviour' is positioned (incorrectly) as a bullet point, to be understood alongside the other (bullet point) behaviour types such as physical or sexual abuse, or psychological abuse. This makes no sense – as was explained in chapter 1 coercive control is a strategy that brings particular meaning to all of the other behaviour types listed.

Section 1 DAA does contain some improvements. The types of abusive behaviour that are listed in the definition explicitly define economic abuse for the first time, replacing the more narrow 'financial abuse' with the more accurate 'economic abuse' terminology. This is welcome. The concept of 'personally connected' is thankfully defined to include ex-partners. Section 68, as explained above, amends section 76 to include ex-partners and bring it in line with the new DAA, s 1 definition of domestic abuse.

Conclusion

Section 76 brings challenges even as it creates opportunities. The first challenge is the further fragmentation of domestic abuse, as police and prosecutors are expected to use section 76 to capture psychological aspects of abuse alongside the existing offences against the person regime, a consequence of the Attorney General's construction of 'controlling or coercive behaviour' via a focus on the "gap" in the law.

A second challenge is the emphasis on the response of the victim – the harm she experiences – and the inadequate/inappropriate articulation of what constitutes that harm to the victim. This makes section 76 uniquely challenging to investigate and prosecute, and creates a more traumatic courtroom experience for survivors. Both of these challenges, the fragmentation of coercive control and the consequences of focusing on the victim's response to the abuse, formed a central plank of Scottish governments extensive (six-year) consultation into domestic abuse law reform. In the following chapter I turn to this consultation, and to the resulting DASA, which has been heralded by Evan Stark as the 'Gold Standard' of domestic abuse legislation.[166] It could be that the DASA points the way to the future of domestic abuse law reform in England and Wales.

Notes

1 Evan Stark, *Coercive Control: How Men Entrap Women in Personal Life* (Oxford University Press 2007).
2 Deborah Tuerkheimer, 'Recognizing and Remedying the Harm of Battering: A Call to Criminalize Domestic Violence' (2004) 94(4) Journal of Criminal Law and Criminology 959, 980.
3 Libby Brooks, 'Scotland Set to Pass "Gold Standard" Domestic Abuse Law' *The Guardian* (London 1 February 2018) available at <https://www.theguardian.com/society/2018/feb/01/scotland-set-to-pass-gold-standard-domestic-abuse-law> accessed 28 March 2018.
4 Justice Unions' Parliamentary Group, 'Independent Parliamentary Inquiry into Stalking Law Reform: Main Findings and Recommendations' (2012) available at

<http://www.dashriskchecklist.co.uk/wp-content/uploads/2016/09/Stalking-Law-Reform-Findings-Report-2012.pdf> accessed 9 May 2017.

5 Jessica Harris, *An Evaluation of the Use and Effectiveness of the Protection from Harassment Act 1997* (Home Office Research Study 203, Home Office 2000) 24.

6 Interview with Detective Constable Shell (4 December 2017) 9.

7 Ibid. more empirical work urgently needs to be done with magistrates on this issue.

8 Justice Unions' Parliamentary Group, Independent Parliamentary Inquiry n4 12.

9 Justice Unions' Parliamentary Group, Independent Parliamentary Inquiry n4 2.

10 Ibid. 11.

11 Ibid.

12 Tuerkheimer, Recognizing and Remedying the Harm of Battering n2.

13 Emily Finch, *The Criminalisation of Stalking: Constructing the Problem and Evaluating the Solution* (Cavendish 2001).

14 Protection of Freedoms Act 2012, s 111.

15 My emphasis.

16 Neil Addison and Jennifer Perry, 'Will the New Stalking Legislation Deliver for Victims?' (2013) 177 Criminal Law and Justice Weekly 53.

17 Ibid. 54.

18 Ibid. 54.

19 Ibid. 54.

20 Home Office Circular 018/2012 available at <https://www.gov.uk/government/publications/a-change-to-the-protection-from-harassment-act-1997-introduction-of-two-new-specific-offences-of-stalking> accessed 26 July 2017.

21 Ibid.

22 Home Office 'Cross-Government Definition of Domestic Violence a Consultation' (December 2011) available at <https://www.gov.uk/government/uploads/system/uploads/attachment_data/file/157798/dv-definition-consultation.pdf> accessed 2 February 2018.

23 Ibid. 6.

24 Ibid. 5.

25 AVA against Violence and Abuse, 'AVA's Response to Cross-Government Definition of Domestic Violence: A Consultation' (document on file with me) 2.

26 Ibid.

27 Home Office, 'New Definition of Domestic Violence' (19 September 2012) available at <https://www.gov.uk/government/news/new-definition-of-domestic-violence> accessed 12 September 2017.

28 I deal with this in more detail in the section on the Government Consultation of 2014–15 below.

29 Home Office, 'Strengthening the Law on Domestic Abuse Consultation Summary of Responses' (December 2014) 5 available at <https://www.gov.uk/government/uploads/system/uploads/attachment_data/file/389002/StrengtheningLawDomesticAbuseResponses.pdf> accessed 31 July 2017; email from Evan Stark to me (2 February 2018).

30 Ibid.

31 'Even where stalking and harassment legislation may be the appropriate tool to tackle domestic abuse, Court of Appeal case law is an unhelpful barrier.' (R v Curtis 1 Cr. App. R.31, and R v Widdows (2011) 175J.P. 345).' Home Office, Summary of Responses n28 11.

32 Home Office, 'Strengthening the Law on Domestic Abuse: A Consultation' [2014] 9 available at <https://www.gov.uk/government/uploads/system/uploads/attachment_data/file/344674/Strengthening_the_law_on_Domestic_Abuse_-_A_Consultation_WEB.PDF> accessed 28 March 2018.

33 Julia Quilter, 'Evaluating Criminalisation as a Strategy in Relation to Non-Physical Family Violence' in Marilyn McMahon and Paul McGorrery (eds), *Criminalising Coercive Control* (Springer 2020) 112.

34 This included a consultation, public evidence from senior police, prosecutors, academics and survivors groups taken at six different meetings over a two month period, written evidence and private testimony from survivors of domestic abuse. See the Justice Committee, *Stage One Report on the Domestic Abuse (Scotland) Bill* (SP Paper 198, 16th Report, 2017) 47. See also my interview with Marsha Scott, Chief Executive of Women's Aid (1 December 2017).

35 Home Office, Strengthening the Law on Domestic Abuse: A Consultation n32 5.

36 Ibid. 8 (my emphasis).

37 Home Office, Summary of Responses n29 5.

38 Ibid.

39 Quilter, Evaluating Criminalisation as a Strategy n33 124.

40 Liz Kelly and Louise Westmarland, 'Time for a Rethink. Why the Current Government Definition of Domestic Violence Is a Problem.' (2014) available at <http://www.troubleandstrife.org/2014/04/time-for-a-rethink-why-the-current-government-definition-of-domestic-violence-is-a-problem/> accessed 25 October 2017.

41 Quilter, Evaluating Criminalisation as a Strategy n33 125.

42 Gov.uk, 'Guidance Domestic Violence and Abuse' (2018) available at <https://www.gov.uk/guidance/domestic-violence-and-abuse> accessed 28 March 2018.

43 Vanessa Bettinson and Charlotte Bishop, 'Is the Creation of a Discrete Offence of Coercive Control Necessary to Combat Domestic Violence' (2015) 66(2) Northern Ireland Legal Quarterly 179, 184.

44 Evan Stark, 'Introduction to the Second Edition' in Evan Stark, *Coercive Control and the Criminal Law* (Oxford University Press 2022) 7.

45 Home Office, Summary of Responses n29 11.

46 In a study in Maine, stalking was found to occur within 80% of domestic abuse cases: Michael Sazl, 'The Struggle to Make Stalking a Crime: A Legislative Road Map of How to Develop Effective Stalking Legislation in Maine' (1998) 23 Seton Hall Legislative Journal 57. This finding was mirrored by Jane Monkton-Smith in the UK: see Jane Monkton-Smith et al, 'Exploring the Relationship between Stalking and Homicide' (Suzy Lamplugh Trust 2017) and also by Charlotte Barlow et al, 'Putting Coercive Control into Practice: Problems and Possibilities' (2020) 60(1) British Journal of Criminology 160.

47 HC Deb, 20 January 2015, Vol 591, Col 171.

48 HC Deb, 20 January 2015, Vol 591, Col 172.

49 Ibid.

50 Ibid.

51 Joanne Clough, 'Criminal Law Legislation Update' [2016] Journal of Criminal Law 3, 3.

52 Serious Crime Bill 2014–2015, Notices of Amendment 7 January 2015, House of Commons Public Bill Committee; Serious Crime Bill 2014–2015 Written Evidence (22 January 2015) SC12 as cited in Bettinson and Bishop, Discrete Offence n42 191.

53 Charlotte Bishop, 'Domestic Violence: The Limitations of a Legal Response' in Sarah Hilda and Vanessa Bettinson (eds), *Interdisciplinary Perspectives on Protection, Prevention and Intervention* (Palgrave Macmillan 2016) 68.

54 Karl Laird, 'Parts 5 and 6 of the Serious Crime Act 2015 – More than Mere Miscellany' [2015] Criminal Law Review 789, 800.

55 Tanya Palmer, 'Failing to See the Wood for the Trees: Chronic Sexual Violation and the Criminal Law' 2020 84(6) The Journal of Criminal Law 573–573.

56 Paul McGorrery and McMahon, 'Criminalising "the Worst" Part: Operationalising the Offence of Coercive Control in England and Wales' (2019) 11 Criminal Law Review 957, 963.

57 Interview with Judge Little (20 March 2018) 3.

58 Bishop, Domestic Violence n53 68.

59 Bettinson and Bishop, Discrete Offence n43 192.

60 Stark, Coercive Control n1 228.

61 Cassandra Wiener, 'Seeing What Is Invisible in Plain Sight: Policing Coercive Control' (2017) 56(4) Howard Journal of Crime and Justice 500. See also Iain Brennan, 'Service Provider Difficulties in Operationalizing Coercive Control' (2019) 25(6) Violence against Women 635.

62 HC Deb, 20 January 2015, Vol 591, Col 172.

63 Stark, Introduction to the Second Edition n44.

64 Michael Johnson, *A Typology of Domestic Violence Intimate Terrorism, Violent Resistance and Situational Couple Violence* (University Press 2008).

65 Home Office, 'Controlling or Coercive Behaviour in an Intimate Relationship Statutory Guidance Framework' (Home Office December 2015) available at <https://assets.publishing.service.gov.uk/government/uploads/system/uploads/attachment_data/file/482528/Controlling_or_coercive_behaviour_-_statutory_guidance.pdf> accessed 7 May 2021.

66 [2017] EWCA Crim 1631.

67 [2017] EWCA Crim 2450 [26].

68 [2019] EWCA Crim 916.

69 Ibid 4.

70 Ibid 8.

71 Ibid 18.

72 See, for example, *Ramskill* [2021] EWCA Crim 61; *Dalgarno* [2020] EWCA Crim 290; *Holden* [2019] EWCA Crim 1885 and *Berenger* [2019] EWCA Crim 1842.

73 Tuerkeimer, Recognizing and Remedying the Harm of Battering n2 980.

74 [2019] EWCA Crim 1842.

75 Ibid [3].

76 Ibid [12].

77 Ibid [22].

78 Palmer, Failing to See the Wood for the Trees n55 573.

79 Palmer, Failing to See the Wood for the Trees n55 573.

80 Adrienne Barnett, '"Greater than the Mere Sum of Its Parts": Coercive Control and the Question of Proof' [2017] Child and Family Law Quarterly 379, 380.

81 McGorrery and McMahon, Criminalising "the Worst" Part n56 964.

82 Ibid.

83 Ibid.

84 Ibid.

85 Ibid.

86 Home Office, *Review of the Controlling or Coercive Behaviour Offence* (Home Office Research Report 122, Home Office 2021) 26.

87 Ibid.

88 Ibid.

89 Ibid.

90 Ibid. 11.

91 Michele Burman and Oona Brooks-Hay, 'Aligning Policy and Law? The Creation of a Domestic Abuse Offence Incorporating Coercive Control' (2018) 18(1) Criminology & Criminal Justice 67, 78.

92 Ibid.

93 See n34, in particular Justice Committee, Stage One Report n33 para 47. See also interview with Marsha Scott, Chief Executive of Women's Aid (Edinburgh, 22 October 2019).

94 Deborah Tuerkheimer, 'Breakups' (2013) 25 Yale Journal of Law and Feminism 51; interview with Karen (6 October 2016); interview with Kim (24 November 2016); interview with Sarah (29 June 2016) 1.

95 Sarah, Survivors Focus Group (8 September 2016).

96 Karen n94 1.
97 Tuerkheimer, Breakups n94 15.
98 Interview with Judge Harwood (21 May 2018) 9.
99 McGorrery and McMahon, Criminalising "the Worst" Part n56.
100 Hansard HL Deb 5 Jan 2021, vol 809, col 100.
101 Home Office, Review n86 23.
102 See Detective Constable James' comments on the difficulties of trying to use s. 76 to prosecute in the context of a difficult mother-daughter relationship: Police Focus Group (30 November 2016) 3.
103 Crown Prosecution Service, 'Man Sentenced for Controlling and Coercive Behaviour against His Mother' (26 March 2019) available at <https://www.cps.gov.uk/london-north/news/man-sentenced-controlling-and-coercive-behaviour-against-mother> accessed 26 June 2019; Andrew Bardsley, 'This Bully Terrorized His Adoptive Mother and Demanded Booze Money' *Greater Manchester News* (Manchester 26 February 2019) available at <https://www.manchestereveningnews.co.uk/news/greater-manchester-news/daniel-beech-openshaw-manchester-court-15885131> accessed 26 June 2019; Emily Walker, 'Crawley Man Banned from Seeing Mother after Months of Bullying' *The Argus* (Brighton 19 March 2018) available at <https://www.theargus.co.uk/news/16097510.crawley-man-banned-from-seeing-mother-after-months-of-bullying/> accessed 26 June 2018; Stuart Able, 'The Evil Grandson Who Controlled His Own Family and How They Got Him Back' *The Plymouth News* (Plymouth 6 June 2018) available at <https://www.plymouthherald.co.uk/news/plymouth-news/evil-grandson-who-controlled-family-1647659> accessed 26 June 2019.
104 The Scottish Government, 'A Criminal Offence of Domestic Abuse Scottish Consultation Paper' (Scottish Government, March 2015) available at <https://www2.gov.scot/Resource/0049/00491481.pdf> accessed 28 June 2019, 6.
105 Sara Simmons et al, 'Long-Term Consequences of Intimate Partner Abuse on Physical Health, Emotional Well-Being and Problem Behaviors' (2018) 33(4) Journal of Interpersonal Violence 540; see also Wiener, Seeing What Is Invisible in Plain Sight n61.
106 Marilyn McMahon and Paul McGorrery, 'Criminalising Emotional Abuse, Intimidation and Economic Abuse in the Context of Family Violence: The Tasmanian Experience' (2016) 35(2) University of Tasmania Law Review 1; Sandra Walklate and Kate Fitz-Gibbon, 'The Criminalisation of Coercive Control: The Power of Law?' (2019) 8(4) International Journal for Crime, Justice and Social Democracy 94.
107 Tuerkheimer, n1 980.
108 McGorrery and McMahon, Criminalising the "Worst" Part n56.
109 Mary Ann Dutton, 'Understanding Women's Responses to Domestic Violence: A Redefinition of Battered Woman Syndrome' (1992) 21 Hofstra Law Review 1191, 1208.
110 Susan Edwards, 'Coercion and Compulsion – Re-imagining Crimes and Defences' [2016] Criminal Law Review 876.
111 Interview with Detective Constable Canford (20 November 2017) 4.
112 Stark, Coercive Control n1 5.
113 Alafair Burke, 'Domestic Violence as a Crime of Pattern and Intent: An Alternative Reconceptualization' (2007) (75) George Washington Law Review 558, 602.
114 Bettinson and Bishop, Discrete Offence n43 194. Jennifer Youngs, 'Domestic Violence and the Criminal Law: Reconceptualising Reform' (2015) 79(1) Journal of Criminal Law 55.
115 Judge Harwood n98 4.
116 Jeremy Armstrong, 'Violent Boyfriend Is Cleared after Judge Says Partner Is 'Too Strong' to Be Victim' *The Mirror* (London 23 November 2018).
117 Ibid.

118 Suzanne Jacob, 'Yes, You Can Be "Strong" and Still Be a Victim of Coercive Control' *The New Statesman* (London 27 November 2018).

119 Ibid.

120 Home Office, Review n86 (my brackets).

121 Julia Tolmie, 'Coercive Control: To Criminalize or Not to Criminalize?' (2018) 18(1) Criminology and Criminal Justice 50, 9.

122 Judge Little n57 1.

123 Ibid. 2.

124 Ibid. 1.

125 Antonia Cretney and Gwynn Davis, 'Prosecuting "Domestic" Assault' [1996] Criminal Law Review 162.

126 Louise Ellison and Vanessa Munro, 'Taking Trauma Seriously: Critical Reflections on the Criminal Justice Process' (2017) 21(3) International Journal of Evidence and Proof 183.

127 Vanessa Bettinson, 'Adding to the Domestic Abuse Criminal Law Framework: The Domestic Abuse Act 2021' (2022) Criminal Law Review 92.

128 For a full discussion of the impact of the way in which a victim, post trauma, gives evidence on a jury see Louise Ellison and Vanessa Munro, 'Reacting to Rape Exploring Mock Jurors' Assessments of Complainant Credibility' (2009) 49 British Journal of Criminology 202.

129 Ellison and Munro, Taking Trauma Seriously n126, 192.

130 Tolmie, Coercive Control n121 7.

131 For a discussion of the effect of trauma on evidence giving generally see Ellison and Munro, Taking Trauma Seriously n126.

132 Ibid.

133 Martha Mahoney, 'Legal Images of Battered Women: Redefining the Issue of Separation' (1991) 90(1) Michigan Law Review 90, 161.

134 Stark, Introduction to the Second Edition n44 30.

135 Bettinson and Bishop, Discrete Offence n43 194.

136 Interview with Jen (15 January 2016) 14.

137 Survivors Focus Group (8 September 2016).

138 Ibid.

139 Interview with Judge Fern (6 March 2018) 1.

140 Mahoney, Legal Images of Battered Women n133; Dutton, Understanding Women's Responses n109; Cathy Humphreys and Ravi Thiara, 'Neither Justice Nor Protection: Women's Experiences of Post-Separation Violence' (2003) 25(3) Journal of Social Welfare and Family Law 195; Stark, Coercive Control n1; Vanessa Bettinson and Charlotte Bishop, 'Evidencing Domestic Violence, Including Behaviour That Falls under the New Offence of 'Controlling or Coercive Behaviour' (2018) 22(1) The International Journal of Evidence and Proof 3.

141 Stark, Coercive Control n1; Bettinson and Bishop, Evidencing Domestic Violence n140.

142 Charlotte Bishop, 'Why It Is So Hard to Prosecute Cases of Controlling or Coercive Behaviour' *The Conversation* (2016) available at <http://theconversation.com/why-its-so-hard-to-prosecute-cases-of-coercive-or-controlling-behaviour-66108> accessed 1 August 2019.

143 Tolmie, Coercive Control n121 55.

144 Finch, Criminalisation of Stalking n13.

145 Sally Kyd et al, *Clarkson and Keating: Criminal Law* (Sweet and Maxwell 2020) 146.

146 Meghan Bumb, 'Domestic Violence Law, Abusers' Intent, and Social Media: How Transaction-Bound Statutes Are the True Threats to Prosecuting Perpetrators of Gender-Based Violence' (2017) 82(2) Brooklyn Law 917, 925.

147 Victor Tadros, 'Rape without Consent' (2006) 26(3) Oxford Journal of Legal Studies 515, 524.

148 Tuerkheimer, Recognising and Remedying the Harm of Battering n1 959; Burke, Domestic Violence n113 558.
149 Burke, Domestic Violence n113 556.
150 Tuerkheimer, Recognizing and Remedying the Harm of Battering n1 1022, her emphasis.
151 Bettinson and Bishop, A Discrete Offence n43 195; Youngs, Domestic Violence and the Criminal Law n114.
152 Bettinson and Bishop, A Discrete Offence n32 195.
153 Ibid.
154 Judge Little n57 5.
155 The name of the defendant has been changed to protect the anonymity of Judge Little.
156 Judge Little n57 5.
157 Ibid. 6.
158 It is not possible to cite the Court of Appeal judgment in question as this identifies Judge Little.
159 This approach was approved by the Court of Appeal in cases such as *Chanaa* [2019] EWCA Crim 2335 (where the defendant was convicted of rape and controlling or coercive behaviour); *Cunningham* [2019] EWCA Crim 2101 (four counts of rape and controlling or coercive behaviour) and *Holden* [2019] EWCA Crim 1885 (rape and controlling or coercive behaviour).
160 *Parkin* [2018] EWCA Crim 2764.
161 Ibid. [39].
162 Serious Crime Act 2015, s 11.
163 Judge Little n57; Judge Harwood n98.
164 Domestic Abuse (Scotland) Act 2018, s 8.
165 Bettinson, Adding to the Domestic Abuse Criminal Law Framework n127.
166 Libby Brooks, Scotland Set to Pass "Gold Standard" Domestic Abuse Law n3.

Bibliography

Able S, 'The Evil Grandson Who Controlled His Own Family and How They Got Him Back' *The Plymouth News* (Plymouth 6 June 2018) available at <https://www.plymouthherald.co.uk/news/plymouth-news/evil-grandson-who-controlled-family-1647659> accessed 26 June 2019.

Addison N and Perry J, 'Will the New Stalking Legislation Deliver for Victims?' (2013) 177 Criminal Law and Justice Weekly 53.

Armstrong J, 'Violent Boyfriend Is Cleared after Judge Says Partner Is "Too Strong" To Be Victim' *The Mirror* (London 23 November 2018).

AVA against Violence and Abuse, 'AVA's Response to Cross-Government Definition of Domestic Violence: A Consultation' (document on file with me).

Bardsley A, 'This Bully Terrorized His Adoptive Mother and Demanded Booze Money' *Greater Manchester News* (Manchester, 26 February 2019) available at <https://www.manchestereveningnews.co.uk/news/greater-manchester-news/daniel-beech-openshaw-manchester-court-15885131> accessed 26 June 2019.

Barlow C, Johnson K, Walklate S and Humphries L, 'Putting Coercive Control into Practice: Problems and Possibilities' (2020) 60(1) British Journal of Criminology 160.

Barnett A, '"Greater than the Mere Sum of Its Parts": Coercive Control and the Question of Proof' (2017) Child and Family Law Quarterly 379.

Bettinson V, 'Adding to the Domestic Abuse Criminal Law Framework: The Domestic Abuse Act 2021' (2022) Criminal Law Review 92.

Bettinson V and Bishop C, 'Is the Creation of a Discrete Offence of Coercive Control Necessary to Combat Domestic Violence' (2015) 66(2) Northern Ireland Legal Quarterly 179.

Bettinson V and Bishop C, 'Evidencing Domestic Violence, Including Behaviour That Falls under the New Offence of 'Controlling or Coercive Behaviour' (2018) 22(1) The International Journal of Evidence and Proof 3.

Bishop C, 'Domestic Violence: The Limitations of a Legal Response' in Hilda S and Bettinson V (eds), *Interdisciplinary Perspectives on Protection, Prevention and Intervention* (Palgrave Macmillan 2016).

Bishop C, 'Why It Is So Hard to Prosecute Cases of Controlling or Coercive Behaviour' *The Conversation* (2016) available at <http://theconversation.com/why-its-so-hard-to-prosecute-cases-of-coercive-or-controlling-behaviour-66108> accessed 1 August 2019.

Brennan I, 'Service Provider Difficulties in Operationalizing Coercive Control' (2019) 25(6) Violence against Women 635.

Brooks L, 'Scotland Set to Pass "Gold Standard" Domestic Abuse Law' *The Guardian* (London 1 February 2018) available at <https://www.theguardian.com/society/2018/feb/01/scotland-set-to-pass-gold-standard-domestic-abuse-law> accessed 28 March 2018.

Bumb M, 'Domestic Violence Law, Abusers' Intent, and Social Media: How Transaction-Bound Statutes Are the True Threats to Prosecuting Perpetrators of Gender-Based Violence' (2017) 82(2) Brooklyn Law 917.

Burke A, 'Domestic Violence as a Crime of Pattern and Intent: An Alternative Reconceptualization' (2007) 75 George Washington Law Review 558.

Burman M and Brooks-Hay O, 'Aligning Policy and Law? The Creation of a Domestic Abuse Offence Incorporating Coercive Control' (2018) 18(1) Criminology & Criminal Justice 67.

Clough J, 'Criminal Law Legislation Update' (2016) 80(6) Journal of Criminal Law 3.

Cretney A and Davis G, 'Prosecuting "Domestic" Assault' (1996) Criminal Law Review 162.

Crown Prosecution Service, 'Man Sentenced for Controlling and Coercive Behaviour against His Mother' (26 March 2019) available at <https://www.cps.gov.uk/london-north/news/man-sentenced-controlling-and-coercive-behaviour-against-mother> accessed 26 June 2019.

Dutton M, 'Understanding Women's Responses to Domestic Violence: A Redefinition of Battered Woman Syndrome' (1992) 21 Hofstra Law Review 1191.

Edwards S, 'Coercion and Compulsion – Re-imagining Crimes and Defences' (2016) Criminal Law Review 876.

Ellison L and Munro V, 'Reacting to Rape Exploring Mock Jurors' Assessments of Complainant Credibility' (2009) 49 British Journal of Criminology 202.

Ellison L and Munro V, 'Taking Trauma Seriously: Critical Reflections on the Criminal Justice Process' (2017) 21(3) International Journal of Evidence and Proof 183.

Finch E, *The Criminalisation of Stalking: Constructing the Problem and Evaluating the Solution* (Cavendish 2001).

Gov.uk, 'Guidance Domestic Violence and Abuse' (2018) available at <https://www.gov.uk/guidance/domestic-violence-and-abuse> accessed 28 March 2018.

Harris J, *An Evaluation of the Use and Effectiveness of the Protection from Harassment Act 1997* (Home Office Research Study 203, Home Office 2000).

HC Deb, 20 January 2015, Vol 591, Col 171.

HC Deb, 20 January 2015, Vol 591, Col 172.

HL Deb, 5 January 2021, Vol 809, Col 100.

Home Office, 'Cross-Government Definition of Domestic Violence a Consultation' (December 2011) available at <https://www.gov.uk/government/uploads/system/uploads/attachment_data/file/157798/dv-definition-consultation.pdf> accessed 2 February 2018.

Home Office, 'Circular 018/2012' available at <https://www.gov.uk/government/publications/a-change-to-the-protection-from-harassment-act-1997-introduction-of-two-new-specific-offences-of-stalking> accessed 26 July 2017.

Home Office, 'New Definition of Domestic Violence' (19 September 2012) available at <https://www.gov.uk/government/news/new-definition-of-domestic-violence> accessed 12 September 2017.

Home Office, 'Strengthening the Law on Domestic Abuse Consultation Summary of Responses' (December 2014) 5 available at <https://www.gov.uk/government/uploads/system/uploads/attachment_data/file/389002/StrengtheningLawDomestic AbuseResponses.pdf> accessed 31 July 2017.

Home Office, 'Strengthening the Law on Domestic Abuse: A Consultation' (2014) 9 available at <https://www.gov.uk/government/uploads/system/uploads/attachment_data/file/344674/Strengthening_the_law_on_Domestic_Abuse_-_A_Consultation_WEB.PDF> accessed 28 March 2018.

Home Office, 'Controlling or Coercive Behaviour in an Intimate Relationship Statutory Guidance Framework' (Home Office December 2015) available at <https://assets.publishing.service.gov.uk/government/uploads/system/uploads/attachment_data/file/482528/Controlling_or_coercive_behaviour_-_statutory_guidance.pdf> accessed 7 May 2021.

Home Office, *Review of the Controlling or Coercive Behaviour Offence* (Home Office Research Report 122, Home Office 2021).

House of Commons Public Bill Committee Serious Crime Bill 2014–2015 Written Evidence (22 January 2015) SC12.

Humphreys C and Thiara R, 'Neither Justice nor Protection: Women's Experiences of Post-Separation Violence' (2003) 25(3) Journal of Social Welfare and Family Law 195.

Jacob S, 'Yes, You Can Be "Strong" and Still Be a Victim of Coercive Control' *The New Statesman* (London 27 November 2018).

Johnson M, *A Typology of Domestic Violence Intimate Terrorism, Violent Resistance and Situational Couple Violence* (University Press 2008).

Justice Committee, *Stage One Report on the Domestic Abuse (Scotland) Bill* (SP Paper 198, 16th Report, 2017).

Justice Unions' Parliamentary Group, 'Independent Parliamentary Inquiry into Stalking Law Reform: Main Findings and Recommendations' (2012) available at <http://www.dashriskchecklist.co.uk/wp-content/uploads/2016/09/Stalking-Law-Reform-Findings-Report-2012.pdf> accessed 9 May 2017.

Kelly L and Westmarland L, 'Time for a Rethink. Why the Current Government Definition of Domestic Violence Is a Problem.' (2014) available at <http://www.troubleandstrife.org/2014/04/time-for-a-rethink-why-the-current-government-definition-of-domestic-violence-is-a-problem/> accessed 25 October 2017.

Kyd S, Eliott T and Walters M, Clarkson and Keating: *Criminal Law* (Sweet and Maxwell 2020).

Laird K, 'Parts 5 and 6 of the Serious Crime Act 2015 – More than Mere Miscellany' (2015) Criminal Law Review 789.

Mahoney M, 'Legal Images of Battered Women: Redefining the Issue of Separation' (1991) 90(1) Michigan Law Review 90.

McGorrery P and McMahon M, 'Criminalising "the Worst" Part: Operationalising the Offence of Coercive Control in England and Wales' (2019) 11 Criminal Law Review 957.

McMahon M and McGorrery P, 'Criminalising Emotional Abuse, Intimidation and Economic Abuse in the Context of Family Violence: The Tasmanian Experience' (2016) 35(2) University of Tasmania Law Review 1.

Monckton Smith J, Szymanska K and Haile S, *Exploring the Relationship between Stalking and Homicide* (Report by the Homicide Research Group, University of Gloucestershire, 2017) available at <http://eprints.glos.ac.uk/4553/> accessed 2 October 2017.

Palmer T, 'Failing to See the Wood for the Trees: Chronic Sexual Violation and the Criminal Law' (2020) 84(6) The Journal of Criminal Law 573.

Quilter J, 'Evaluating Criminalisation as a Strategy in Relation to Non-Physical Family Violence' in Marilyn McMahon and Paul McGorrery (eds), *Criminalising Coercive Control* (Springer 2020).

Sazl M, 'The Struggle to Make Stalking a Crime: A Legislative Road Map of How to Develop Effective Stalking Legislation in Maine' (1998) 23 Seton Hall Legislative Journal 57.

Scottish Government, 'A Criminal Offence of Domestic Abuse Scottish Consultation Paper' (Scottish Government, March 2015) available at <https://www2.gov.scot/Resource/0049/00491481.pdf> accessed 28 June 2019.

Simmons S, Knight K and Manard S, 'Long-Term Consequences of Intimate Partner Abuse on Physical Health, Emotional Well-Being and Problem Behaviors' (2018) 33(4) Journal of Interpersonal Violence 540.

Stark E, *Coercive Control How Men Entrap Women in Personal Life* (Oxford University Press 2007).

Stark E, 'Introduction to the Second Edition' in Stark E (ed) *Coercive Control and the Criminal Law* (Oxford University Press 2022).

Tadros V, 'Rape without Consent' (2006) 26(3) Oxford Journal of Legal Studies 515.

Tolmie J, 'Coercive Control: To Criminalize or Not to Criminalize?' (2018) 18(1) Criminology and Criminal Justice 50.

Tuerkheimer D, 'Recognizing and Remedying the Harm of Battering: A Call to Criminalize Domestic Violence' (2004) 94(4) Journal of Criminal Law and Criminology 959.

Tuerkheimer D, 'Breakups' (2013) 25 Yale Journal of Law and Feminism 51.

Walker E, 'Crawley Man Banned from Seeing Mother after Months of Bullying' *The Argus* (Brighton 19 March 2018) available at <https://www.theargus.co.uk/news/16097510.crawley-man-banned-from-seeing-mother-after-months-of-bullying/> accessed 26 June 2018.

Walklate S and Fitz-Gibbon K, 'The Criminalisation of Coercive Control: The Power of Law?' (2019) 8(4) International Journal for Crime, Justice and Social Democracy 94.

Wiener C, 'Seeing What Is Invisible in Plain Sight: Policing Coercive Control' (2017) 56(4) Howard Journal of Crime and Justice 500.

Youngs J, Domestic Violence and the Criminal Law: Reconceptualising Reform (2015) 79(1) Journal of Criminal Law 55.

Cases

Barratt [2017] EWCA Crim 1631.
Berenger [2019] EWCA Crim 1842.
Challen [2019] EWCA Crim 916.

Chanaa [2019] EWCA Crim 2335.
Conlon [2017] EWCA Crim 2450.
Cunningham [2019] EWCA Crim 2101.
Curtis [2010] EWCA Criminal 123.
Dalgarno [2020] EWCA Crim 290.
Holden [2019] EWCA Crim 1885.
Parkin [2018] EWCA Crim 2764.
Ramskill [2021] EWCA Crim 61.
Widdows (2011) 175 JP 345.

Legislation

Domestic Abuse Act 2021.
Domestic Abuse (Scotland) Act 2018.
Offences against the Person Act 1861.
Protection of Freedoms Act 2012.
Protection from Harassment Act 1997.
Serious Crime Act 2015.
Sexual Offences Act 2003.

6

THE SCOTTISH APPROACH

Introduction

On 1 February 2018, a unanimous vote by the Scottish Parliament passed the Domestic Abuse (Scotland) Bill 2018 into law. This is an important moment for everyone all over the world with an interest in domestic abuse and the criminal law: Scotland has done things differently. Scotland has a distinctive approach to what it frames as 'gender-based violence'.[1] Devolution in 1999 highlighted that there were significant differences between England/Wales and Scotland in relation to the organisation of policy responses to social problems.[2] A Scottish approach to domestic abuse emerged, as devolution allowed for an accompanying decentralisation of policy – allowing the women's sector and newly elected members of a supportive Scottish Parliament to work together to prioritise violence against women.[3] In particular, the women's sector moved to implement a national partnership approach which, crucially, was based on *gendered* understandings of domestic abuse.

The academic debate on the relationship between gender and abuse was the subject of a detailed analysis in chapter 1. In that chapter I explained that an (admittedly tentative) international consensus has been reached around Evan Stark's conceptualisation of coercive control. As I explained in chapter 1, my position is in alignment with Stark and Michael Johnson. I accept that men and women in intimate relationships can abuse each other in the absence of an imbalance of power between them (Johnson calls this kind of abuse 'common couple violence' or 'situational couple violence').[4] But coercive control is, as Stark says, domestic abuse at its most dangerous and insidious and is perpetrated mainly by men against women.

Scotland has been much more prepared than England and Wales to adopt the distinctions between coercive control and situational couple violence at a policy,

DOI: 10.4324/9780429201844-7

and then legislative, level and it is this more than any other fact that explains the more progressive aspects of the Domestic Abuse Scotland Act (2018) (the DASA). This chapter is divided into three parts. I begin with an analysis of the Scottish context, which I argue is critical to what became possible in terms of later legislation. I go on to review the Scottish Consultation process, before turning to the DASA itself. I finish with an update on implementation, and conclude that while it is too early to give definitive answers about the efficacy of this progressive approach, the early figures are encouraging.

The Scottish Context

Dr Marsha Scott, (CEO of Scottish Women's Aid), points out that the definition of domestic abuse in policy documents in Scotland has been, from the beginning, based on gendered notions of abuse. It was restricted to partners and ex-partners, and taken from the UN 1993 Declaration on the Elimination of Violence against Women. This anchoring in international rights-based understandings of violence against women, Scott thinks, is fundamental to why the women's sector in Scotland is different – in her view it is more connected. She said to me that:

> This is one of the things that makes the policy context in Scotland so different. Which is that you have this internationally connected women's centre … our links and expertise and recognition and influence are in Europe, are in the UN. And they have been since 2000. So we have a women's community, a women's expert group of international links.[5]

In 2000, the year after devolution, the Scottish Executive[6] published a 'keystone'[7] *National Strategy to Address Domestic Abuse in Scotland*.[8] This National Strategy, which established the Scottish Executive's first national group focusing on domestic abuse (the Scottish Partnership on Domestic Abuse),[9] promoted the early adoption of a working definition of domestic abuse which is progressive in three ways – it foregrounds gender, it restricts abuse to partners and ex-partners, and frames abuse as controlling behaviour:

> Domestic abuse (as gender based abuse) can be perpetrated by partners or ex-partners and can include physical abuse (assault and physical attack involving a range of behaviour) sexual abuse (acts which degrade and humiliate women and are perpetrated against their will (including rape) and mental and emotional abuse (such as threats, verbal abuse, racial abuse, withholding money and other types of controlling behaviour such as isolation from family or friends).[10]

The framing of domestic abuse as a gendered issue is a core assumption that underpins the National Strategy document. The introduction begins with the observation that, 'Domestic abuse *is one aspect of a range of forms of violence against women*, all of which must be tackled in Scotland'.[11] Commentators observe that this gendered framing of domestic abuse which began with the National Strategy document 'has formed the basis of Scottish initiatives ever since'.[12]

In 2000, this gendered definition of abuse was adopted widely across the government and the criminal justice system. Page 8 of the National Strategy document makes it clear that 'This strategy is aimed at politicians, policy makers, service providers and the public in Scotland, all of whom have a role in the elimination of domestic abuse and in supporting women or children who experience this'.[13] Specifically included on page 8 as relevant service providers who need to take account of the policy are police, legal professionals, social work services, the Crown Office and Procurator Fiscal Service (COPFS), housing services, court services and the Scottish Prison Service.[14] Interestingly one of the 'specific initiatives' identified in the action plan set out in the National Strategy Document is the setting up of a working group consisting of the Scottish Executive and the voluntary sector to consider, 'the consideration of the resource implications of new legislation and the implications for other aspects of policy/legislation'.[15]

A legal definition of domestic abuse has been incorporated into English/Welsh law[16] via the Domestic Abuse Act 2021 (the 'DAA'), section 1, which I discussed in some detail in the previous chapter. This DAA, section 1 definition is explicitly gender-free and includes 'family members' in the abuse. It lists what it frames as 'controlling or coercive behaviour' as one bullet point in a list of behaviours alongside physical and sexual violence, for example. The difference, in my view, between the two approaches is that in Scotland, the focus since at least 2000 has been on coercive control, whereas the DAA, section 1 definition does not frame domestic abuse around a power imbalance. This distinction – between centring coercive control (Scotland) and listing behaviours under one umbrella with no recognition of the significance of a power imbalance (the DAA, section 1) – explains much of the differences in approach in Scotland and England/Wales that followed.

As Scott points out, 'Scotland was an early adopter of Evan Stark's critique of the violent-incident model of domestic violence and his paradigm of coercive control'.[17] Stark had strong links with the women's sector in Scotland, and the Women's Support Project in Glasgow brought Stark to speak at a seminar even before his groundbreaking book was published in 2007.[18] He was invited to Edinburgh to speak at Scottish Women's Aid's national conference in 2007, just as his book was being published. Scott explains: 'That appearance by Evan Stark was the first of many all over Scotland in the ten years that followed, including a three-month stint as Leverhulme Vising Professor at the University of Edinburgh in 2014'.[19]

Stark's book achieved a paradigm shift worldwide in the context of the conceptualisation of domestic abuse but his influence in Scotland, (and I return to this below), has been particularly fundamental. Scott explains that there was a keen desire to understand the growing number of cases going through Scotland's court. In particular, Stark (and the work of Michael Johnson) was helpful in explaining why official figures, which conflated situational couple violence (one-off incidents of violence) with coercive control, had significant numbers of female perpetrators.

Separating those one-off incidents from the course of conduct offence (coercive control) allowed a very different picture of offending to emerge. In 2015, the COPFS invited Johnson to speak to attendees at its Prosecution College. Since then, Scott observes, 'references to "situational couple violence" can be found in numerous COPFS speeches and protocols'.

It is against this backdrop of devolution and a Stark informed approach that the sensational Bill Walker case highlighted the limitations of the legislative status quo. Just as in England and Wales, prior to the DASA, Scotland did not have a specific offence of domestic abuse. Domestic abuse in Scotland was prosecuted using a mostly familiar mix of associated common law and statutory offences, including (as in England and Wales) common assault, sexual offences and (unique to Scotland), 'threatening or abusive behaviour', further to section 38 Criminal Justice and Licensing (Scotland) Act 2010.[20]

In July 2012, Bill Walker, who was the former MSP for Dunfermline, was charged in the specialist domestic abuse court in Edinburgh of 23 counts of assault and one count of breach of the peace. These charges involved a 28-year history of abuse against his three ex-wives and a step-daughter. Much of his behaviour fits the model of control outlined in chapter 1: his third wife Diana Walker, for example, told of how he recorded all of her phone calls, and made her sign an agreement to do household chores in their home.[21] Sheriff Kathrine Mackie found Walker guilty of all charges and correctly sentenced him to the maximum permitted: one years' imprisonment. When she sentenced him, Sheriff Mackie observed that the evidence showed him to be 'controlling, domineering, demeaning and belittling' towards his former partners.[22]

It is fair to say that 'calls for the criminalisation of coercive control gained a new momentum following the Walker case'.[23] One week after Walker was sentenced, Lesley Thomson QC, then Solicitor General for Scotland, appointed Anne Marie Hicks to a newly created post of National Prosecutor for Domestic Abuse. Her responsibilities included: coordinating the prosecution services' response to domestic abuse cases across Scotland, reviewing prosecution policy with regard to domestic abuse crimes, and engaging with stakeholders to strengthen the collective response to domestic abuse cases, and working to raise awareness among prosecutors and the police.[24] The following year, on 8 May 1014, speaking at the annual COPFS conference, Thomson called on the Scottish Parliament to consider the creation of a bespoke offence of domestic abuse. She commented that:

> The patterns and consequences of coercive control so often experienced by victims of domestic abuse are simply not on the court's radar in any formal manner. Of course individual Sheriffs and Judges trained in this area will recognise these patterns from the evidence presented but there will be no charge before them requiring them to deal with this aspect of the accused's behaviour. Instead it is for them to sentence the accused on the basis of the crime that is proved − an assault, a statutory breach of the peace or some

other offence. Each incident is treated in isolation and the cumulative harm to the victim is not recognised, instead such an episodic approach leads to the minimisation of abuse by the criminal justice system.[25]

Thomson concluded her speech with a call to arms: 'in my personal view, there are strong arguments in favour of creating a new bespoke criminal offence of domestic abuse'.[26]

The Scottish Consultation(s)

The Scottish Parliament rose to Thomson's challenge, and there were, in fact, two public consultations in the time period March 2015 to August 2016. The first consultation ran for 16 weeks, from March to June 2015. Entitled *Equally Safe – Reforming the Criminal Law to Address Domestic Abuse and Sexual Offences*, it explored the need for a specific offence.[27]

I said in the preceding chapter that the remit of the one (eight week) English/ Welsh consultation *Strengthening the Law on Domestic Abuse*[28] that took place in 2014 was unfortunately narrow. In particular I pointed out that there was a failure to consider how, or to what extent the existing laws were capturing domestic abuse. In many ways the labelling of the reviews is instructive: the English/Welsh consultation is narrowed to looking at strengthening existing law even before it has begun. The possibility that existing law might be in need of *reforming* is overlooked. Furthermore, the wording of the Scottish title *Equally Safe* frames the investigation within the equality, (and therefore gender), agenda – an emphasis that is avoided by England/Wales altogether.

In the introduction to the first consultation the Scottish Government explains:

> A commitment was given to a "whole systems" review of the approach taken to these issues within the justice system. The review includes consideration of the criminal law relating to sexual offences and domestic abuse: the support available for victims, the time taken to complete cases through the justice system and the impact of justice interventions in changing perpetrator behaviour and wider public attitudes.[29]

It continues:

> The question of whether the current criminal law reflects the true experience of victims of long-term domestic abuse, including coercive control, and whether a specific domestic abuse offence would improve the ability of people to access justice through effective prosecution of domestic abuse.[30]

Later on, under the heading 'Current Legal Framework', on page 9 of the first consultation, the Scottish Government conducts exactly the review of the existing legal infrastructure that I said was missing from the English consultation. One of the conclusions drawn is the observation that 'Even victims whose cases are successfully prosecuted can be left thinking that their experience as a victim of domestic abuse has not been fully recognised by the courts'.[31] This, the Government states, is in part because

> The severity of the specific incidents of violence or threatening behaviour for which the abuser is prosecuted can only be fully understood against the background of on-going psychological abuse and controlling behaviour. However, at present, it is not formally recognised by the courts and judges and sheriffs must sentence the offender on the basis of the offences which were proven in that particular case.[32]

At the outset of the consultation process, therefore, the Scottish Government is aware that the context can render domestic violence offences different in a way that means the wrong and the harm are not captured by the existing criminal law on violence against the person. This realisation paved the way for the more progressive reform that followed.

The Scottish Government Consultation Paper, *A Criminal Offence of Domestic Abuse*, firstly sets out the responses to that first consultation. An overwhelming majority (93%) of respondents felt that the existing criminal law 'does not re-cognise the particular nature and consequences of domestic abuse sufficiently'.[33] Having established the need for a new offence, *A Criminal Offence* then launches a second consultation by setting out a further set of questions directed at different ways that the new offence could or should be drafted. *An Analysis of Consultation Responses*, which collates the responses to the second consultation, was published in August 2016. On 17 March 2017 the Domestic Abuse (Scotland) Bill was officially announced in Parliament and allocated to the Justice Committee for the Scottish parliamentary scrutiny process.

The Justice Committee thus oversaw the formal evidence-gathering process from March 2017 onwards. The Justice Committee issued a call for evidence on the Bill and received 45 responses. It took public evidence at six meetings in May and June 2017. It also heard private testimony from survivors at three concurrent meetings. In addition, throughout the drafting period, members of the Government's Bill team corresponded regularly with policy experts in Scottish Women's Aid, who tested the bill language with survivors and service users. Focus groups were held by Scottish Women's Aid in a number of areas of Scotland to support the work of the Justice Committee by gathering survivor expert input on the proposals.

The Domestic Abuse (Scotland) Act 2018

The Domestic Abuse (Scotland) Act 2018 (DASA) came into force two years later on 1 April 2019. Section 1 creates the new offence:

1. A person commits an offence is −

    a. The person ("A" engages in a course of behaviour which is abusive of A's partner or ex-partner ("B") and

    b. Both of the further conditions are met.

2. The further conditions are −

    a. That a reasonable person would consider the course of behaviour to be likely to cause B to suffer physical or psychological harm,

    b. That either −

        i. A intends by the course of behaviour to cause B to suffer physical or psychological harm, or

        ii. A is reckless as to whether the course of behaviour causes B to suffer physical or psychological harm.

3. In the further conditions, the references to psychological harm include fear, alarm and distress.

Section (2) defines what constitutes abusive behaviour:

1. Subsections (2) to (4) elaborate on section 1(1) as to A's behaviour.

2. Behaviour which is abusive of B includes (in particular) −

    a. Behaviour directed at B that is violent, threatening or intimidating,

    b. Behaviour directed at B, at a child of B or at another person that either −

        i. Has as its purpose (or among its purposes) one or more of the relevant effects set out in subsection (3), or

        ii. Would be considered by a reasonable person to be likely to have one or more of the relevant effects set out in subsection (3).

3. The relevant effects are of −

    a. Making B depend on, or subordinate to, A,

    b. Isolating B from friends, relatives or other sources of support,

    c. Controlling, regulating or monitoring B's day-to-day activities,

    d. Depriving B of, or restricting B's, freedom of action,

    e. Frightening, humiliating, degrading or punishing B.

4. In subsection (2)

    a. In paragraph (a) the reference to violent behaviour includes sexual violence as well as physical violence,

    b. In paragraph (b), the reference to a child is to a person who is under 18 years of age.

I use the rest of this chapter to reflect on what Scotland has done differently. In essence, Scotland took three steps into the unknown. The most radical is the decision to cover physical and sexual violence as well as psychological control within the same offence. Equally as important is the removal of harm to the victim as a constituent part of the offence. Also radical and progressive is the way that controlling behaviours are captured by the Act. Just as with the preceding chapter, I draw on interviews with the judiciary to report on how the DASA has been working in the courts thus far. Unlike the previous chapter, it is also possible with the DASA to draw on the extensive consultation process, and on my interviews with the COPFS (the English/Welsh equivalent, the Crown Prosecution Service (the 'CPS') were unfortunately unable to take part in the research project). Unfortunately, however, this chapter does not benefit from an analysis of early cases – there are no reported DASA cases at the time of writing, and my plans to observe early trials have been thwarted by the covid-19 pandemic which has severely restricted my ability to travel and the courts' accessibility to observers during 2020–2021. This will be an important future project.

Treating It 'All of a Piece'[34]

This vital question, of whether and to what extent the new law should include previously criminal behaviour is the central preoccupation of the first consultation. The Scottish Government realised immediately that it had two options. Option one was to follow the English/Welsh approach, i.e. 'to create an offence which is specifically limited in scope to dealing with psychological abuse and coercive and controlling behaviour in a relationship which is of a kind that could not necessarily be prosecuted under the existing criminal law'.[35] Option two, which is significantly more radical, and for which there was no precedent, was 'to provide for a general offence of "domestic abuse" that covers the whole range of conduct that can make up a pattern of abusive behaviour within a relationship'.[36]

At this early stage, the overwhelming response from respondents was to take the second approach and have the one, all-inclusive offence.[37] The Scottish Government agreed. The reason given is instructive:

> Our reason for taking this second approach is that, where the criminal conduct in question consists of an on-going "campaign" of abuse which may comprise physical and/or sexual assaults, threats, the placing of unreasonable restrictions of the victim's day-to-day life and acts intended to humiliate or degrade the victim, we consider there is a strong case for allowing the prosecution the flexibility to treat it as all "of a piece" and enabling the entire ambit of an offender's abusive behaviour to be libelled within a single offence, where considered appropriate to do so. The alternative would require that certain aspects of a course of conduct amounting to domestic abuse must be libelled as separate offences because they fall outwith the scope of the "domestic abuse" offence.[38]

This paragraph of *A Criminal Offence* shows the importance of an understanding of the different typologies of abuse at a governmental and policy level. The reason, *A Criminal Offence* explains, for choosing to create the one offence is that it gives the prosecution flexibility. Where it is 'appropriate' (where there is an abusive course of conduct, i.e. coercive control) the prosecution can use the one offence, to prosecute the offending behaviour 'all of a piece'.[39] It is still open to the prosecution to use the existing offences against the person regime to prosecute violence that is situational. But, critically, the Scottish Government realised that if it were to follow the Serious Crime Act 2015, s 76 ('section 76') route and create a limited "psychological abuse" type offence, then this would result in fragmentation. It would "require", in other words, that that part of the course of conduct be prosecuted separately, just as is the case currently in England and Wales.

Interestingly, some of the respondents to this early consultation expressed a concern that serious instances of sexual violence and/or physical harm may have to be charged separately.[40] There was also resistance (although only from one respondent to the second consultation) to the notion that it is possible to distinguish between different types of domestic abuse in the criminal law. This respondent commented, 'Embodying a distinction between common couple violence and coercive control in a workable definition of a crime is extremely challenging'.[41]

Challenging it may be, but that this was to be the preferred approach is then confirmed by the *Justice Committee Stage One Report* published on 21 December 2017:

> The new offence provides for a definition of abuse expressly encompassing both physical and psychological abuse … The Scottish Government took the decision to include both physical and psychological abuse within the new offence in order to enable prosecutors to include all acts of abuse in a single charge as evidence of a course of conduct, rather than having to bring a separate charge for the physical aspect of the abuse.[42]

The Scottish Government, having listened to the experiences of survivors of domestic abuse, decided to give the prosecution the flexibility to include the 'ambit of an offender's abusive behaviour to be labelled within a single offence'[43] specifically to address the fragmentation issue caused by the separation of physical and psychological aspects of domestic abuse. A single offence is better able to reflect harm that is experienced as a continuum: 'The rationale for merging all abusive behaviours into one criminal charge is a recognition that abuse is often experienced as a continuum'.[44]

Police and prosecutors, when giving evidence to the Justice Committee as part of the Stage one scrutiny of the bill, agreed that a new law should be the preferred approach. Paragraph 35 of the *Stage One Report* records that Anne Marie Hicks, the National Prosecutor for Domestic Abuse, told the Committee that:

The essence of the current law was that prosecutors were, in effect, restricted to prosecuting offences that "attack someone's physical integrity" … they could not prosecute controlling behaviour amounting to an abuse of power. For prosecutors, this was a gap in the law with real-life consequences. The current law, with its emphasis on particular acts, also prevented what she called "the bigger picture" behind an abusive relationship being put before the court. This she said, "cannot be right".

Detective Superintendent Lesley Boal of Police Scotland supported her on this. He added that, 'The gap in the law sometimes meant that "horrific" behaviour could not be addressed adequately by the criminal law'.[45]

One key advantage to this approach is the flexibility it offers prosecutors. The progressive, Stark informed approach that has been adopted throughout the criminal justice system is reflected in the training giving to the COPFS. The COPFS explained to me that being able to distinguish the typologies of abuse is critical to good prosecutorial decision-making. It said:

> The DASA is an Act that creates an offence that deals with the coercive behaviour. And it is important for prosecutors when they are analysing police reports to be able to identify the difference between what is coercive control and what is individual acts of situational couple violence. If there is domestic abuse that does not form part of a coercive abusive behaviour, then we would prosecute under the old regime, using current previously existing single stand-alone charges or breaches of the peace. The training was very much designed to allow them to identify and recognise where there is a course of abusive behaviour rather than individual situational couple violence so that it can be prosecuted correctly.[46]

The Stark informed approach, identifying that coercive control needs specific legislative treatment, further narrows the gap between life and law that has been a consistent theme for survivors of abuse throughout this book. The DASA makes this possible.

It is interesting that the DASA, while being the best example anywhere in the world of the translation of Stark's coercive control paradigm into law, does not use the wording 'coercive control' in the offence. In the first consultation response paragraph 2.5 explains that Stark's work is a 'starting point' for the new offence:

> In framing any offence, a number of respondents referenced the work on "Coercive Control" by Professor Evan Stark and suggested it would provide a useful starting point for deciding which behaviours that are not currently criminalised should be covered by any offence. A number of respondents identified a range of core principles that should be applied when developing any legislation. These included that it should be gender-based in line with

the Scottish Government's commitment to preventing and eradicating violence against women and girls'.[47]

However, by the time of the second consultation it had become clear that it was felt that the label 'coercive control' was not that helpful ... 'it was suggested that the "abusive behaviour" term is useful in dispensing with the complexities surrounding the terms "coercion" and "control"'.[48] In fact, it's likely that the difficulty for the criminal law with the term "coercive control" is the need for the criminal law to distinguish between abusive behaviour and its impact. Coercive control, as I explained in chapter 1, covers both perpetrator behaviour and the victim's response (harm). The criminal law needs to distinguish 'behaviours from their impacts'.[49]

This does not matter – what is important is that the DASA captures the nuances of coercive control. From a prosecution perspective it means that, finally, the crown can get evidence of the abusive relationship in front of the jury. As a prosecutor explained to me the shift in emphasis allowed by the 'abusive behaviour' term is critical. He said:

> Historically, you were only interested in what happened immediately surrounding an incident. Whereas now, it allows for a victim to come and explain how the relationship was, explain how things happened and why they might have been fearful, on the basis of all of the things that were going on.[50]

'Explaining how the relationship was', in other words, is what matters, and the 'abusive behaviour' wording allows this to happen.

No Need to Prove Harm Happened

Next to the decision to include the whole range of abusive conduct within the one offence, the second most radical decision made by the Scottish Government was to abandon harm to the victim as a constituent part of the offence. Instead, there is a 'reasonable person' test. In the first consultation, the Scottish Government explained that this is an important trade-off. It said, 'We consider the advantage of having a reasonable person ("objective") test is that the court will not require to hear evidence relating to the reaction of the victim'.[51] The Scottish Government thought that it would be better to avoid the necessity of a victim giving evidence as to her subjective experience of the abuse in court. It also feared that with the subjective approach, 'where a victim is stoical and does not exhibit obvious distress (even where it would be quite reasonable for them to do so) a court may not feel able to convict'.[52]

This aspect of the offence is the one that generated the most concern in the second consultation. The advantages of the approach were recognised: namely that there would be less pressure on the victim to give difficult evidence in court, and that where victims have been coerced into believing that perpetrators are not at fault, the 'reasonable person' test will help give them confidence that this is not the case. The concerns raised by respondents included the fact that as the character-istics of the victim would have to be taken into account there is a necessarily subjective element to the assessment of harm, and that in general, this test is too innovative (not readily recognised in the criminal law) and required too much interpretation.[53]

Another concern expressed is that the test would not be subjective enough – in other words, that judgments being made on the basis of what a 'reasonable' response would be, is difficult if the person making the judgment has never experienced domestic abuse. The contextual nature of abuse can make it seem innocuous and therefore 'reasonable', and juries would need to be able to understand 'the subtle and cumulative nature of abuse and that the threatening environment created by the perpetrator is the context for what otherwise may appear to a reasonable person to be benign, non-malignant behaviour'.[54] Other concerns raised are that it is not a feature of proof for other crimes of violence or abuse and that it therefore adds unreasonably to the burden of proof. Finally, it is argued, the 'reasonable person' test would already have been met in terms of defining abusive behaviour.[55]

By the time of the *Justice Committee Stage One Report* the Scottish Government's mind was made up. The harm experienced by the victim would not feature as a constituent part of the new offence:

> It is the Scottish Government's view that proving a crime was committed should not depend on demonstrating in court that the complainer suffered harm. The Scottish Government considers that this reduces the likelihood of the trial process being traumatic for the victim (by forcing them to "re-live" the experience of the abuse in order to establish that the crime was committed) … Instead the focus is on what the individual actually did (or failed to do), on whether they had the requisite mental element of recklessness or intent, and on an objective assessment of what the outcome for the victim would likely have been.[56]

Section 4 of the DASA makes it clear that the commission of an offence, 'does not depend on the course of behaviour actually causing B to suffer harm'.[57] There is no doubt that the objections put forward by respondents to the second con-sultation have merit. But this is a reflection, I think, of the fact that there is no perfect solution to the prosecution of domestic abuse within an adversarial court of law.

It is not possible to avoid the victim's experience being part, (even in an in-direct way), of the evidence before the court, and an element of subjectivity is essential in the context of criminal behaviour that is contextual and bespoke. I think that the Scottish consideration of the victim's courtroom experience, and determination to focus on the perpetrator's actions and state of mind, is a pro-gressive compromise and to be preferred. The COPFS is not anticipating victimless prosecutions will be possible.[58] To the extent that the victim experience can be taken into account, however, it should be. The Scottish approach means that victims might not face cross-examination in relation to the most personal aspects of their story, their response to the abuse they have experienced.[59] The argument that juries need to be able to understand the complexities of domestic abuse has little merit in the context of legislation that works hard to capture those complexities from a doctrinal perspective. The subtle and cumulative nature of the abuse is more likely to be before the court than ever before. Finally, on the "resilient victim" point: the English experience has shown that including the harm as a constituent part of the offence does mean that people with an unusual capacity for resilience (like Lauren Smith in the Paul Measor case in the preceding chapter) do get unfairly penalised.

The Definition of 'Abusive Behaviour'

Both consultations asked respondents to consider what specific types of behaviour should be included in the new offence. Respondents came back with:

- Deprivation of liberty;
- Isolating an individual from friends, family and wider society;
- Withholding or controlling access to resources, including money;
- Psychological control and manipulation;
- Threats and creation of a climate of fear, including threats towards children; and
- Controlling or withholding access to health care, education or employment opportunities.[60]

This feedback from the respondents mostly made it into the final draft of the bill. Section (2) defines abusive behaviour as follows:

1. Behaviour which is abusive of B includes (in particular) −

    a. Behaviour directed at B that is violent, threatening or intimidating,
    b. Behaviour directed at B, at a child of B or at another person that either −

        i. Has as its purpose (or among its purposes) one or more of the relevant effects set out in subsection (3), or
        ii. Would be considered by a reasonable person to be likely to have one or more of the relevant effects set out in subsection (3).

2. The relevant effects are of −

    a. Making B depend on, or subordinate to, A,
    b. Isolating B from friends, relatives or other sources of support,
    c. Controlling, regulating or monitoring B's day-to-day activities,

    d.   Depriving B of, or restricting B's, freedom of action,

    e.   Frightening, humiliating, degrading or punishing B.

3.   In subsection (2)

    a.   In paragraph (a) the reference to violent behaviour includes sexual violence as well as physical violence,

    b.   In paragraph (b), the reference to a child is to a person who is under 18 years of age.

As the list included in section (2) is not exhaustive, and as the notes which accompany the DASA make clear, all of the specific types of behaviour listed by the respondents could be prosecuted further to the DASA, whether or not they are specifically listed in section (2).

Scott describes section 2 as 'extensive but 'not exhaustive" and this, indeed, is its great strength.[61] Scott was pleased that this section of the DASA in particular draws heavily on the language and experiences of the survivors who were consulted.[62] Phrases such as 'depriving B of, or restricting B's, freedom of action' come from the consultations, and the Explanatory Notes that accompany the DASA provide further, survivor-informed examples of what constitutes abuse.[63]

Final Points

Restricting the Offence to Partners/Ex-partners

The Scottish Government was influenced by early findings that suggested that the remit of the offence should be narrow. The responses to the first consultation suggested that the majority of respondents:

> Thought that "domestic abuse" should be restricted to people who are partners or ex-partners. Those who thought that the offence should be restricted most frequently pointed to the dynamics of an intimate partner relationship being different to that of other relationships. A number also felt that it was important to keep a clear focus on domestic abuse within the broader understanding of gender inequality and control. A concern was that extending the legislation to cover other familial relationships could lead to a dilution and diminution of the understanding of and response to domestic abuse.[64]

Thus this is the position that was adopted from the start: that the offence should be restricted to partners or ex-partners, and the second consultation merely confirmed that this should be so. The chief concern was that, 'An offence that seeks to include all forms of relationships where abusive behaviour is used may become unwieldy'.[65] There was some resistance,[66] but the by the time of the *Justice Committee Stage One Report* the case had been made:

At the start of oral evidence-taking, Scottish Government officials informed the Committee that, in prior Government consultations the question of what types of relationship to include in legislation had been put and that "there was strong support for an offence that relates to partners and ex-partners, because there is such a particular dynamic to that type of abuse."[67]

This decision was not revisited. In particular, there was never any discussion around restricting the offence to current partners. Instead, there is awareness of the vulnerability of survivors at the point of separation. As a prosecutor explained to me: 'the point of separation becomes the most dangerous time. And immediately after that …'.[68]

Mens Rea

From the start, the Scottish Government was determined to avoid what they saw as the pitfalls of a *mens rea* of intent. This is because:

In some abusive relationships, the accused may argue, and indeed may genuinely believe, that they did not intend to harm their partner. Where the accused's actions are such that, irrespective of their intent, they were clearly reckless as to whether their actions would cause physical or psychological harm, the prosecution would not be required to prove that it was the accused intent to cause such harm.[69]

Early objections to the suggested *mens rea* of either intent or recklessness included concerns on legal certainty – did the combination of the possibility of a wholly objective *mens rea* and the breadth of behaviours that could constitute abuse together disrupt the requirement for legal certainty in a criminal offence? Other early feedback agreed that a *mens rea* of intent only would be too high a threshold and/ or inappropriate in the context of an offence where by definition, 'Many perpetrators will argue that they did not intend to cause the harm and therefore a recklessness alternative will avoid the offence failing. Including recklessness decreases their opportunity to dismiss, deflect and minimise their behaviour'.[70] Another commentator pointed to the need for a capacity-based exception – if 'the perpetrator lacks capacity to understand the results of their behaviour'.[71]

Section 1(2) of the DASA contains the *mens rea* for the offence. The Scottish Government agreed that it was necessary to include recklessness as a potential *mens rea* – 'It was considered necessary to include recklessness as intention could be difficult to prove in cases where the prosecution case rests of proof of coercive and controlling behaviour'.[72] A must intend, or be reckless as to, whether the course of behaviour causes the victim to suffer physical or psychological harm. Recklessness in Scotland can be assessed either subjectively or objectively. So section 1(2) of the DASA, just like section 76, has the possibility of a wholly objective *mens rea*. Just as with section 76, there is no capacity-based exception.

The Definition of a 'Course of Behaviour'

This is the only aspect of the DASA that I think is actually less progressive than its English/Welsh equivalent (section 76). When deciding how to particularise abuse in the new offence, the Scottish Government followed the approach of the existing Scottish stalking laws and their English equivalent - the Protection from Harassment Act 1997 (the 'PHA'). This has the benefit of familiarity, but the same issues crop up as with the PHA which was the subject of analysis in chapter 3. The DASA, s 1 creates an offence where A engages in a 'course of behaviour' which is abusive of B. Section 10(4) of the DASA states that 'a course of behaviour involves *behaviour on at least two occasions*'. This follows existing Scottish stalking laws with which police and prosecutors in Scotland are familiar: section 39 of the Criminal Justice and Licensing (Scotland) Act 2010 criminalises stalking, and section 39(6) states that a 'course of conduct' requires *conduct on* 'at least two occasions'. As set out in chapter 3, the PHA defines a 'course of conduct' as offending that must involve 'conduct *on at least two occasions*'.[73]

As I have said previously, the question of how to particularise behaviour that is ongoing rather than incident-specific goes to the root of what is difficult about domestic abuse and the criminal law. Domestic abuse is ongoing. It does not occur as a 'series of discrete events'.[74] I explained in chapter 3 how Tuerkheimer's conceptualisation of the way in which reality comes to bear on legal structures via a series of pressure points promotes 'movement and resistance' in the criminal law.[75] I explained how this was a helpful framework within which to understand how the PHA constructed stalking as a 'course of conduct' offence. Constructing stalking by reference to two related but separate incidents instead of just one incident did not "move" the transactional nature of the legal structure very far. Police complained that it had the unintended effect of increasing the incident-specific focus yet delaying a police response, and commentators observed that 'judicial decisions interpreting the Act … lapse back into an examination of individual incidents'.[76] Section 76 abandons the reference to incidents altogether and criminalises instead behaviour that is 'ongoing'. To date, I reported in the last chapter that this seems to be working well.

Unfortunately, in Scotland, the assumption was made early on to stick with the idea of a "course" of behaviour, that would constitute at least two "incidents" of abuse. The second consultation, for example, specifically asked respondents to address the question of what should constitute a "course of behaviour". Concerns were expressed as to how the two separate occasions needed to be connected. For example, did they need to be of the same behaviour? Or could there be two incidents of abusive, but potentially different, behaviour? Would there need to be two separate police reports, or would one report covering multiple instances be enough? Will there be a restrictive timeframe? How far back will police/prosecutors be able to go? Would previous convictions be considered? Would the two incidents have to involve the same victim?[77] But the assumption throughout, that defining a "course" around at least two "incidents" was the best way of conceptualising the new domestic abuse offence was never interrogated.

The Scottish Government decided to leave the question of what, exactly, constitutes or can constitutes two incidents to the courts. It explains in the *Justice Committee Stage One Report*:

> A "course of behaviour" consists of behaviour on at least two occasions. No time period is specified in the Bill. In theory, it therefore appears that these two (or more) instances could be separated by minutes, or, conversely by years. The Policy Memorandum notes that "two isolated incidents occurring far apart in time" are perhaps unlikely to be considered a "course of behaviour", but says that ultimately this would be a matter for the court to determine in each given case.[78]

Sheriffs told me that they had been advised to look to the PHA caselaw as guidance on how to determine in each given case whether two incidents constitute the necessary course of conduct.[79] It remains to be seen whether and to what extent the definition of "course of behaviour" and the accompanying focus on incidents interferes with the progressive new relational focus of the DASA.

Another layer of complication is added to the "course of behaviour" construct by the (unique) Scottish evidential principle of corroboration, which requires two separate and independent sources of evidence to establish (a) that the crime was committed and (b) that it was the defendant who committed it. Corroboration is needed in the case of each of the two incidents, and only in each of the two incidents, that are required to establish proof of the 'course of behaviour'.[80] There are some exceptions to this principle – a detailed examination of the Scottish law on the doctrine of mutual corroboration is outside the scope of this book – but it is likely that the scope to apply the doctrine of mutual corroboration in respect of DASA charges is limited. It is unlikely, in other words, that evidence of one type of offending behaviour (for example an assault) could corroborate another (for example stalking).

One concern raised early on by the judiciary is that despite the fact that one type of offending behaviour cannot corroborate another, technically the fact that only two "incidents" need corroborating leaves open the possibility that a defendant might get a long prison sentence in respect of an uncorroborated serious assault. As one senior Sheriff explained to me:

> But what a lot of the judges were concerned about was whether it was competent to include an uncorroborated serious sexual or violent offence in the middle of an otherwise corroborated course of conduct? Which is not even close to the same magnitude. So you could end up with two summary breaches of the peace, and a serious sexual assault. And the guy gets six years in a jail. Because of the serious sexual assault. But it wasn't corroborated.[81]

The early solution to this is that the COPFS have confirmed that, 'As a matter of practicality they will not charge uncorroborated serious sexual or violent offending unless it is much of a muchness with the rest of the corroborated evidence'.[82] This appears to give the COPFS options. Rape and serious physical assault can always be charged separately. Yet, if it forms part and parcel of the coercive control, it can be charged as part of a section one offence. One respondent to the second consultation pointed out that legislators should not place too much "trust" in prosecutors. Instead 'legislators should try to get the law right in the first place'.[83] Corroboration is a uniquely Scottish problem, and not therefore necessarily of concern to legislators around the world. But this key question, of what to do with serious physical and sexual assault – whether and when they should be charged separately, and if this decision can or should be left to prosecutors – needs to be revisited as the early DASA cases come through the courts.

Sentencing

The original proposed maximum penalty for the offence was ten years.[84] This was felt in December 2015 to be appropriately severe, reflecting as it did 'the fact that it may be appropriate to try the most serious cases of abuse in the High Court'.[85] The majority of respondents to the later consultation (August 2016) agreed. At this stage (August 2016) the suggestion was also made that non-harassment orders should be a routine consideration at sentencing. Also, it was suggested that on indictment the court should not be limited to ten years. The possibility was also raised that a serious sexual offence might need to be libelled separately.[86]

As explained in the section on corroboration, above, it is the intention that there is flexibility to libel serious sexual and violent offences separately. In the end, the maximum penalty included in section 9(b) of the DASA is imprisonment (on indictment) for a term not exceeding 14 years. It is not clear when it was decided that the original proposal should be increased, but the COPFS explained to me that the inclusion of a high maximum sentence was to ensure that:

> This is an offence that can include within it the serious sexual assaults and serious violence, it is not an offence that is just limited to summary offending. Because there is the option of a 14-year prison sentence that covers anything pretty much up to murder. So the view is that this is an offence that can be used for the serious offending.

It is too early to draw any conclusions on how sheriffs are sentencing further to a DASA conviction. There are no reported cases at the time of writing. Early concerns have been expressed by commentators that, 'Physical assaults, more readily understood and evidenced, are likely to remain privileged in a hierarchy of harms in the minds of sentencing judges'.[87] We will have to wait and see if this is indeed the case.

Conclusion

There is much that will be learned in the first decade of the DASA. This is to be expected: it is in many ways a progressive step into the unknown. In particular, there are questions around when serious physical and sexual violence should be charged separately, and how sheriffs are sentencing the new offence. How and to what extent victim testimony will still be needed in court, and whether (and to what extent) the incident-specific focus introduced by the "course of behaviour" construct will interfere with the more relational focus of the new offence are also important.

Statistics for the first year of the operation of the new offence are positive. Around 3.5% of domestic abuse charges were brought under the DASA, and of those 96% were prosecuted. In England and Wales, only 155 cases in total were prosecuted in the first year of section 76. This amounts to 0.0001% of the ap-proximately 1.3 million women who experience domestic abuse in England and Wales each year. The numbers in England and Wales are improving year on year, the most recent figures show that 24,856 section 76 offences were recorded in the year ending March 2020. This still only amounts to 0.02% of the 1.3 million women in England and Wales who experienced domestic abuse during that time period.[88]

On 1 February 2018, as it passed into law, Michael Matheson MSP closed the debate on the DASA with the words of a survivor of abuse, saying:

> At the very heart of this new legislation is the voices of those women who have experienced domestic abuse. And I want to draw this debate to a close by finishing their voice. The voice of Nichola Borthwick. Who said: "Life as an abused woman was dangerous. Terrifying and exhausting. I had no freedom, no escape and no voice. After fleeing I remained in hiding. I have spoken and been heard at our nation's Parliament. I have given personal evidence to support this domestic abuse bill. This is a precious memory, that will stay with me for the rest of my life. To transform the legacy of abusive deeds from merely damaging into something positive, contributing to safety from domestic abuse for others, is incredibly rewarding and fulfilling".[89]

In a dramatic moment MSPs rose to their feet, turned to the public gallery and gave a standing ovation to Dr Marsha Scott, CEO of Scottish Women's Aid, and all of the survivors who were sitting there with her. The passage of the DASA is indeed a memorable and emotional moment. The next few years will show whether it can live up to its early promise.

Notes

1 Michele Burman and Jenny Johnstone, 'High Hopes? The Gender Equality Duty and Its Impact on Responses to Gender-Based Violence' (2015) 43(1) Policy & Politics 45, 46.
2 Ibid.
3 Michele Burman and Oona Brooks-Hay, 'Aligning Policy and Law? The Creation of a Domestic Abuse Offence Incorporating Coercive Control' (2018) 18(1) Criminology & Criminal Justice 67.

4 Michael Johnson, 'Patriarchal Terrorism and Common Couple Violence: Two Forms of Violence against Women' (1995) 57(2) Journal of Marriage and the Family 283; Michael Johnson, *A Typology of Domestic Violence Intimate Terrorism, Violent Resistance, and Situational Couple Violence* (University Press 2008).

5 Interview with Marsha Scott (22 October 2019) 8.

6 The 'Scottish Executive' was the post devolution name given to the Scottish Government. It rebranded itself as the Scottish Government in 2007. See BBC News, 'Scottish Executive Renames Itself' available at <http://news.bbc.co.uk/1/hi/scotland/6974798.stm> accessed 26 May 2021.

7 Burman and Brooks-Hay, Aligning Policy and Law n3 70.

8 Scottish Executive, 'National Strategy to Address Domestic Abuse in Scotland' (Scottish Executive 2000) available at <www.gov.scot/Resource/Doc/158940/0043185.pdf> accessed 26 May 2021).

9 Ibid. 17.

10 Ibid.

11 Ibid. 3 (my italics).

12 Burman and Brooks-Hay, Aligning Policy and Law, n3 70.

13 Scottish Executive, National Strategy n8 8.

14 Ibid. 8.

15 Ibid. 19.

16 The DAA extends to England and Wales but not Scotland, see the DAA, section 89.

17 Marsha Scott, 'The Making of the Gold Standard' in Marilyn McMahon and Paul McGorrery (eds), *Criminalising Coercive Control* (Springer 2020) 2.

18 Evan Stark, *Coercive Control: The Entrapment of Women in Personal Life* (Oxford University Press 2007).

19 Scott, Gold Standard n17 2.

20 This adapted the so called common law 'breach of the peace' offence so that it did not need a 'public element' thereby making it appropriate for the prosecution of domestic abuse – see Scottish Government Consultation Paper, *Equally Safe– Reforming the Criminal Law to Address Domestic Abuse and Sexual Offences* (March 2015) 11.

21 Simon Johnson, 'Wife-Beater Former MSP Bill Walker Jailed for a Year' *The Telegraph* (19 September 2014) available at <https://www.telegraph.co.uk/news/uknews/scotland/10322765/Wife-beater-former-MSP-Bill-Walker-jailed-for-a-year.html> accessed 24 May 2021.

22 Ibid.

23 Burman and Brooks Hay, Aligning Policy and Law n3 72.

24 Scottish Government, Equally Safe n20 8.

25 Lesley Thomson QC, COPFS Conference on Domestic Abuse Ministerial Address (May 2014) available at <https://www.copfs.gov.uk/images/Documents/Our%20Priorities/Domestic%20abuse/Sol%20Gen%20Speech%20-%20COPFS%20Domestic%20Abuse%20Conference%208%20May%202014.pdf> accessed 24 May 2021, 3.

26 Ibid. 4.

27 Scottish Government, Equally Safe n20.

28 Home Office, 'Strengthening the Law on Domestic Abuse: A Consultation' (2014) 9 available at <https://www.gov.uk/government/uploads/system/uploads/attachment_data/file/344674/Strengthening_the_law_on_Domestic_Abuse_-_A_Consultation_WEB.PDF> accessed 28 March 2018.

29 Ibid. 6.

30 Ibid.

31 Scottish Government, Equally Safe n20 1.26.

32 Ibid. 1.28.

33 Scottish Government, A Criminal Offence of Domestic Abuse (December 2015) available at <https://consult.gov.scot/criminal-law-and-sentencing-team/criminal-offence-domestic-abuse/user_uploads/00491481.pdf-1> accessed 24 May 2021.

34 Scottish Government, A Criminal Offence n33 3.10.
35 Ibid. 3.8.
36 Ibid. 3.9.
37 Lucy Robertson, 'Criminal Offence of Domestic Abuse Analysis of Consultation Responses' (Scottish Government August 2016) available at <https://www.gov.scot/publications/criminal-offence-domestic-abuse-analysis-consultation-responses/> accessed 24 May 2021.
38 Scottish Government, A Criminal Offence n33 3.10.
39 Ibid. n32 3.10
40 Robertson, Analysis of Consultation Responses n37 12.
41 Ibid.
42 Justice Committee, 'Stage 1 Report on the Domestic Abuse (Scotland) Bill' (Scottish Parliament September 2017) para 16. For academic commentary see Emma Forbes, 'The Domestic Abuse (Scotland) Act 2018: The Whole Story?' (2018) 22 Edinburgh Law Review 406.
43 Scottish Government, A Criminal Offence n33 para 3.1.
44 Forbes, The Domestic Abuse Scotland Act n42 406.
45 Justice Committee, Stage One Report n42 35.
46 Interview with the COPFS (22 October 2019).
47 Scottish Government, A Criminal Offence n33 2.5.
48 Lucy Robertson, Analysis of Consultation Responses n37 22.
49 Burman and Brooks Hay, Aligning Policy and Law n3 73.
50 Interview with COPFS n46 4.
51 Scottish Government, A Criminal Offence n33 3.13.
52 Ibid.
53 Robertson, Analysis of Consultation Responses n37 14.
54 Ibid. 16.
55 Ibid. 15.
56 Justice Committee Stage One Report n42 para 17.
57 Domestic Abuse (Scotland) Act 2018 s. 4(1).
58 Interview with COPFS, n46 6.
59 Forbes, The Domestic Abuse Scotland Act 2018 n42 407.
60 Scottish Government, *A Criminal Offence* n33 2.6. More suggestions as to additional elements to be included in the definition were listed in the later (August 2016) Robertson, Analysis of Consultation Responses n37 23.
61 Interview with Marsha Scott, n5.
62 Ibid.
63 Domestic Abuse (Scotland) Act 2018 Explanatory Notes available at <https://www.legislation.gov.uk/asp/2018/5/notes> accessed 28 May 2022.
64 Scottish Government, A Criminal Offence n33 2.7.
65 Robertson, Analysis of Consultation Responses n37 27.
66 Ibid.
67 Justice Committee, Stage One Report n42 para 74.
68 Interview with COPFS, n46 6.
69 Scottish Government, A Criminal Offence n33 3.14.
70 Robertson, Analysis of Consultation Responses n37 18.
71 Ibid.
72 Justice Committee, Stage One Report n42 para 63.
73 S 7(3) Protection from Harassment Act 1997.
74 Mary Ann Dutton, 'Understanding Women's Responses to Domestic Violence: A Redefinition of Battered Woman Syndrome' (1992) 21 Hofstra Law Review 1191, 1208.
75 Deborah Tuerkheimer, 'Recognising and Remedying the Harm of Battering: A Call to Criminalize Domestic Violence' (2004) 94(4) Journal of Criminal Law and Criminology 959, 990.

76 Charlotte Bishop, 'Domestic Violence: The Limitations of a Legal Response' in Sarah Hilda and Vanessa Bettinson (eds), *Interdisciplinary Perspectives on Protection, Prevention and Intervention* (Palgrave Macmillan 2016) 68.
77 Lucy Robertson, Analysis of Consultation Responses n37 17.
78 Justice Committee, Stage 1 Report n42.
79 Interview with Sheriff Matthews (25 November 2019).
80 Livingstone v JH [2021] Scot D 17/10.
81 Interview with Sheriff Dunhill, 23 October 2019 7.
82 Ibid.
83 Justice Committee, Stage One Report n42 paragraph 50.
84 Scottish Government, A Criminal Offence n33 3.22.
85 Ibid.
86 Robertson, Analysis of Consultation Responses n37 30.
87 Forbes, The Whole Story n42 410.
88 Office for National Statistics, 'Domestic Abuse Prevalence and Victim Characteristics' available at <https://www.ons.gov.uk/peoplepopulationandcommunity/crimeandjustice/datasets/domesticabuseprevalenceandvictimcharacteristicsappendixtables> accessed 28 May 2022.
89 Michael Matheson SMP, 'Closing Address to the Scottish Parliament' available at <https://www.bbc.co.uk/news/live/uk-scotland-scotland-politics-42858902> accessed 4 June 2021.

Bibliography

BBC News, 'Scottish Executive Renames Itself' available at <http://news.bbc.co.uk/1/hi/scotland/6974798.stm> accessed 26 May 2021.

Bishop C, 'Domestic Violence: The Limitations of a Legal Response' in Sarah Hilda and Vanessa Bettinson (eds), *Interdisciplinary Perspectives on Protection, Prevention and Intervention* (Palgrave Macmillan 2016).

Burman M and Brooks-Hay O, 'Aligning Policy and Law? The Creation of a Domestic Abuse Offence Incorporating Coercive Control' (2018) 18(1) Criminology & Criminal Justice 67.

Burman M and Johnstone J, 'High Hopes? The Gender Equality Duty and Its Impact on Responses to Gender-Based Violence' (2015) 43(1) Policy & Politics 45.

Dutton M, 'Understanding Women's Responses to Domestic Violence: A Redefinition of Battered Woman Syndrome' (1992) 21 Hofstra Law Review 1191.

Forbes E, 'The Domestic Abuse (Scotland) Act 2018: The Whole Story?' (2018) 22 Edinburgh Law Review 406.

Home Office, 'Strengthening the Law on Domestic Abuse: A Consultation' (2014) available at <https://www.gov.uk/government/uploads/system/uploads/attachment_data/file/344674/Strengthening_the_law_on_Domestic_Abuse_-_A_Consultation_WEB.PDF> accessed 28 March 2018.

Johnson M, 'Patriarchal Terrorism and Common Couple Violence: Two Forms of Violence against Women' (1995) 57(2) Journal of Marriage and the Family 283.

Johnson M, *A Typology of Domestic Violence Intimate Terrorism, Violent Resistance, and Situational Couple Violence* (University Press 2008).

Johnson S, 'Wife-Beater Former MSP Bill Walker Jailed for a Year' *The Telegraph* (19 September 2014) available at <https://www.telegraph.co.uk/news/uknews/scotland/10322765/Wife-beater-former-MSP-Bill-Walker-jailed-for-a-year.html> accessed 24 May 2021.

Justice Committee, 'Stage 1 Report on the Domestic Abuse (Scotland) Bill' (Scottish Parliament September 2017).

Michael Matheson SMP, 'Closing Address to the Scottish Parliament' available at <https://www.bbc.co.uk/news/live/uk-scotland-scotland-politics-42858902> accessed 4 June 2021.

Office for National Statistics, 'Domestic Abuse Prevalence and Victim Characteristics' available at <https://www.ons.gov.uk/peoplepopulationandcommunity/crimeandjustice/datasets/domesticabuseprevalenceandvictimcharacteristicsappendixtables> accessed 28 May 2022.

Robertson L, 'Criminal Offence of Domestic Abuse Analysis of Consultation Responses' (Scottish Government August 2016) available at <https://www.gov.scot/publications/criminal-offence-domestic-abuse-analysis-consultation-responses/> accessed 24 May 2021.

Scott M, 'The Making of the Gold Standard' inMarilyn McMahon and Paul McGorrery (eds), *Criminalising Coercive Control* (Springer 2020).

Scottish Executive, 'National Strategy to Address Domestic Abuse in Scotland' (Scottish Executive 2000) available at <www.gov.scot/Resource/Doc/158940/0043185.pdf> accessed 26 May 2021).

Scottish Government Consultation Paper, *Equally Safe – Reforming the Criminal Law to Address Domestic Abuse and Sexual Offences* (March 2015).

Scottish Government, 'A Criminal Offence of Domestic Abuse' (December 2015) available at <https://consult.gov.scot/criminal-law-and-sentencing-team/criminal-offence-domestic-abuse/user_uploads/00491481.pdf-1> accessed 24 May 2021.

Stark E, *Coercive Control: The Entrapment of Women in Personal Life* (Oxford University Press 2007).

Thomson L, COPFS Conference on Domestic Abuse Ministerial Address (May 2014) available at <https://www.copfs.gov.uk/images/Documents/Our%20Priorities/Domestic%20abuse/Sol%20Gen%20Speech%20-%20COPFS%20Domestic%20Abuse%20Conference%208%20May%202014.pdf> accessed on 24 May 2021.

Tuerkheimer D, 'Recognising and Remedying the Harm of Battering: A Call to Criminalize Domestic Violence' (2004) 94(4) Journal of Criminal Law and Criminology 959.

Cases

Livingstone v JH [2021] Scot D 17/10.

Legislation

Criminal Justice and Licensing (Scotland) Act 2010.
Domestic Abuse (Scotland) Act 2018.
Protection from Harassment Act 1997.
Serious Crime Act 2015.

7

CONCLUSION

In this book I answer the question: what is the best way to criminalise coercive control? As the world wakes up to the magnitude of the damage caused by domestic abuse and coercive control, it is unsurprising that the criminalisation of coercive control is moving up policy agendas around the world. Using existing criminal law infrastructure to prosecute domestic abuse *just like any other violent crime* was hailed as a significant achievement towards the end of the last century. But as it becomes apparent that the harms caused by coercive control are unfortunately *unique*, existing criminal law doctrine everywhere is coming under scrutiny. It is hard to avoid the conclusion that prosecuting domestic abuse effectively is impossible without a specific consideration of coercive control.

How you consider coercive control is key. The recent steps taken in all of the jurisdictions of the United Kingdom and Ireland have therefore quite rightly been the focus of considerable international attention. The reform programmes in England/Wales and Ireland were similar. However, Scotland and Northern Ireland, while taking paths similar to each other, took a different approach to England/Wales and Ireland. In this book, I use England/Wales to represent the first approach, and Scotland the second. The ensuing different outcomes for the new law in the different jurisdictions shows that *how the law is drafted* has significant repercussions later on for the efficacy of the police and prosecutors that work to enforce it. This is why "knowing what matters" from a doctrinal perspective is important for the jurisdictions around the world which are considering this step.

The Mismatch: Coercive Control and the Criminal Law

One of the key themes of this book has been the recognition that there are conflicts between the traditional specificity requirements of the criminal law, and what we now know about coercive control. This mismatch makes the

DOI: 10.4324/9780429201844-8

criminalisation of coercive control an especially delicate exercise. My background is in criminal law doctrine, and as I learnt about coercive control, I began to appreciate that it does not respect the kind of boundaries and binaries that the traditional criminal law uses as its building blocks.

For example: existing criminal law lexicons use categories of offending. We talk about 'violent offences', 'sexual offences', 'offences against the person' and 'harassment' or 'stalking'. Those categories of offences are further organised into groups of 'violent' or 'non-violent' offences, 'sexual' or 'non-sexual' offences. Perpetrator behaviours in coercive control, on the other hand, cannot be so contained. They are at the same time, physical *and* non-physical; they are simultaneously sexually, physically *and* psychologically abusive. Perpetrator behaviours in coercive control cross over, interconnect, and in fact cannot even be located in time and space as they respect the boundaries of neither. Exactly the same can be said of the harm experienced by the victims of coercive control, which can be emotional, which can have an impact on mental health as well as physical health, which can erode sexual as well as physical and economic autonomy.

I explained in chapter 1 how Tanya Palmer articulates sexual violence as 'chronic' or 'acute'.[1] Sexual violence that is acute is incident-specific and limited in time, duration, place. It is rapid in onset, and short in duration. Violence that is relational on the other hand is chronic. A victim's autonomy is 'gradually eroded over a longer period of time'.[2] This is useful terminology for articulating the conflict between the criminal law and coercive control. The criminal law traditionally deals in acute incidents. The perpetrator behaviours *in*, and the harm caused *by* coercive control, on the other hand, are relational rather than incident-specific, chronic rather than acute. As I said above this creates a problem: how do you satisfy the criminal law's insistence of specificity, in the context of an amorphous domination strategy and resulting damage, that uses a lack of respect for traditional boundaries as its insidious raison d'etre?

"Fragmentation" Vis a Vis 'All of a Piece'[3]

When considering how to draw normative boundaries around behaviour that is relational, pervasive and amorphous, there are options. In England/Wales the decision was made to take what I have referred to in this book as the "fragmentation" approach. The Government chose to conceptualise coercive control as an additional bullet point, in a list of perpetrator behaviours that make up domestic abuse. It decided (wrongly) that the majority of those perpetrator behaviours were accommodated by the existing regime. It thus focused on bulleting the one aspect of coercive control ("psychological abuse") that it felt was not adequately captured by the existing criminal law framework. It then created a fragment of law (Serious Crime Act 2015, s 76 ('section 76')) to "plug" that specific "gap".

Scotland started from a very different place. Since at least 2000, Scotland has focused on the significance of gender in relation to coercive control. In particular, Stark's work (and the work of Michael Johnson) was used to reframe official statistics, which, just as is the case in England/Wales, conflate situational violence (one-off incidents) with coercive control. Once these two strands of offending are separated a more accurate picture of domestic abuse-related offending begins to emerge. In 2015 the Crown Office Procurator Fiscal Service, (the 'COPFS'), invited Johnson to speak to attendees at its Prosecution College. Since then, COPFS and Police Scotland have taken what could be termed a control-informed response to domestic abuse.

Police and COPFS in Scotland are trained to recognise, in other words, that *coercive control is not a bullet point, it's a paradigm shift*. This shift allows for the recognition of traits – that coercive control is gendered, (situational abuse is not), that coercive control is relational and chronic (situational abuse is one-off, incident-specific). When, in the wake of the Bill Walker debacle, Scotland began to think about a new offence, it began from the premise that existing, traditional criminal law legislation on physical and sexual abuse was crafted with situational incidents in mind. There was awareness that while these statutes work well in the context of abuse that is situational, they do not lend themselves to the prosecution of coercive control.

In Scotland, therefore, rather than fragmenting coercive control into its constituent parts, the decision was made to take a step back, and review how the existing criminal law infrastructure was being used to prosecute coercive control. From this perspective, it became clear that rather than a specific fragment of law to "plug" a "gap", what was needed was a radical new law to allow for the paradigm shift – for the prosecution of coercive control 'all of a piece'.[4]

Fragmentation - A Closer Look

The definition of domestic abuse in English law that was introduced by the Domestic Abuse Act 2021 (the 'DAA'), s 1 reflects the "bullet point" understanding of coercive control referred to above. The DAA, s 1 constructs domestic abuse as an umbrella term with six different behaviour types sitting under it in a bullet point list. 'Controlling or coercive behaviour' is itemised as one of those six behaviours. As a bullet point, 'controlling or coercive behaviour' is conceptualised as something separate to, alongside and also equivalent to 'physical abuse', 'sexual abuse', 'threatening behaviour', 'economic abuse' or 'psychological, emotional or other abuse'. It is not then defined further.

Section 76 makes 'Controlling or coercive behaviour' (the bullet point) a criminal offence. It does not define 'controlling or coercive behaviour' any further. The intention is/was for section 76 to be charged alongside existing criminal law offences to prosecute coercive control. The six bullet points in the definition are therefore prosecuted mostly separately, as fragments. Physical assaults are charged as offences against the person,[5] sexual assaults as sexual offences,[6] threatening behaviour as stalking and harassment.[7] This means that much of coercive control in England and Wales, despite the introduction of section 76, is still prosecuted under the old set of non-bespoke criminal law statues. 'Controlling or coercive behaviour' is framed as a type of non-physical, non-sexual psychological abuse which often accompanies but which is somehow separate from (exists alongside) the other fragments of abuse.

In fact, listing coercive control as one of six behaviour types is misleading. It suggests an equivalence between 'controlling or coercive behaviour', 'sexual abuse', 'physical abuse' 'economic abuse' and 'emotional/psychological abuse' which is inaccurate. Coercive control is not one of five behaviour types that make up domestic abuse. It is the wrapper that gives meaning to other the four behaviour types in the list. Coercive control, where it exists, is a domination strategy *consisting of* the sexual, physical, emotional and economic abuse which function as instruments in its toolbox.

The repercussions of this mis-framing are still playing out in England and Wales to the detriment of the prosecution of domestic abuse. The most immediate problem, from a doctrinal perspective, is what I have referred to elsewhere in this book as 'cloaking'.[8] If chronic controlling physical abuse is prosecuted, say, alongside rather than as part of coercive control, much of what makes it wrong is missed. The non-bespoke offences, the Offences against the Person Act 1861, the Sexual Offences Act 2003 and even the Protection from Harassment Act 1997, that end up getting used alongside the coercive control law, were not, as I explained in detail in preceding chapters, drafted with coercive control in mind.

Take the Offences against the Person Act 1861. It is not surprising that legal provisions introduced in the nineteenth century 'to address bar brawls and street fights'[9] are ill-suited for the prosecution of coercive control well over a 100 years later. The non-fatal offences against the person regime reflects a Victorian preoccupation with 'men's security of property and persons',[10] and rests on assumptions that are not appropriate in the context of coercive control. A transactional focus places an emphasis on the boundary preservation of property or a person. The crime is conceived of as an acute violation of that boundary that is located in time and space.[11] Harm is conceived of as physical harm to person or to property. This emphasis on transactional specificity and physical harm means that much of the violence and the harm experienced by survivors of coercive control is excluded altogether. Trying to capture that strategic intent and harm as fragments, and prosecuting them together, but as somehow separate to the physical violence, means that what Deborah Tuerkheimer refers to as the 'disconnect between life and law'[12] persists for survivors of domestic abuse.

The same 'cloaking'[13] applies in the context of the sexual offending that so often forms part of a perpetrator's controlling strategy. The Sexual Offences Act 2003 is also transactional and incident-specific and targets acute, one-off incidents of sexual violation, using the 'moral magic'[14] of "consent" to separate behaviour that is abusive from that which is not. The structuring of the sexual offences around the consent construct was not drafted with coercive control in mind. Even survivors struggle to articulate their experiences of controlling sexual abuse in the language of the Sexual Offences Act 2003, preferring to talk about "unwanted sex" or "forced sex" rather than "rape".

'All of a Piece'[15] – A Closer Look

As has been pointed out, 'Scotland was an early adopter of Evan Stark's critique of the violent-incident model of domestic violence and his paradigm of coercive control'.[16] There was awareness from the beginning that the challenge of coercive control extends beyond a "gap" in the law around psychological abuse. Stark's critique was better understood: Stark does not focus on a gap. Instead, he points out the inadequacies touched on in this chapter, that statutes drafted in Victorian times to deal with street fights and pub brawls are not equipped to deal with coercive control. Scotland understood that the existing infrastructure, and not a gap, was the problem.

This recognition prompted a whole systems review[17] that was not undertaken in England and Wales. The resulting piece of law, the Domestic Abuse Scotland Act 2018 (the DASA), has been crafted to reflect a paradigm shift – it allows police and prosecutors to expose all behaviour that is coercive, whether it is sexual assault or stalking, whether it is a low-level push or a shove, or a denial of access to money – *for what it really is*. This allows, in other words, for the telling of a more accurate story about domestic abuse in court, one which makes more sense to judges, to juries, and most importantly to the survivors themselves.

The DASA, s 2 defines what constitutes 'abusive behaviour'. It is behaviour that is 'violent, threatening, or intimidating' that has as its purpose creating dependence, isolation, control, deprivation, fear, humiliation or punishment. Violence includes sexual violence as well as physical violence. This means that the Scottish offence is radical in a number of ways – it covers physical and sexual violence as well as psychological abuse in the same offence. It removes harm to the victim as a constituent part of the offence. And it draws on survivor experience to accurately capture what coercive control looks like.

The repercussions of those progressive decisions are discussed in more detail below. But it is important to point out that the immediate effect of the DASA is that it allows the COPFS and police to take an appropriately control-informed approach to the investigation and prosecution of domestic abuse. Domestic abuse that is situational can still be prosecuted using the old statutory framework which resembles the regime in England and Wales. Where there is coercive control – a pattern of abuse defined by the perpetrator's malignant controlling intent – then this behaviour can be prosecuted 'all of a piece'[18] using the bespoke DASA. This is not an option open to the Crown Prosecution Service, who still mostly use the Offences against the Person Act 1861 and the Sexual Offences Act 2003 to prosecute sexual and physical violence alongside section 76 for the psychological aspects of coercive control.

Repercussions

The practical repercussions that follow from the fragmentation approach have been the subject of much of this book. They are myriad and complex, and affect every aspect of the prosecution of domestic abuse from the beginning (for example the survivor's decision to report to police) to the end (the sentencing exercise carried out by the criminal law judges). There is not space to cover all of the repercussions again here, but some are more significant than others. I am going to focus on the ones that matter most, at sites of importance to survivors of abuse that choose to engage with criminal justice: the police station and the court room.

The Police Station

As I explained in chapter 2, one of the most fundamental consequences of the incorrect framing of coercive control in England and Wales is the effect that this has on the ability of the police to assess risk. As stated above, the bullet point approach uses domestic abuse as an umbrella term, which lists controlling or coercive behaviour as a bullet point alongside sexual and physical violence. Critically no consideration is given to whether any sexual and physical violence that is present is part of a controlling strategy or not. The Crown Prosecution Service charging guidelines reinforce this by *conflating* control with domestic abuse in a way that is confused and confusing for officers making delicate safeguarding decisions in highly emotive situations. Wording such as, 'domestic abuse is rarely a one-off incident and is the cumulative and interlinked physical, psychological, sexual, emotional or financial abuse that has a particularly da-maging effect on the victim',[19] assumes domestic abuse *is the same thing as coercive control* – which it is not.

I used the case of Caroline Flack in Chapter 2 to demonstrate how this con-flation of domestic abuse with coercive control can backfire – it is likely that the poor charging and safeguarding decisions in her case contributed to the failing mental health which cost her her life. This is an example of what can happen if situational violence is not recognised for what it is. The failure to identify the *absence* of control in Caroline's case, and the assumption, encouraged by guidelines such as the one quoted above, that because she was in a relationship and had assaulted her boyfriend, she must be a high-risk perpetrator, lead to an inflated assessment both of the harm she caused and the risk that ensued.

This has even worse repercussions the other way around. A failure to identify coercive control where it does exist at the earliest opportunity often has tragic consequences. Senior police explained to me that cases that end in a domestic homicide are often assessed incorrectly initially as low risk because the coercive control lens is missing. The bullet point approach means that police still use si-tuationally specific law (the old regime) to prosecute many of the constituent parts of coercive control. This forces them down situation-specific rabbit holes. Using law that requires evidence of location in time and place, in other words, means that they still focus on "individual" "acute" "incidents" of violation. In coercive control, the cumulative nature of the harm/risk is much greater than the sum of its "low-risk" parts. Conceptualising coercive control as a fragment of offending behaviour rather than a paradigm shift is responsible for this muddle.

The way that the criminal law is structured in England and Wales, therefore, has a significant, direct impact on risk assessment. Feeding into this impact on the risk assessment process is also a harder to quantify indirect impact on the ability of police to empathise with victims of coercive control. Focusing on incidents leads to 'the assumption [by police] that victims ... exercise decisional autonomy "between" episodes'.[20] This means that victims who fail to capitalise on that (assumed) autonomy can be perceived as responsible, at least in part, for the on-going abuse that they experience. Being *trapped*, in other words, is misconstrued as a *decision* to stay. An understanding of the coercive control paradigm shift would allow police to understand that each acute, violent incident is, to many women, relatively unimportant in the context of the chronic 'state of siege'[21] imposed by their abuser – and that escape is neither possible, nor, necessarily, a route to safety.

The Court Room

Much has been written in the literature on criminal justice process about the fraught nature of the "responsibilisation" of the domestic abuse victim as prosecution witness.[22] My interest in this book has been on the contribution made by the criminal law itself. The introduction of section 76 in England/Wales has resulted in two repercussions for the victim giving evidence that are particularly significant. The first is as a result of the (by now) familiar mismatch between law that is acute and behaviour that is chronic. The second relates to how and to what extent section 76 defines harm.

I have said that the bullet point approach adopted in England and Wales means that non-bespoke statutes are used to prosecute many of the coercive controlling behaviours experienced by victims. Non-bespoke statutes introduce the need for *evidence* that is singularly inappropriate in the context of coercive control. For example, I have said that the Offences against the Person Act 1861 demands that assaults are framed in an incident-specific way. From an evidential perspective, this means locating attacks in time and space. Survivors understandably find this difficult. It is hard to pinpoint chronic abuse to specific dates on which particular assaults took place. Locating attacks in other words, that are experienced as continuous is a difficult and frustrating exercise. It allows defence barristers to attack victims' credibility in a way that is distressing for victims but which is entirely reasonable in light of the evidential requirements of the Offences against the Person Act 1861.

Some of the evidential difficulties introduced by the Sexual Offences Act 2003 have already been touched on, above. I said that the Sexual Offences Act 2003 is transactional and incident-specific and targets acute, one-off incidents of sexual violation, using the 'moral magic'[23] of "consent" to separate behaviour that is abusive from that which is not. Exactly the same problem with times and dates occurs therefore in the context of *sexual* abuse which is ongoing and chronic. But the Sexual Offences Act 2003 creates additional hurdles for the survivor. Juries struggle to accept that sexual contact is unwanted in the context of consensual contact that might take place before, or after, the abuse. Juries also struggle to assess the extent to which a perpetrator had a 'reasonable belief' in the victim's consent in the context of evidence of the kind of gradual erosion of a victim's sexual autonomy that takes place in coercive control.

Another way in which section 76 creates difficulties for survivors giving evidence in court is to do with the way in which it uses and articulates harm. Section 76 is drafted as what in criminal law is termed a "result" crime, because the harm experienced by the victim is a constituent part of the offence. Section 76(1) (c) states that the 'controlling or coercive behaviour' is an offence *only* where it has a 'serious effect' on the victim. 'Serious effect' is defined in subsection (4): if it causes the victim to fear, on at least two occasions, that violence will be used against the victim or if it causes the victim serious alarm and distress which has a substantial adverse effect on her usual day-to-day activities. If there is no fear of physical violence, or if the victim manages to carry on with her day-to-day activities as usual, then there is no offence.

One unintended consequence of defining and centralising the harm in this way is the discriminative effect it has on the 'resilient' victim. I described in chapter 5 how Paul Measor subjected his partner Lauren Smith to horrific abuse, teaching their toddler son to tell her to "fuck off" and spitting in her face. Nevertheless, District Judge Helen Cousins correctly acquitted him, ruling that 'there's no doubt the victim is a strong and capable woman. It is to her credit that I cannot find his behaviour had a serious effect on her in the context of the guidelines'.[24] Penalising resilience is not a good courtroom optic. Worse, though, is what the focus on harm does more generally to the victim in the courtroom.

Adversarial justice is not known for its sensitivity to the needs of victims experiencing trauma.[25] Victims tell us that testifying against an abusive perpetrator who still has access to her outside the courtroom is, anyway, a truly terrifying experience. Making the harm she suffers a constituent part of the offence makes a conviction heavily dependent on her account (under cross-examination) of the most intimate details of her emotional state. Police officers that give evidence in court are trained to do so, and they are necessarily detached from material to which they have a professional, not emotional, commitment. Nevertheless, they tell us they find this difficult.[26] An abused woman is not trained to give evidence, traumatised, and speaking publicly (often for the first time) about some of the most difficult and personal emotional experiences she has ever had. If she cannot perform, the prosecution falls at the first hurdle. But if she performs too well, juries mistrust her.

The DASA gets around this problem in two ways. Firstly, I explained in the preceding chapter that much of the wording on harm in the DASA was taken from survivors' accounts of abuse. The DASA articulates harm as the experiences of dependence, isolation, control, deprivation, fear, humiliation or punishment that survivors tell us are the hallmarks of coercive control. This much more accurately reflects how survivors tell us they experience control, and thus narrows the 'life/law' gap, making the courtroom experience an easier one. Secondly, the existence of this harm is NOT a constituent part of the offence. The focus is on what the perpetrator has done, and not on how that made the victim feel, or on what it made the victim do. To be clear this does not do away with the need for victim testimony necessarily, although it makes a victimless prosecution more possible as an option. But it shifts the focus from 'how-she-feels' to 'what-he-did' in a way that survivors tell us is helpful for them.

The Impact on Sentencing

The sentencing difficulties experienced by judges in the context of a section 76 conviction are the ultimate practical repercussion of the bullet point approach. Section 76 is rarely, if ever, charged alone; the most common accompanying counts are, as is to be expected, offences against the person and sexual offences. The difficulty for the sentencing judge is how to separate out the different strands of the offending behaviour while avoiding the possibility of double counting. As is to be expected there is a lack of consistency between judges. Some decide to use the section 76 offence as the principal offence to reflect the totality of the offending for the sentence on that count, and to make the sentencing for the associated charges concurrent. If there is a significant one-off incident of sexual or physical violence (for example a rape, or the causing of grievous bodily harm) then the judge will tend to use that charge as the principal offence and to make the sentencing of the section 76 offence concurrent.[27] In these cases the distinct harm of coercive control does not get enough recognition.[28]

Neither approach is ideal. Separating the strands is an artificial exercise and raises the inevitable spectre of double counting. And using violence as the "principal sentence" means we are still left with the hierarchy of harms that places physical violence at the top, which is not the way that survivors articulate their experiences of abuse. The "mismatch" between life and law, in other words, continues.

Unfortunately, the low maximum sentence of imprisonment for controlling or coercive behaviour (five years) adds to the perception of a hierarchy of harms.[29] Judges interviewed for this project agreed that this is too low.[30] The low sentencing threshold contributes to a perception of a hierarchy of harm that places physical violence at the top, which is not how survivors articulate the harms they have experienced. Furthermore, it does not reflect the severity of coercive control. Dealing with it 'all of a piece',[31] (the DASA), and incorporating the violent and non-violent behaviours into a single offence allowed Scotland to introduce a maximum penalty on conviction on indictment of 14 years imprisonment.[32]

Final Thoughts

In light of the difficulties introduced by what I have referred to in this book as "fragmentation", it is perhaps not surprising that the uptake of section 76 in England and Wales has been disappointing. Firstly, the data suggest that only a fraction of cases involving coercive control are being investigated as such by the police in England and Wales. Data obtained by the BBC, for example, from 33 police forces in England and Wales show that while there were 7,034 arrests in the time period January 2016–July 2018, there were only 1,157 cases that ended up with a perpetrator facing charges.[33] This finding is supported by a Freedom of Information request issued by the Bureau of Investigative Journalism which showed some forces in England and Wales recording as few as five charges over a 12-month period.[34]

The conclusion thus reported in the press – that coercive control is, in England and Wales, still going under the radar – is substantiated in the academic literature. One recent study showed that of the nearly 19,000 domestic abuse offences recorded by one police force during a recent 18-month period less than 1% were recorded as coercive control.[35] The authors of the study conclude that 'This number is considerably low, particularly when compared with other offences'.[36] Another study found that the rate of charge for controlling or coercive behaviour was half that for other domestic abuse offences.[37] And finally, this position is supported by the government's own statistics: in the year ending 2018, 4,686 defendants were prosecuted further to section 76 – this is 0.004% of an estimated 1.3 million women experiencing domestic abuse during that time period.[38] By contrast, in Scotland, the early signs are that the implementation of the DASA has gone relatively smoothly. In 2020–21 1,581 charges were reported accounting for 4.7% of all domestic abuse charges.[39]

Secondly, the data show difficulties in England and Wales with evidencing section 76 charges. In Scotland in 2020–21, 95% of charges reported were prosecuted.[40] A Home Office early review of section 76 reports that in England and Wales, 85% of section 76 offences in 2018/19 were 'finalised' (which means discontinued) due to 'evidential difficulties'.[41] An independent academic study found that the likelihood that a case would be discontinued for evidential reasons was over 50% higher than for other domestic abuse-related offences.[42] Criticism that police and prosecutors in England and Wales are not pursing enough section 76 cases is therefore 'regular and ongoing'; also apparent is that police understanding of coercive control in England and Wales is poor, and that this is hampering their ability to investigate.[43]

To conclude: section 76 *is* imperfect in execution. It contributes to, rather than resolves, the fragmentation of coercive control into its constituent parts. This makes it harder to investigate, prosecute and sentence the coercive control than it would be if there was one domestic abuse offence. It quite possibly makes the experience of criminal justice a more difficult and traumatic one for the survivors of domestic abuse than it needs to be.

Domestic abuse that is coercive control is a wrong like no other crime. This is why it requires a bespoke criminal offence dealing with all of its various manifestations – the sexual abuse, the physical abuse, the stalking, the emotional abuse – in one place.

There is no "perfect" way to criminalise coercive control and every jurisdiction will work within the socio-legal confines of what is politically possible. It is, anyway, early days for the criminalisation project: as has been said 'the incorporation and use of coercive control in an adversarial context is relatively uncharted territory'.[44] To the extent that there is room for manoeuvre, there are useful lessons to be learnt from the decisions made in England/Wales and Scotland. Legal reform is always a work in progress. While section 76 marks progress, it is clear that in England and Wales at least there is more work to be done.

Notes

1 Tanya Palmer, 'Failing to See the Wood for the Trees: Chronic Sexual Violation and the Criminal Law' 2020 84(6) The Journal of Criminal Law 573.
2 Ibid 573.
3 Scottish Government, 'A Criminal Offence of Domestic Abuse' (December 2015) para 3.10 available at <https://consult.gov.scot/criminal-law-and-sentencing-team/criminal-offence-domestic-abuse/user_uploads/00491481.pdf-1> accessed 24 May 2021.
4 Ibid.
5 Offences against the Person Act 1861.
6 Sexual Offences Act 2003.
7 Protection from Harassment Act 1997.
8 Deborah Tuerkheimer, 'Recognizing and Remedying the Harm of Battering: A Call to Criminalize Domestic Violence' (2004) 94(4) Journal of Criminal Law and Criminology 959, 980.
9 Charlotte Bishop, 'Domestic Violence: The Limitations of a Legal Response' in Sarah Hilda and Vanessa Bettinson (eds), *Interdisciplinary Perspectives on Protection, Prevention and Intervention* (Palgrave Macmillan 2016) 66.
10 Nagire Naffine, *Criminal Law and the Man Problem* (Hart 2019) 23.
11 See also Vanessa Bettinson and Charlotte Bishop, 'Evidencing Domestic Violence, Including Behaviour That Falls under the New Offence of "Controlling or Coercive Behaviour"' (2017) 22(1) The International Journal of Evidence and Proof 3, for an English perspective.
12 Tuerkheimer, Recognizing and Remedying the Harm of Battering, n8 980.
13 Tuerkheimer, Recognizing and Remedying the Harm of Battering n8 980.
14 Heidi Hurd, 'The Moral Magic of Consent' (1996) 2(2) Legal Theory 121.
15 Scottish Government, A Criminal Offence of Domestic Abuse n3.
16 Marsha Scott, 'The Making of the Gold Standard' in Marilyn McMahon and Paul McGorrery (eds), *Criminalising Coercive Control* (Springer 2020) 2.
17 Scottish Government, *Equally Safe – Reforming the Criminal Law to Address Domestic Abuse and Sexual Offences* (March 2015).
18 Scottish Government, A Criminal Offence of Domestic Abuse n3.
19 Crown Prosecution Service, 'Domestic Abuse Legal Guidance' available at <https://www.cps.gov.uk/legal-guidance/domestic-abuse> accessed 7 April 2022.
20 Ibid. 200.
21 Mary Ann Dutton, 'Understanding Women's Responses to Domestic Violence: A Redefinition of Battered Woman Syndrome' (1992) 21 Hofstra Law Review 1191, 1208.
22 Charlotte Barlow et al., 'Putting Coercive Control into Practice: Problems and Possibilities' (2020) 60(1) British Journal of Criminology 160; Louise Ellison and Vanessa Munro, 'Taking Trauma Seriously: Critical Reflections on the Criminal Justice Process' (2017) 21(3) The International Journal of Evidence and Proof 183.
23 Hurd, The Moral Magic of Consent n14.
24 Jeremy Armstrong, 'Violent Boyfriend Is Cleared after Judge Says Partner Is 'Too Strong' to Be Victim' *The Mirror* (London 23 November 2018).

25 Ellison and Munro, Taking Trauma Seriously n22.

26 Ibid.

27 This approach was approved by the Court of Appeal in cases such as *Chanaa* [2019] EWCA Crim 2335 (where the defendant was convicted of rape and controlling or coercive behaviour); *Cunningham* [2019] EWCA Crim 2101 (four counts of rape and controlling or coercive behaviour) and *Holden* [2019] EWCA Crim 1885 (rape and controlling or coercive behaviour).

28 See, for example *Parkin* [2018] EWCA Crim 2764.

29 Serious Crime Act 2015, s 11.

30 See, for example, interview with Judge Little (20 March 2018); interview with Judge Harwood (21 May 2018).

31 Scottish Government, A Criminal Offence of Domestic Abuse n3.

32 Domestic Abuse (Scotland) Act 2018, s 8.

33 Patrick Cowling, 'Domestic Abuse: Majority of Controlling Cases Dropped' *BBC News Services* (4 December 2018) available at <https://www.bbc.co.uk/news/uk-46429520> accessed 28 June 2019.

34 Maeve McClenaghan and Charles Boutard, 'Questions Raised over Patchy Take-up of Domestic Violence Law' (Bureau of Investigative Journalism 24 November 2017) available at <https://www.thebureauinvestigates.com/stories/2017-11-24/coercive-control-concerns> accessed 15 November 2019.

35 Ibid.

36 Barlow et al., Putting Coercive Control into Practice: Problems and Possibilities n22 166.

37 Ian Brennan and Andy Myhill, 'Coercive Control: Patterns in Crimes, Arrests and Outcomes for a New Domestic Abuse Offence' 2022 22(2) The British Journal of Criminology 468.

38 Only 235 defendants were convicted: Office for National Statistics, 'Domestic Abuse in England and Wales: Year ending March 2018' para 11 available at <https://www.ons.gov.uk/peoplepopulationandcommunity/crimeandjustice/articles/domesticabusefindingsfromthecrimesurveyforenglandandwales/yearendingmarch2018> accessed June 27 2019. This number is improving year on year, see Office for National Statistics 'Domestic Abuse in England and Wales: Year ending March 2021' <https://www.ons.gov.uk/peoplepopulationandcommunity/crimeandjustice/articles/domesticabuseprevalenceandtrendsenglandandwales/yearendingmarch2021> accessed 13 May 2021.

39 Crown Office and Procurator Fiscal Service, 'Domestic Abuse and Stalking Charges in Scotland 2021' available at <https://www.copfs.gov.uk/media-site-news-from-copfs/1976-domestic-abuse-and-stalking-charges-in-scotland-2020-21#:~:text=The%20Domestic%20Abuse%20%28Scotland%29%20Act%202018%20came%20into,4.7%20percent%20of%20all%20domestic%20abuse%20charges%20reported>accessed 29 May 2022.

40 Ibid.

41 Home Office, *Review of the Controlling or Coercive Behaviour Offence* (Home Office Research Report 122, Home Office 2021).

42 Brennan and Myhill, Coercive Control n37.

43 Cassandra Wiener, 'Seeing What Is Invisible in Plain Sight: Policing Coercive Control' (2017) 56(4) 500; Paul McGorrery and Marilyn McMahon, 'Criminalising "the Worst" Part: Operationalising the Offence of Coercive Control in England and Wales' (2019) 11 The Criminal Law Review 957, 963; Barlow et al, Putting Coercive Control into Practice n22.

44 Michele Burman and Oona Brooks-Hay, 'Aligning Policy and Law? The Creation of a Domestic Abuse Offence Incorporating Coercive Control' (2018) 18(1) Criminology & Criminal Justice 67, 74.

Bibliography

Armstrong J, 'Violent Boyfriend Is Cleared after Judge Says Partner Is "Too Strong" to Be Victim' *The Mirror* (London 23 November 2018).

Barlow C, Johnson K, Walklate S and Humphries L, 'Putting Coercive Control into Practice: Problems and Possibilities' (2020) 60(1) *British Journal of Criminology* 160.

Bettinson V and Bishop C, 'Evidencing Domestic Violence, Including Behaviour That Falls under the New Offence of "Controlling or Coercive Behaviour"' (2017) 22(1) *The International Journal of Evidence and Proof* 3.

Bishop C, 'Domestic Violence: The Limitations of a Legal Response' in Sarah Hilda and Vanessa Bettinson (eds), *Interdisciplinary Perspectives on Protection, Prevention and Intervention* (Palgrave Macmillan 2016).

Brennan I and Myhill A, 'Coercive Control: Patterns in Crimes, Arrests and Outcomes for a New Domestic Abuse Offence' (2022) 22(2) *The British Journal of Criminology* 468.

Burman M and Brooks-Hay O, 'Aligning Policy and Law? The Creation of a Domestic Abuse Offence Incorporating Coercive Control' (2018) 18(1) *Criminology & Criminal Justice* 67.

Cowling P, 'Domestic Abuse: Majority of Controlling Cases Dropped' *BBC News Services* (4 December 2018) available at <https://www.bbc.co.uk/news/uk-46429520> accessed 28 June 2019.

Crown Office and Procurator Fiscal Service, 'Domestic Abuse and Stalking Charges in Scotland 2021' available at <https://www.copfs.gov.uk/media-site-news-from-copfs/1976-domestic-abuse-and-stalking-charges-in-scotland-2020-21#:~:text=The%20Domestic%20Abuse%20%28Scotland%29%20Act%202018%20came%20into,4.7%20percent%20of%20all%20domestic%20abuse%20charges%20reported> accessed 29 May 2022.

Crown Prosecution Service, 'Domestic Abuse Legal Guidance' available at <https://www.cps.gov.uk/legal-guidance/domestic-abuse> accessed 7 April 2022.

Dutton M, 'Understanding Women's Responses to Domestic Violence: A Redefinition of Battered Woman Syndrome' (1992) 21 *Hofstra Law Review* 1191.

Ellison L and Munro V, 'Taking Trauma Seriously: Critical Reflections on the Criminal Justice Process' (2017) 21 (3) *The International Journal of Evidence and Proof* 183.

Home Office, *Review of the Controlling or Coercive Behaviour Offence* (Home Office Research Report 122, Home Office 2021).

Hurd H, 'The Moral Magic of Consent' (1996) 2(2) *Legal Theory* 121.

McClenaghan M and Boutard C, 'Questions Raised over Patchy Take-up of Domestic Violence Law' (Bureau of Investigative Journalism 24 November 2017) available at <https://www.thebureauinvestigates.com/stories/2017-11-24/coercive-control-concerns> accessed 15 November 2019.

McGorrery P and McMahon M, 'Criminalising "the Worst" Part: Operationalising the Offence of Coercive Control in England and Wales' (2019) 11 *The Criminal Law Review* 957.

Naffine N, *Criminal Law and the Man Problem* (Hart 2019) 23.

Office for National Statistics, 'Domestic Abuse in England and Wales: Year ending March 2018' available at <https://www.ons.gov.uk/peoplepopulationandcommunity/crimeandjustice/articles/domesticabusefindingsfromthecrimesurveyforenglandandwales/yearendingmarch2018> accessed June 27 2019.

Office for National Statistics 'Domestic Abuse in England and Wales: Year ending March 2021' <https://www.ons.gov.uk/peoplepopulationandcommunity/crimeandjustice/articles/domesticabuseprevalenceandtrendsenglandandwales/yearendingmarch2021> accessed 13 May 2021.

Palmer T, 'Failing to See the Wood for the Trees: Chronic Sexual Violation and the Criminal Law' (2020) 84(6) *The Journal of Criminal Law* 573.

Scott M, 'The Making of the Gold Standard' in Marilyn McMahon and Paul McGorrery (eds), *Criminalising Coercive Control* (Springer 2020) 2.

Scottish Government, 'A Criminal Offence of Domestic Abuse' (December 2015) available at <https://consult.gov.scot/criminal-law-and-sentencing-team/criminal-offence-domestic-abuse/user_uploads/00491481.pdf-1> accessed 24 May 2021.

Scottish Government, *Equally Safe – Reforming the Criminal Law to Address Domestic Abuse and Sexual Offences* (March 2015).

Tuerkheimer D, 'Recognizing and Remedying the Harm of Battering: A Call to Criminalize Domestic Violence' (2004) 94(4) *Journal of Criminal Law and Criminology* 959.

Wiener C, 'Seeing What Is Invisible in Plain Sight: Policing Coercive Control' (2017) 56(4) *The Howard Journal of Crime and Justice* 500.

Cases

Chanaa [2019] EWCA Crim 2335.
Cunningham [2019] EWCA Crim 2101.
Holden [2019] EWCA Crim 1885.
Parkin [2018] EWCA Crim 2764.

Legislation

Offences against the Person Act 1861.
Protection from Harassment Act 1997.
Serious Crime Act 2015.
Sexual Offences Act 2003.

INDEX